This is the
Henry Holt Walks Series,
which originated with
PARISWALKS *by Alison and Sonia Landes.*
Other titles in the series include:

LONDONWALKS *by Anton Powell*

JERUSALEMWALKS *by Nitza Rosovsky*

FLORENCEWALKS *by Anne Holler*

ROMEWALKS *by Anya M. Shetterly*

VIENNAWALKS *by J. Sydney Jones*

VENICEWALKS *by Chas Carner and Alessandro Giannatasio*

RUSSIAWALKS *by David and Valaria Matlock*

BARCELONAWALKS *by George Semler*

BEIJINGWALKS *by Don J. Cohn and Zhang Jingqing*

NEW YORKWALKS *by The 92nd Street Y*

MADRIDWALKS *by George Semler*

BERLINWALKS *by Peter Fritzsche and Karen Hewitt*

PRAGUEWALKS *by Ivana Edwards*

PARISWALKS

REVISED EDITION

Alison and Sonia Landes

*Photographs by Myrna Patterson,
Anne Peretz, and Templeton Peck*

An Owl Book

Henry Holt and Company • New York

Henry Holt and Company, Inc.
Publishers since 1866
115 West 18th Street
New York, New York 10011

Henry Holt® is registered trademark of
Henry Holt and Company, Inc.

Photographic Credits:

Myrna Patterson: frontispiece, pages ii, 26, 69, 80, 127, 148, 159,
165, 170, 210, 218, 223, 229, 232, 240, 249, 252, 254, 258, 279
Templeton Peck: pages 67, 88, 94, 97, 106, 284
Anne Peretz: pages xii, 8, 21, 23, 48, 53, 56, 57, 102,
112, 113, 132, 155, 157, 178, 183, 193, 202

Library of Congress Cataloging-in-Publication Data
Landes, Alison, 1953–
Pariswalks / Alison and Sonia Landes ;
photographs by Myrna Patterson. — Rev. ed.
p.   cm.
Includes index.
ISBN 0-8050-6127-4 (pbk. : alk. paper)
1. Paris (France)—Tours.   2. Walking—
France—Paris—Guidebooks.
I. Landes, Sonia, 1925–   . II. Title.
DC707.L28   1999
914.4'36104839—dc21 98-42822

First Owl Book Edition 1981
Revised Edition 1999

Maps by Jeffrey L. Ward

Printed in the United States of America
All first editions are printed on acid-free paper.∞
3 5 7 9 10 8 6 4

To David, *père de famille,*
and to Nicholas, Rebecca, and Elana

Contents

Acknowledgments

We would like to thank all of our friends who came to visit and were dragged willingly or unwillingly into the streets of Paris to test our walks. Also, we thank all those who read the manuscript for their encouragement and helpful advice. We have received many wonderful letters from readers and walkers, with valuable information and suggestions. We are most indebted to Jacques Hillairet, author of *Dictionnaire Historique des Rues de Paris*, the foundation work for the history of the streets of Paris.

Thanks to Elise Proulx, our editor, who has shown real interest and energy in getting this latest edition of *Pariswalks* off and running. Thanks to three photographers: to Myrna Patterson for new photos and new information, to Anne Peretz for the original photographs, and to Templeton Peck, who replaced lost photographs at the last minute.

This book has become a family affair. Susannah Landes Foster, granddaughter and niece, with her friend Caroline Katzen, walked the entire book last summer and made excellent suggestions and changes. This winter, Rebecca walked with her mother, Alison, and helped decide the final changes to the manuscript. *Un grand merci* to our spouses: to Nicholas, for saving us from computer disasters, and to David, for reading almost every word with a discerning eye.

MONTMARTRE
CEMETERY

PLACE PIGALLE

PARC MONCEAU

GARE ST. LAZARE

PLACE CHARLES DE GAULLE
(ETOILE)

BLVD. HAUSSMANN

AVE. FOCH

Arc de Triomphe

RUE DU FAUBOURG ST. HONORE

PLACE
MADELAINE

Opéra

AVE. DES CHAMPS-ELYSEES

ROND POINT
DES CHAMPS-ELYSEES

PLACE
VENDOME

AVE. DE L'OPERA

PLACE DU TROCADERO

JARDINS DU
TROCADERO

PLACE DE LA CONCORDE

RUE   DE   RIVOLI

JARDINS DES
TUILERIES

Palais
Chaillot

Seine

Louvre

Tour Eiffel

PARC DU
CHAMP DE MARS

Hôtel des
Invalides

WALK 3

BLVD. RASPAIL

BLVD.
ST. GERMAIN
DES PRES

RUE DE RENNES

ODEON

JARDINS DU
LUXEMBOURG

RUE   DE   VAUGIRARD

MONTPARNASSE

GARE
MONTPARNASSE

MONTPARNASSE
CEMETERY

PLACE DENFERT
ROCHEREAU

BLVD.

WALKS AND MAIN SIGHTS
Central Paris

Walk 1: St. Julien le Pauvre
Walk 2: La Huchette
Walk 3: St. Germain des Prés
Walk 4: Mouffetard
Walk 5: Place des Vosges
Walk 6: Rue des Francs-Bourgeois
Walk 7: Bastille to Eglise Saint-Gervais

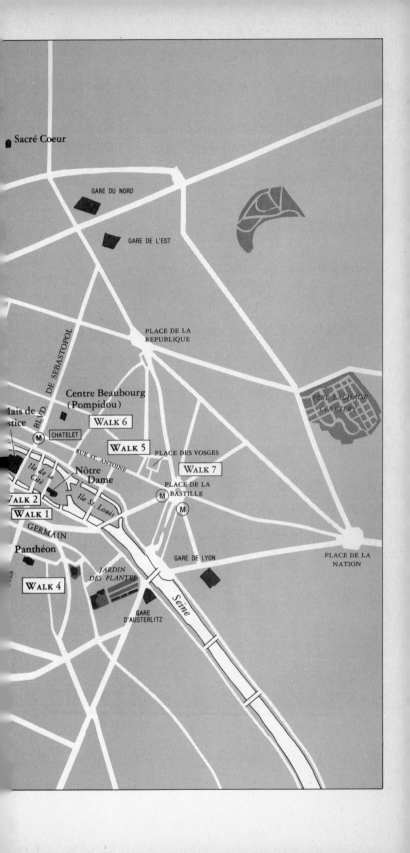

Introduction

In this book, we offer you step-by-step tours of seven of the oldest and most fascinating neighborhoods of Paris. On the Left Bank, Saint-Julien-le-Pauvre, La Huchette, Saint-Germain-des-Prés, and Mouffetard. On the Right Bank, the Marais, including the Place des Vosges, the Rue des Francs-Bourgeois, and the Bastille.

These morning or afternoon walks, which cover no more than five to ten blocks each, will make you a connoisseur of these areas. What is hidden to the casual observer becomes the key to Paris. Through the signs and stories of the past, the architectural details, and the life of today, the city unveils itself. This knowledge makes you a friend and possessor of the *quartier* forever.

We feel that this book represents a significantly different approach to travel. After seeing Paris in the large—the obligatory monuments and sights—you must see Paris in its detail to feel, even for a short time, a part of the city. Our approach, which we call "close-up tourism," allows you to get to know a piece of the city intimately, house by house, shop by shop. Here, there are no long walks to get from one site to another. Paris has something to show off at every step, and we have found it for you.

We have chosen for this purpose *quartiers* where many of the streets are still the narrow, irregular, meandering paths of medieval and early modern times. These seven neighborhoods have, in part, been preserved by the accidents of history, though repeatedly threatened by the hammers and shovels of urban planners and boulevard builders.

No matter how often we researched our walks, we never failed to make new discoveries, even for this, the sixth edition of *Pariswalks*. One friend said she would never walk down a street in the same way again. We expect this to happen to you, and we would be pleased to hear about your discoveries.

On these walks you may sit, stand, snack, lunch, or dine. Eating places have been carefully chosen for their interest as well as their cuisine. The walks are free. They are designed to be comfortable, nonstrenuous, and fun. Most of the people in the area know us well, and if you show them *Pariswalks*, they will be happy to speak with you. Our maps and pictures should guide you without difficulty.

It is wise to read each walk before setting out, in order to plan your day more effectively. We advise morning walking; more courtyards are open for mail and deliveries. You will not be disturbing anyone by walking into courtyards or by peering through glass windows. Paris is for everyone. Press the main button on the door keypad to enter. Not all are locked.

A few words about how we came to write this book. One summer before leaving to spend the year in Paris, we (Sonia, mother, and Alison, daughter) decided that since we were already a sort of agency for advice about the city, we ought to put it in writing. We felt eminently qualified: we had lived in Paris on and off for many years; the children had gone to school there; one was even born there. We had first gone as a family in 1948 because David, the *père de famille*, was writing his thesis in French history. That was when Pierrette, a French Breton lady, came to live with us. She still does. She has kept the French feeling alive in the household ever since. That was the beginning. Since then, the pleasures of Paris and friends, David's research, educating our grandchildren in French schools for a term each, and revising this book have taken us back countless times.

Everyone remains surprised that a mother and daughter have been able to work together so easily and successfully for the last twenty-five years. We are often asked, "Do you still talk to each other?" "Who did the writing?" "Who did the research?" and so on. Yes, we still talk all the time, and we share all the work. Although our styles differ—one of us is more friendly and will talk to anyone, while the other is a stickler for accuracy in every statement—we have continued in all the later editions to combine our efforts by dint of give-and-take, and lots of laughing.

Brief Chronology
of Paris

B.C. 52	Roman invasion of Lutetia
A.D. 360	City receives the name of Paris
481–511	Reign of Clovis, who makes Paris the capital
511–588	Reign of Childebert I, son of Clovis
885	Norman invasion of the capital
1000	Church of Saint-Germain-des-Prés begun
1180–1223	Reign of Philippe Auguste
1226–1270	Reign of Saint Louis; Sorbonne founded
1380–1422	Reign of Charles VI
1420s	Paris under English occupation
1547–1559	Reign of Henri II and Catherine de Médicis
1574–1589	Reign of Henri III, their son
1589–1610	Reign of Henri IV, married to "*chère* Margot," his cousin Marguerite de Valois, sister of Henri III; then, in 1600, to Marie de Médicis. Henry was accidentally killed in a jousting tournament celebrating his daughter's marriage.
1605	Place des Vosges started
1610–1643	Reign of Louis XIII, following murder of Henri IV by a mad cleric. Place des Vosges inaugurated April 5, 6, and 7, 1612. Richelieu was Louis's first minister, from 1624 to 1642.
1643–1715	Reign of Louis XIV, called *le Roi Soleil* (the Sun

King). He reigned for sixty years and is remembered for the slogan *l'état, c'est moi* (the state, that's me). He turned a hunting lodge into the palace at Versailles. His eight children by Mme de Montespan were tutored by Mme de Maintenon, whom Louis secretly married after the death of his wife, Queen Marie-Thérèse (1683).

1715–1774	Reign of Louis XV left France almost bankrupt. He was known for saying *Après moi, le déluge* (after me, the flood).
1774–1792	Reign of Louis XVI, with Marie Antoinette. They were attacked at Versailles and taken to Paris. They were guillotined in 1793.
1789–1799	French Revolution. The revolutionary government guillotined Louis and Marie Antoinette in the Place de la Concorde.
1793–1794	The Terror. In 421 days, 2,669 people were condemned and executed. Robespierre, revolutionary leader and member of the Committee of Public Safety, was chiefly responsible.
1795–1799	Directory
1799–1804	Consulate under Napoléon Bonaparte
1804–1814	Empire, with Napoléon as emperor
1852–1870	Reign of Napoléon III. Georges Haussmann was his city planner.
1910	Great Paris flood
1914–1918	World War I
1939–1945	World War II. German occupation from 1940
1962	Malraux law decrees Paris buildings must be cleaned every twelve years.
1968	*Evénements de mai* (events of May): serious student riots in Paris
1980–1989	A period of historical building in Paris: the Louvre Pyramid, the Pompidou Center, the Arc de la Défense, the Orsay Museum, the Très Grande Bibliothèque, the Opéra-Bastille
1981	François Mitterrand begins his first term as president of the French Republic.
1992	The date of the realization of the European Economic Community. Common Market becomes a single unit. European internal borders collapse.
1995	Jacques Chirac elected president of the Republic.
1999	The common currency, the euro, is introduced.

Tips

- Use your bank's ATM card to get French money from the automatic teller machines. They all take any card on the Cirrus or Plus system. You will get the bank exchange rate of the day with only a small transaction service charge. Forget the traveler's checks.

- Buy a *carnet*, booklet, of ten *métro* and/or bus tickets at a time to save money (52 francs). Have tickets for the bus before you get on—the bus driver charges more. You can buy them at a *tabac* or a *métro* station.

- Beware of pickpockets on the *métro* and at the Place de l'Opéra.

- Taxis begin at 13 francs and take no more than three persons at a time. *Tariff* B is used outside of Paris and between 10 P.M. and 6 P.M.

- Order the *menu conseillé*, recommended menu, at restaurants to save money.

- Dinner is served from 7:30 P.M. on. If you are a nonsmoker, dine on the early side. There will be fewer people at the restaurant.

- Reserve at least a month in advance at famous restaurants and always reconfirm. Call the same day for other restaurants.

- A 15 percent service charge is already included in your restaurant bill. You may leave small change. Check on service charges at your hotel.

- A good *café crème* tastes better than a latte, and although the French only drink it in the morning, don't be shy about ordering it whenever you want.

- Bring plastic plates, silverware, and a corkscrew and buy some of your meals to eat in the park or your hotel room. *Charcuteries,* delicatessens, sell prepared dishes.

- Buy a *télécarte* from the post office, a newspaper store, or a *tabac* for use in public telephones. To call the United States, dial 001 and the number. Try to have the U.S. connection call you at your hotel. They dial 011-331 and your number. It's much less expensive to call from the United States.

- Buy *The International Tribune* every day even though it costs $2. Buy *Pariscope*, the activities-of-the-week booklet with an English section. It comes out on Wednesdays. In the movie listings, "v.o." means the movie is in its original language.

- For house-call doctors, call S.O.S., 01-4707-7777. The cost is $60. Pharmacists also are very helpful.

- Students and senior citizens should inquire about reduced fees at museums and movies.

- McDonald's has the best public bathrooms in Paris, but the public toilets on the streets are automatically disinfected after every use.

Walk · 1

Saint-Julien-le-Pauvre

"Shakespeare and Co. Kilometer Zero Paris."

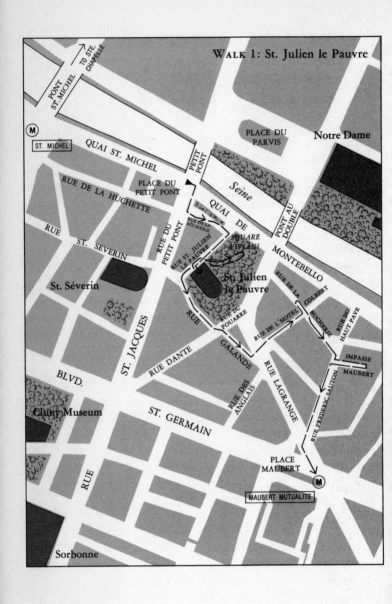

WALK 1: St. Julien le Pauvre

Notre Dame

PLACE DU PARVIS

M ST. MICHEL

QUAI ST. MICHEL

PONT ST. MICHEL

TO STE. CHAPELLE

PETIT PONT

Seine

PLACE DU PETIT PONT

RUE DE LA HUCHETTE

RUE DE LA BÛCHERIE

QUAI DE

PONT AU DOUBLE

RUE ST. SEVERIN

RUE DU PETIT PONT

SQUARE VIVIANI

MONTEBELLO

St. Séverin

St. Julien le Pauvre

RUE ST. JULIEN LE PAUVRE

RUE DE LA COLBERT

RUE DU HAUT PAVE

RUE DU FOUARRE

RUE DE L'HOTEL

BÛCHERIE

RUE

RUE ST. JACQUES

RUE DANTE

GALANDE

IMPASSE MAUBERT

BLVD.

Cluny Museum

RUE DES ANGLAIS

RUE LAGRANGE

RUE FREDERIC SAUTON

ST. GERMAIN

RUE

PLACE MAUBERT

M

MAUBERT MUTUALITE

Sorbonne

Starting Point: The corner of the Petit Pont and the Quai de Montebello, 5th arrondissement
Métro: Saint-Michel, RER
Buses: 24, 27, 47, 63, 86, 87

Here you are in the heart of Paris, looking at Notre-Dame on the Ile de la Cité, where the Parisii, the tribe for whom the city was named, originally settled long before Caesar came here in 52 B.C. (The Romans stayed four hundred years.) At that time there were eight or nine islands in this region of the Seine; now there are only two—this one and, behind it, the Ile Saint-Louis.

The Place du Parvis, the square in front of Notre-Dame, is the official center of France; stone markers along the French roadside mark the kilometers to this spot. This walk will not take you farther than "0 kilometers Paris," but there is much to see.

The Seine in prehistoric times was a wide, slow-flowing river more than a hundred feet higher than it is today. The river meandered all over the area between Mont Sainte-Geneviève to the south (take a look about five blocks down and you will see the hill) and Montmartre, one mile away to the north.

Even Parisians forget the river was so wide, but in 1910

an extraordinary flood in the month of January reminded them of the tributaries of the Seine still flowing underground. The subterranean waters welled to the surface and swept through the city. From the present course of the river to the Place de l'Opéra and from the Gare Saint-Lazare to the suburbs of the north, the secret Seine came up from hiding and took possession of the city once again.

Postcards depicting the flood show men and women rowing around Paris at the level of street signs. A great many important historical records were lost, including those of some of the major libraries and banks. Deep cellars in this area are still cemented in mud from the flood, and excavations constantly unearth buried architecture and artifacts.

For ancient Paris, this sprawling river, whose waters were sweet and clean enough to drink, was a boon. Because of it, the Parisii felt safe from surprise attacks; an enemy would have to cross large stretches of swamp to reach the island. The river was also an excellent highway for trade, as it still is today. By Gallic times the Seine had already dug its present channel, but the banks to either side, especially the Right Bank, remained swampy and uninhabitable.

The first part of the mainland to be settled was the south or Left Bank, where the ground rose more sharply than on the marshy Right Bank called the Marais, or marsh. (See Walk 5, page 171). If you look up the Rue du Petit Pont with your back to the bridge, you will see, about two hundred yards away and beyond what is now the Rue des Ecoles, the College of France on the left side and the observatory tower of the Sorbonne on the right.

Two thousand years ago, Roman baths stood on these sites, for it was on this hill that the ancient residents finally got far enough above the water line to build important structures. The remains of the baths still exist under the College of France. Other ruins close by, unearthed as recently as 1946, can be seen in the garden of the Cluny Museum. The area between this high-water line and the river, the area you are visiting today, was settled much later.

The site of the present church of Saint-Séverin, the back of which you can see down the Rue du Petit Pont on the right, was a small dry hillock where a hermit chose to settle in the fifth century. Later, as the Seine continued to dig itself a deeper channel, the area between high ground and the river filled with houses and narrow paths.

Even as late as the Middle Ages, the street level was thirty feet (three stories) lower than it is today. This is why three levels of cellar still exist in the seventeenth-century buildings you see in the area. Until the middle of the nineteenth century the streets and alleys of the *quartier* ran steeply down to the river's edge.

The present ground-floor shops (the café Le Notre-Dame and Optique, for example) are on what was once the second floor of these buildings. Notice the thirty-foot embankment that rises from the Seine; where that stands, houses once stood.

The first bridge connecting the Ile de la Cité to the mainland, the present Petit Pont, was built here because at this point the island is closest to the Left Bank. A little fortress, Le Petit Châtelet, which doubled as a tollhouse, stood at the end of the bridge on the spot where you are now. It was the custom then, as it is today on some bridges, to pay a toll in order to pass in and out of the city.

Another, larger, fortress, Le Grand Châtelet, stood on the right bank of this part of the Seine at the Pont Saint-Michel. Both these bastions were used as prisons during the French Revolution. With the help of underground passageways to many points in the vicinity, prison affairs could easily be carried on in secret.

The Petit Pont was not only a passageway; two- and three-story houses and shops lined either side, making it the busiest street in town. In the Middle Ages the picturesque aspect of this bridge, really a street thrown across the river, was enlivened by philosophers offering their intellectual wares, by jugglers, singers, and dog and bear trainers. During the day it was a paradise for cut-purses, at night for cutthroats. The bridge was rebuilt after fire, flood, and attack more times than the French care to count. Fire was the most common cause of destruction, until the eighteenth century, when the bridge was finally rebuilt in stone.

In the Middle Ages people believed that bodies of those drowned in the Seine could be located by setting a votive candle on a wooden disc afloat in the river and noting where it stopped or went out. It was doubly important to find drowned bodies before the authorities did, because a huge fee of 101 *écus*, the equivalent of a year's pay for a manual laborer, is said to have been charged for the delivery of a loved one from the morgue at the Châtelet.

One story about this bridge and its fires has it that a poor old widow whose son had drowned set a candle afloat in hopes of finding his body. The candle floated close to a straw-laden barge, setting it on fire. The barge touched the wooden scaffolding of a pillar of the bridge, and from there the flames spread to the bridge itself. In three days, the raging fire destroyed the bridge and the houses on it.

If you like, climb down the steps on the island side of the channel near the Petit Pont or on the Left Bank toward the Pont au Double, and look at the Seine close up. You will be in the company of fishermen who catch live, though small, fish; of *clochards*, tramps, who find this spot slightly warmer and more private for sleeping than the streets; and of lovers of all ages expressing various degrees of affection.

The Quai de Montebello, the street that runs along the riverside in front of you and is packed with cars (we say this with absolute confidence after having watched the street over an entire year at all hours of the day and night), was built by Baron Georges Haussmann. He was the famous city planner of Napoléon III who, in the 1850s and 1860s, built most of the avenues and boulevards that have fortunately and unfortunately saved Paris for the automobile.

Cross the *quai* with the light (watch for turning cars).

The small strip of park before you was once covered by the Petit Châtelet. Later, an annex of the Hôtel-Dieu hospital was located here. The park was finally cleared in the early 1920s. This little park with benches and the park of Saint-Julien-le-Pauvre to your left (with your back to the river) are the only pieces of green along the Seine, the only spots in Paris as far downstream as the Eiffel Tower that the French have allowed to lie fallow. This pocket-sized park, which once belonged to vagrants and *boule* (bocci) players has now been redesigned and modernized.

Place du Petit Pont

The street that leads out from the bridge is called the **Place du Petit Pont**. At the next crossing its name changes to the Rue du Petit Pont. In both places, the street is the same width. If you look closely at the buildings on either side of the Rue du Petit Pont, you will probably be able to work out why the *rue* is as wide as the *place*.

The apartment houses on the left side of the street were built in the seventeenth century. They are straight buildings with slim rectangular windows, free of ornamentation except for iron grillwork on the windows. On the right side of the street are nineteenth-century buildings, built two hundred years later, and heavy with curves, carvings, protuberances, and balconies. They stand on ground cleared when the street was widened and rebuilt in 1857.

The Rue du Petit Pont lasts one short block, then becomes the Rue Saint-Jacques. From prehistoric times this road, which climbs straight up the gentle hill in front of you, was the main road from Paris to the south.

When the Romans first came to Lutetia, which was what Paris was then called, they came this way. Soon after, they transformed the dirt road into a paved road nine meters (twenty-nine feet) wide. Two huge stones from this construction were found below the surface in 1926; you will see them later in the parvis of Saint-Julien-le-Pauvre. Elephant remains have also turned up, which will give you an appreciation of how the Romans thought big and built big, and why we still speak with admiration and awe of Roman roads.

As early as 1230 the Rue Saint-Jacques was given its present name because the famous pilgrimage to the shrine of Saint James (Saint Jacques) of Compostela traveled south along it. Santiago (Spanish for Saint James) de Compostela, a city near the Atlantic coast of Spain, was rich in scallop shells, *coquilles,* which the pilgrims were quick to gather and bring back as proof of their voyage and their devotion. The pilgrims displayed the shells whenever and wherever possible, and as a result the shells have come to be a common symbol even to this day. Shell Oil uses its name to signify its role as a refueling stop for us on our modern pilgrimages; we eat coquilles Saint Jacques; and shell designs are common as a decoration on buildings and churches, and in wood on furniture.

Rue de la Bûcherie

Turn left into the Rue de la Bûcherie, the street facing the small park, pass the café, **Le Petit Pont**, a good place for a light lunch and a most pleasant spot on a sunny day, and stop at the restaurant **La Bûcherie**.

A *bûcherie* is a storehouse for wood. It was on this street that barges loaded with logs for heating deposited their goods. This restaurant remembers its past, not only in its name, but with a wood fire, which burns on a hearth in the center of the room. It was, and still is, a hangout for actors and politicians, though the celebrities themselves change. The restaurant is expensive, but the quality is always high. A specialty is sole with lobster-and-basil butter.

If you choose not to dine here, peer in at the window

to look at the back wall. It is covered with a piece of tapestry woven for the restaurant by Lurçat, the famous reviver of the ancient art and modern tapestry-maker.

Lurçat used to live upstairs, and wove this wall of tapestry in lieu of paying rent. The entire wall was once covered with Lurçat's work, but the rest is now in the owner's home to protect it from cigarette smoke. In France art and food are closely linked, and in view of this the restaurant owner, M. Bosque, engages an art advisor to help decorate his walls. Paintings by Miró and Jean Hélion (the ex-husband of Peggy Guggenheim) are among the collection.

The house next door, **no. 39**, is most amazing. The houses we have been looking at are mostly seventeenth-century; this one was built in the early sixteenth. It is a small two-story wooden structure, the kind that was typical five hundred years ago and can still be seen in towns like Riquewihr in Alsace, or Conques in southern France, but has almost vanished from most European cities. The building once served as an inn and was hidden from sight for most of its long history. **Le Petit Châtelet**, as the inn was called—after the fortress it stood behind, and to whose employees it gave meat and drink over the centuries—was tucked away until 1909, when the ground was cleared between the Rue de la Bûcherie and the river. This building had been closed for many years, but Chantal Silly, the building owner, restored it, and because of the enormous time and money required, is not cleaning out the twelfth-century *caves*, cellars, under the building.

The little building is architecturally interesting for several reasons. Almost no wooden structures in Paris have survived; the big enemy has been fire, as evidenced by the history of the Petit Pont. Note the large dormer windows that jut out from the steep roofline and the smaller windows on the attic floor above. Step back and look at the exposed side of the building on its right, and you will see coming out from the exterior wall the ends of the framing

George Whitman in front of his famous bookstore

beams used in its construction hundreds of years ago. These are the wooden joists, half of which one sometimes sees as exposed rafters in a ceiling.

Now look at the exposed side of the half-timbered remains of the building on the left. There you will see one of only three open staircases, *escaliers à claire voie,* left in Paris. This was the typical staircase of the sixteenth century; it was replaced in the seventeenth by the closed *escalier à vis*, corkscrew staircase.

Immediately to the left is **Shakespeare and Company**. You will get a hint of the store's uniqueness from the notice board outside and from the amusing announcements. George Whitman, the owner, doesn't try very hard to sell books; he just likes people who like to read. The ground floor is mainly devoted to books-for-sale of all kinds—old and new, almost all in English. Whitman owns the house next door and keeps his own library and an antiquarian bookshop there. The walls are covered with books he does not sell, including a first edition of James Joyce's *Ulysses*. This is where one gets a feeling of Whitman's unusual personality.

The shop itself is a treasure trove of books and people, and if you nose around long enough and look interested, Whitman might invite you to tea. The front room was once a stone courtyard, into it Whitman has set fragments of marble friezes, tiled borders, and brass plaques. The narrow one-way staircase at the very back of the store leads to a maze of book-lined rooms filled with chairs and couches. You can read the books in these rooms, meet people, even take a nap if you wish, and go to the famous tea parties on Sundays at 4 P.M.

More than a bookseller, Whitman takes in travelers, especially serious writers—a vanishing breed, he feels. If an author notifies him ahead of time, he or she may stay in one of Whitman's rooms free or in exchange for working in the shop for a week or so, until other quarters are found.

Shakespeare and Company has always promoted the literary avant-garde. When the publishing house of the same name was originally founded by Sylvia Beach, it was the only house that would publish James Joyce's *Ulysses*. Now Whitman gives young writers a chance to be heard at poetry readings in his library every Monday night at eight and to be published in his review.

Give this store some browsing time. It is generally open from noon to midnight, or one to one. If you want a souvenir of Paris, buy a book and get it stamped here. The inscription around the head of William reads, "Shakespeare and Co. Kilometer Zero Paris."

Notice the Wallace fountain near the corner. See Walk 4, page 133.

Rue Saint-Julien-le-Pauvre

Go around the corner to the right into the **Rue Saint-Julien-le-Pauvre**. **Nos. 4–8** on your right are all owned by the same people. The **Esmeralda Hotel**, **no. 4**, is a hotel named for Victor Hugo's heroine in *The Hunchback of Notre-Dame*. The hotel recently achieved some fame in another book, *Linnea in Monet's Garden,* a children's book written by Christina Björk, and illustrated by Lena Anderson. For connoisseurs of the neighborhood, the details in the book's watercolors will be impressively authentic. The owner of the Esmeralda is, herself, a character for a book. She came to Paris from the provinces and thought that the city was especially beautiful from the Seine. She and her husband went into partnership with a financial backer and, with one decrepit boat, started the **Bateaux Mouches** sight-seeing boats on the Seine. On the first day out the boat malfunctioned, going only in circles. Today, however, this pleasure boat line is a hugely successful tourist attraction, though as a result of her divorce she no longer has any connection to it.

The owner never intended to run a hotel but somehow acquired the building. It had only one bath and was occupied by women who had lived there for forty years and hardly paid any rent. She had to wait for changes in the law before she could evict them, restore the building's seventeenth-century details, and put in all the necessary bathrooms. Today the small rooms are each uniquely decorated with antiques and will fulfill all your dreams of a truly "Left Bank" experience of Paris. Book well in advance.

Notice from across the street the soft-beige stone building, **no. 10**, and, in particular, the ground-floor apartment's elegant windows, which are taller than the others. If you count the panes on each story you will see that with the exception of the second floor, the number of panes decreases and the windows get smaller as you go up. At the very top, almost out of view, the tiny mansard windows (named after their inventor, the architect François

No. 10, Rue Saint-Julien-le-Pauvre: *before the advent of the elevator, the best apartment was on the second floor*

Mansart), which peep out from the sloping roof, are reduced to one small pane. The taller windows of the ground floor mean, of course, higher ceilings, a mark of distinction still dear to the French, especially in old, non-standardized apartments.

The exterior decoration tells the same story. Thus, the iron railings on the protruding sills of the two balconies on this first floor are finer than those on the floor above, after which there are no more balconies or grillwork at all. (Look at other examples of handwrought iron decoration on nineteenth-century houses as well as those of the seventeenth century as you walk around the city.)

It is clear that the first floor above the street was once the coveted apartment, *appartement noble.* The ground floor, called the *rez-de-chaussée*, which means "even with the road," was reserved for the concierge's one or two rooms, the courtyards, and the rubbish. The wealthy nobles and bankers stepped up one flight; the middle-class professionals and shopkeepers climbed two or three; the servants and workers trudged to the top. Apartment buildings, therefore, in all but the poorest neighborhoods, were microcosms of French society.

The advent of the elevator, however, turned this arrangement upside down and made possible the one-class high-rise building. Today the servants' rooms—often used as workshops or extra bedrooms, sleep-in servants being hard to come by—are located on the ground floor alongside the concierge; the apartments cost more the higher you go, and the prize residence is a sunlit, glass-enclosed, terraced retreat at the top, as far as possible from the city's noise and dirt. There are relatively few of these newer apartment buildings on the Left Bank, but the next time you visit the bourgeois neighborhoods of western Paris (the seventh, eighth, and sixteenth arrondissements), take a look at the imposing, prosperous buildings with cut-stone façades, and follow the lines of balconies up to the elegant penthouses at the top.

A very important person lives upstairs in the house at

Themis, the Greek goddess of Justice, at no. 14 Rue Saint-Julien-le-Pauvre

no. 12: the architect Claude Frémin. He is responsible for some of the most remarkable restorations in the area. Frémin's latest project has been the restoration of the street: the wide brick pavements have returned it to their original medieval width.

The **Tea Caddy** at **no. 14** is one of the nicer tea shops in Paris. A stop in this cozy shop is wonderful. Light meals (mainly eggs in various forms), pastries made on the premises, and a wide variety of teas are served. The Tea Caddy was founded in 1928 by Miss Kinklin, an English governess to a Rothschild offspring. The tea shop, which she had always dreamed of, was the family's retirement gift to her.

The Tea Caddy was formerly the stables of the building next door. The entrance of no. 14 is an impressive stone gateway with massive wooden doors. Look above at the pediment where Themis, the Greek goddess of "justice in all its relations to men," sits. She is represented as a dignified and commanding prophetess holding the scales of justice; she is surrounded by olive branches of peace, while a cherub holds an hourglass.

The symbolism of this sculpture was carefully chosen in the early seventeenth century when this entry was added to the official residence of Isaac Laffémas, prefect of police of the Châtelet under Cardinal Richelieu. The prefect was, among other things, the king's prosecutor, and we have cause to wonder how wisely he used those scales. While he and his family lived comfortably above ground, three levels of cellars below were used as a prison. The cellars date from the fourteenth century and were originally used to house the monks from the church of Saint-Julien-le-Pauvre across the street. This prison eventually fell into disuse in the seventeenth century, but 150 years later, in 1793, the Revolution created such an overflow of prisoners in the Petit and Grand Châtelets and everywhere else that these cells were restored to use.

We have it on good authority that instruments of torture, real ones, now rusted, existed in the lowest basement. Hélène, an excellent hairdresser whose salon was just down the street, saw them when she and her husband were on the track of a damaged water pipe: a rack and a devilish seat with a hole in it to allow the heat from boiling oil to cook a bound and helpless victim. In the name of justice, of course.

The house has been converted into apartments whose owners keep the door locked. This is unfortunate because the interior restoration was beautifully done and is a perfect example of how modern additions and restoration can enhance an original fifteenth-century structure. Look over the wall at the façade of the building. It is merely façade. Concealed underneath this trompe l'oeil of plaster cut to look like stone is a fifteenth-century half-timbered wall.

Visit the odd church of **Saint-Julien-le-Pauvre**. Before you is a truncated edifice with a lopsided pediment crowning a flat, improvised façade, the remains of a thirteenth-century pillar, and an iron-caged well flanking the front portal. There is much to tell about Saint Julien himself, and you may wish to sit inside the church (cool in summer, warm in winter) and read his story, which supposedly took place in the first century. The story has been told by Flaubert in his *Trois Contes*.

Julien, the son of a noble family, was an avid hunter. One day he was having excellent luck in the forest. He had killed a doe and her fawn and was about to shoot the stag when the animal turned and spoke to him. "How darest thou kill my family and pursue me, thou who wilt one day kill thine own father and mother?" Julien was staggered by these words and swore a sacred oath that he would never hunt again. To prevent the fulfillment of the prediction, he left his parents' castle and went off to serve the king.

In the course of his duty Julien traveled to distant lands, where he fought so valiantly that the king knighted him and rewarded him with a castle and the hand in marriage of the widow of a rich lord. The couple lived together very happily, except for Julien's irrepressible passion for the hunt. One morning his wife encouraged him to go into the forest, saying that he had abstained long enough and, besides, it could in no way affect his parents. Julien succumbed and set out to hunt. But though he imagined game in every thicket he could kill nothing.

In Julien's absence an old and travel-weary couple arrived at his castle. His wife took them in and, as they conversed, discovered they were Julien's parents, who had searched for him everywhere since his unexplained departure. She welcomed them heartily and invited them to stay, offering them her own bed.

When Julien returned from the hunt, tired and frustrated, he went straight to the bedroom to rest. Opening the door he perceived two figures in his bed and flew into a rage. "This is the reason my wife encouraged me to hunt," he said to himself, and he drew his sword and slew the sleeping figures. At that his wife came to tell him the good news of his parents' arrival. When Julien realized what he had done, he wept bitterly. "What will become of me, most unfortunate man? It is my dear parents I have killed. I have fulfilled the promise of the stag on the very day that I broke my vow never to hunt again. I will enjoy no rest until I know God has accepted my repentance."

With these words he resolved to abandon his estate

Julien and his wife ferrying a beggar across the Seine

and fortune in order to do penance. His wife would not let him leave alone, and so the two settled on the shores of a large river, ferrying people across the water and offering them lodgings in the small guest house that they built on this spot.

One bleak winter night, when Julien had gone to bed exhausted, there was a knock at the door. A hideous stranger, half-frozen and half-dead, stood there asking first for hospitality and then to be rowed across the river. Julien brought him into his own bed and treated him with care. Later, as he was ferrying him across the river, the stranger, who had looked so hideous moments before, was suddenly transformed into a radiant angel. He said, "Julien, the Lord sent me to tell thee that thy repentance hath been accepted and that thy wife and thyself will soon be able to rest in God."

Julien's story is depicted in a remarkable fourteenth-century stone relief, which is now fixed onto the façade of a modern cinema around the corner at no. 42 Rue Galande, which we shall see later.

Not only was the large river where Julien and his wife settled the Seine, but the site of their house later became the junction of the two main Roman roads from Paris to the south: the Rue Saint-Jacques led to Orléans, and the

Rue Galande led to Lyons and Italy. Actual proof of the existence of an oratory and hostelry on this spot dates from the sixth century, when Bishop Gregory of Tours visited the area and the church of Saint-Julien in particular. Records have been found showing that Gregory preached a midnight mass here in 587.

Both the hostelry and oratory were destroyed in 866 by the Norman invaders. The church was rebuilt much later, between 1170 and 1240. Much of that structure remains today, making Saint-Julien the oldest church in Paris. Although Notre-Dame was started a few years earlier, in 1163, it was not completed until 1330. Parts of the church of Saint-Germain-des-Prés—the bell tower, the bases of two towers, and part of the nave—are older, but at the time it was built the church was outside the city walls, so it doesn't count for strict antiquarians. Saint-Julien-le-Pauvre is a poor church in comparison with the other two. It has neither bell tower nor transept, but it does have lots of pillars.

What the church lacks in appearance it makes up for in colorful history. The original center of learning in Paris was Notre-Dame in the Ile de la Cité. It was Peter Abelard, the famous and infamous theologian-philosopher, who broke with established doctrine there at the beginning of the twelfth century and led a massive student exodus to Saint-Julien-le-Pauvre on the Left Bank. Three thousand rebels went along with him, thereby creating what became known as the Latin Quarter, that is, the quarter of Latin-speaking clerics.

Saint-Julien-le-Pauvre became the official seat of the newly chartered University of Paris and enjoyed the privilege of being the site of the election of the *rector magnificus* and of a sermon every two years restating the rights of students and teachers. The church grew rich and built a network of underground cells to house more than a hundred monks. In time, however, the center of instruction shifted south, and by 1449 the monks had been reduced to a lonely three.

In 1524 the church was almost destroyed; the next year it was decided never to hold elections there again. Students, unhappy over the election of a new rector, proceeded to break chairs, windows, furniture, and statues, forcing the church to close. With closure came neglect. An appraiser in 1640 noted that the rain and weather penetrated the building "as if it were open countryside."

This is why the present entrance stands far back from the original front of the church, which stood about where the street runs now. The whole entrance hall was on the point of collapse and had to be removed in the middle of the seventeenth century. All that is left are the ravaged thirteenth-century pillar with thin colonettes above, on the left side, and the twelfth-century flowering well, on the right. Beside the well lies a huge slab of stone that dates from the fourth century but was unearthed only in 1926. These stones formed part of the famous Roman road that became the Rue Saint-Jacques.

After its long period of abandonment, the church and its land were ceded in 1655 to the Hôtel Dieu, the city hospital. The hospital restored the remains of the church sufficiently for it to serve as its chapel as well. During the French Revolution, however, more than a hundred years later, the chapel, along with so many other churches, was shut down.

Saint-Julien continued to suffer ignominy and was used alternatively as a salt storehouse, as fairgrounds for wool merchants, and as a flour granary. Photographs from the nineteenth century show barrels of goods piled on the parvis, the area in front of the entrance. Houses and stores leaned against the church, glad to use its wall as one of their own.

Sometime after the Hôtel Dieu took over Saint-Julien and its property, it built two wide three-story annexes on the Left Bank facing the river, between the Petit Pont and the Pont au Double. These massive additions blocked a view of the river and darkened the streets in this area. Photographs taken from the front of the church looking toward the Seine show a street that looks like a dead end. The buildings were finally taken down in 1877, when the hospital confined itself to its historic location on the Ile de la Cité next to Notre-Dame. The city fathers decided then that no structure would ever again be built on this spot. That is why we are fortunate enough today to have two green pockets on the banks of the Seine on the Quai de Montebello.

It was not a disaster to demolish these squat sick wards. Hospital care in those days was to be avoided like the plague; prayer was said to account for much of what healing did take place. But it would have been a disaster to tear down Saint-Julien itself. That intention seems scarcely credible, but in fact an extension of the Rue Monge (what is now the Rue Lagrange) was planned that would have cut into this area and gone right through the church to the Rue Saint-Jacques. At the last minute, as is so often the case when it comes to saving historical monuments, the plans were revoked, and Saint-Julien and the small neighborhood remained intact.

Look at the uncomplicated interior of the church. You may be surprised to see a rood screen (iconostasis) with three doors and six rows of icons in front of the altar. There is a simple explanation for these unexpected objects. In 1889 the unused church was given by the archdiocese of Paris to the Eastern Catholic community, the Melchites. The service, sung in Greek, can be heard on Sunday mornings.

Most striking is the tremendous number of twelfth-century columns, especially in such a small area. The capitals, like those in Notre-Dame, are decorated with leaf and fern patterns, except for one on the right-hand side nearest the screen. From that one, four harpies, birdlike women with wings, peer down at you, warning perhaps of the wages of sin. Storytelling on capitals was typical of the earlier Romanesque style of architecture for the benefit of the illiterate masses. Notice also the large arabesque iron music stand to your left that faces the screen.

Outside again (with your back to the church entrance), look to your left at the back of a seventeenth-century building covered with fake timbering, nailed on forty years ago to give an appearance of great age, as though three hundred years were not enough. Contrast this with the genuine article, Le Petit Châtelet, on the Rue de la Bûcherie.

The blood-red door belongs to **La Guillotine Pub**, formerly called the Caveau des Oubliettes. The entrance is now around the corner on the Rue Galande. It is an underground cabaret installed in what was once a prison. *Oubliettes,* from the French word meaning "to forget," were cells where prisoners were put away in solitary holes and left there with nothing but a grate above for food to go in and waste to go out. Turnover of occupants was rapid.

The waiters, garbed in medieval costume, will show you old prison holes with fingernail messages scratched by the dying, a guillotine, a chastity belt, and barbaric instruments of torture. But it would seem that the proprietors have allowed themselves some poetic license in these matters. In fact, the cells of the Caveau were used not for prisoners but for monks, while the real *oubliettes* are those we spoke about on the right side of the Rue Saint-Julien-le-Pauvre.

La Guillotine Pub is fun, especially if your French is good enough to follow the words of the entertainers. If not, there are always the gestures. The pub is open every night from nine-thirty to two in the morning.

Before turning into the Rue Galande go into the garden next to Saint-Julien. This is the **Square René-Viviani**, the loveliest park on the banks of the Seine. Eight hundred years ago it was the scene of boisterous, bustling student activity and dormitories. Later it became the site of one of the annexes of the Hôtel Dieu. Forty years ago it was the untended backyard of Saint-Julien. Today it is an oasis amid the concrete, stone, and asphalt of some of the busiest streets in Paris. Here, you will find tired tourists and passersby, couples, mothers and children, and an occasional vagrant. Ordinarily, the French do not allow anyone to walk or play on the grass. But you can in the Square Viviani, because everyone is more relaxed in this part of town.

Paris is filled with parks and small squares, but this one has more to offer than most. It has the great distinction of affording from its benches what may well be the finest view of Notre-Dame. After peering through the trees and changing your seat several times, turn and look at pieces of church sculpture in the park itself. Those odd fragments of broken statuary, worn down by time and weather, were once a part of the Cluny Abbey. When pieces of sculpture decorating churches decay beyond recognition, they are moved to parks and replaced by whole new copies made in restoration workshops behind Notre-Dame.

What passes for the oldest tree in Paris stands in this park, but not without the help of stone buttresses. The acacia (known as a false acacia—*Robinia pseudoacacia*), which still blooms every spring (a miracle of tenacity), was planted in 1680 by a Mr. Robin who brought it from Guyana. Two kinds of props hold it up: the modern straight-lined, buttresslike crutch and the older imitation trunk of ridged stone.

A fascinating sculpture and fountain by Georges Jeanclos, dated 1995, present Julien in all his compassion and caring. He is entwined on a triangular pyramid surrounded by sufferers while water pours from the heads of three stags above. Jeanclos says, "I wanted to express the action of supporting and carrying the bodies of others in an act of love, tenderness, and compassion."

Return to the church and continue walking around it until you reach a sealed window, which is in a lower garden. Directly behind this window is the apse of Saint-Julien; in front there once was a well. It was a mystical well that supposedly cured the crippled and the sick. The window in the apse of the church was turned into a door for easy access to the well. One day the church decided to give the water away free. Suddenly it cured no one. The door was walled over.

Go up the stairs and cross the square to what is now the **Rue Lagrange** (named after the great mathematician and astronomer who helped invent the metric system during the French Revolution), which starts at the *quai* and then bends toward the Place Maubert.

The *rue*, from the *quai* to the bend, adjacent to the park, has swallowed what was once the Rue du Fouarre, of which only a little leg is left, connecting the Rue Lagrange and the Rue Dante. In the Middle Ages this was a narrow way, lined solid with student housing, and its animation and intellectual activity made it one of the most famous streets in Europe. Classes were held in the open air, the students sitting on the ground and not on benches so that, as a bull of Pope Urban V in 1366 put it, "occasion for haughty pride be kept away from youth." The ground was always filthy and often damp, so the students spread straw to sit on. The Old French word for straw is *feurre* or *fouarre*, close to the English word "forage." Hence the name of the street, originally named the Rue des Ecoliers after the students.

Classes were taught by such notables as Peter Abelard and Albertus Magnus. At a later date, Dante, whose street begins where the present Rue du Fouarre ends, studied here. Dante refers to the *vico degli strami* (literally, the road of straws) in his *Paradiso* (10:137) and speaks of the violent discussions he shared in and listened to there.

When the Rue du Fouarre was in effect the campus of the University of Paris, the students lived in dormitories called colleges in the Square Viviani. Each dormitory represented a different "nation," and collectively they constituted the College of Nations. In the thirteenth century these were Normandy, Picardy, France, and England. In time these proliferated, and all European and even some Asian countries were represented in Paris. Thousands of students and hangers-on filled this area.

Vagabonds sleeping on the students' beds during the day and high life among the students and their clashes with the citizens gave the street a bad reputation. In 1358 Charles V, then regent, was forced to chain the street at both ends to keep it closed at night. Today the old road is a wide thoroughfare, and the rush of cars crossing from the Left Bank to the Ile de la Cité is continuous.

Rue Galande

Recross the park, where the colleges stood, and leave it by the gate through which you entered. Go left, past the church, to the corner of the **Rue Galande** and the Rue Saint-Julien-le-Pauvre. This place marks the beginning of the road that led to Lyons and Rome. In 1202 the street took the name Garlande, later Galande, after the name of a family who owned a large enclosure of land here. This was the road that students and teachers took to go from the Ile, or from Saint-Julien, to the Rue du Fouarre, and it remained as important as that little road. In 1672 the street was widened to all of eight meters (twenty-six feet) and became one of the best addresses in Paris, a place where families of the nobility lived. After the Revolution, though, things went downhill, and by 1900 the guidebooks were advertising Galande as one of the seamiest streets in the city. Much restoration, some of the best in the area, has taken place on this street, and we will be able to see several of these magically transformed buildings.

Find the two tiny houses squeezed in against already existing walls. Watch for rooms or houses tucked in between existing walls or roofs; it is an economical way to build. **No. 75** is a wooden house, a rarity, above a restaurant. **No. 77** is a french-fry place from which you can carry off your lunch and eat in the Square Viviani.

The **Trois Mailletz** at **no. 56** has a long history. The stonemasons who were building Notre-Dame came here for drinks and food. After World War II it became known

Sixteenth-century frieze at no. 65 Rue Galande

for its jazz clubs and the torture instruments in the *oubliettes* in the cellar, the same cellar as 14 Rue Saint-Julien-le-Pauvre. In the early 1980s the club was sold to a group of young people who remodeled the building and threw out the torture instruments. When they couldn't pay the rent, they too were thrown out. Today there is an excellent fifties-style classic jazz club on the spot, with food and music until 3 A.M.

At the door of **no. 52** a stone pillar has been uncovered. Curious caryatids adorn the corners of every window of this house, front and back; the neighbors say the figure is Quasimodo. This is the entrance of La Guillotine Pub. Visit **Le Chat Huant, nos. 50–52**, an attractive shop with Asian calligraphy articles, jewelry, and clothes.

Cybele at **no. 65 bis** is a gallery, bookstore, and archaeological treasure trove. The paintings are modern, featured in changing exhibits in the restored, vaulted twelfth-century cellar, while upstairs there is a fine collection of books on the ancient civilizations of Egypt, Greece, and

Twentieth-century frieze at no. 59 Rue Galande

Rome, along with authentic archaeological artifacts in a restored seventeenth-century building.

If you can get into the courtyard of **no. 48**, try to find toward the center back an oval stone which is an entry to an underground cellar. A square stone under the planter on the left opens to a corkscrew staircase descending to the first basement.

No. 65, now restored, was built in the sixteenth century and was occupied by the noble family of Châtillon. The restoration here was undertaken by the City of Paris. The residents moved out during the work period but were given the option to return to this now magnificent building. The rents are low and the tenants have the right to pass on their apartments to their children.

Above the doorway, notice the recently discovered frieze of a woman's head surrounded by garlands of roses and oak leaves. We were the first to get a glimpse of her. One day as we were studying the building something fell at our feet from above the doorway. It was a totally black piece of nineteenth-century plaster of paris, which had covered over the original sixteenth-century stone garland carving. Not as exciting as uncovering Eve at the cathedral of Autun, but on our scale, still pretty terrific.

Garlands of acorn and oak appear above the first-floor windows, rolling waves above the next bank of windows, and rosettes above the next. Garlands of flowers are a fitting decoration for this street, Rue Galande. The two-windowed, rounded gabled roof is crowned by a double ledge extending from the roofline. This sort of gable-front house, with the roof at a right angle to the street, was declared illegal in the sixteenth century because rainwater collected between the buildings. From that time on, the roofline had to be parallel to the street so that the rain would drain into gutters instead of falling on passersby. About thirty gable-front houses still exist in Paris, two farther down a street that we will pass later on. The stone sculpture of garlands and an urn above the entry was also uncovered by the restoration work on the building.

Nos. 61 and **59** look like one building on the outside but hold surprises on the inside; these were not revealed to us until we had walked the street dozens of times. The flowing tresses of the lovely Art Nouveau lady crown the entrance to both buildings here. She is three hundred years younger than the lady to your right. No. 59 was, as it says in the stone, built in 1910, and it and **no. 57** are examples of the brick construction that Paris has used for low-cost houses. Rich and not-so-rich Parisians insist on buildings with cut-stone façades.

Notice that the building is set back about ten feet from its neighbor. This is an example of the fond hope the city had of moving back the building line in order to widen the entire street eventually. As each building was torn down, its replacement had to be set back this prescribed distance. Fortunately, few buildings do come down in Paris, and that explains the ins and outs of Paris sidewalks.

Except for the woman's head, this part of the building is not exceptional. The door here is usually open. If not, open it and walk in. The hall is divided in two; the left side leads to apartments, but down the corridor on the right side you will find an iron-grille door, which opens to an old and beautifully restored house, **no. 61**.

The stairway and stairwell beyond the iron grille are an example of the care taken to bring the building back to its original shape. When Martin Granel and his family bought the place, it was almost impossible to get inside. The wall to the right of the staircase bellied out so far that the pillar of the house on the ground floor had to be reset. The brick-and-wood stairs were redone with old wood that came from the South of France. The banister behind the pillar dates from the time of Louis XIII. Doors, paneling, and rafters were also brought from the south to complete the interior of the house. Every piece has been fitted and finished with great care.

The courtyard to the left of the staircase is filled with curious sights. The stones on the ground come from a former printing establishment next door, and black print and designs, in reverse, are barely legible on the portions of the floor that are not frequently walked on. A once-open staircase, now enclosed behind a wide expanse of beautiful windows, looks down on this green courtyard with its stone fountain. We were fortunate enough to be able to roam the house from top to bottom. Each landing and corner, and there were many, was used to good advantage. Old armoire doors concealed the washer and dryer. Velvet hangings enclosed a bedroom.

In 1198 some of this land on the odd-numbered side of the Rue Galande was given to the Jews for a burial ground. It had once served as such in Gallo-Roman times, from A.D. 270 to A.D. 360. In the twelfth century, Jews were returning from a sixteen-year exile imposed by King Philippe Auguste, one of the many that they suffered in different countries during those years of crusading fervor and intolerance. They came back, of course, to their old neighborhoods at the Petit Pont and the Rue de la Harpe, where they already had a cemetery, though it was no longer available to them. In any event, when Philippe III became king in 1270, he declared that the Jews of Paris could have only one synagogue and only one cemetery, so the one on Rue Galande was given up.

Then, in 1311, another king, Philippe le Bel, expelled the Jews once again, and closed the other cemetery as well. The absence of any trace of tombstones suggests that the Galande ground may have been used by Jews of modest means. The engraved tombstones found in 1849, however, under no. 79 Boulevard Saint-Germain, have generated passionate Hebraic studies.

No. 46 was the **Auberge des Deux Signes**, not only one of the best restaurants in the area but also a masterpiece of discovery and restoration. M. and Mme Dhulster retired on February 27, 1998, after many years of devotion, and it was a sad time for all. They were gracious hosts and preservers of French culture. We can't say what will take the restaurant's place, but we can't imagine that the architectural finds that were made there could be kept from the public.

We shall tell the story of this building as we heard it from the owners, M. and Mme Dhulster. M. Dhulster's father, who came from Auvergne, had a coal and wood business, which he combined, as was customary, with a restaurant-bar to serve the hearty needs of his workers. Because there was no central heating in those days, each flat needed its own fuel; because there were no lifts, haulers had to climb a lot of stairs to deliver these goods. (The zinc counter—one French term for bar is *le zinc*—that once served the workers is gone.)

The coal and wood business turned into a restaurant, and then restoration began. Read about the interior first, and then enter the building, book in hand, no matter who has moved in, and ask to see the treasures.

The uncovering and restoration of no. 46 began when the municipality planned to realign the street and remove part of the building, which dates from the sixteenth century. Because the construction of the house was superior to that of many around it, the owners received permission to let it stand and to restore it. Among their most successful efforts was the cleaning of coat after coat of plaster from the large beige stone pillars in front. These are now separated by sections of plate glass, but earlier these spaces were filled with many smaller panes, and originally there may have been only shutters, open for trade in the daytime, closed at night.

The big surprises lay hidden in the back of the house, where construction from the fourteenth century had been covered. Not afraid of hard work, Dhulster decided in 1962 to dig out a lower level of his basement. Like all the basements in the area, this had been flooded and filled with mud in 1910, and undoubtedly during previous inundations as well.

A few steps down, he began to unearth vaulted arches built six hundred years ago. With the help of his son,

Dhulster carried out twelve thousand coal sacks of dirt and gravel over a period of two years, finally revealing a large vaulted room that had served as a dormitory for a hundred monks from Saint-Julien-le-Pauvre. All of this was done without official permission. When the Dhulsters finally told the proper city officials, the latter yielded to the spectacular evidence, authorized the work, and saw to it that the crumbled arches were reinforced by the most modern techniques and the use of prestressed concrete.

In 1969, while the family was redoing the bedrooms on the second and third floors in the back part of the house, a pick hit some iron and the unveiling of an entire fifteenth-century Gothic window began. Part of Saint-Julien-le-Pauvre, the chapel of Saint Blaise for masons and carpenters once stood here. It was demolished in 1770, obviously not completely, and in 1812 a house was built over and around the wall that remained standing.

This window, a stone *pignon ogival*, pointed gable, had to be completely dismantled (each piece weighed about five hundred pounds) because the floor and ceiling rafters attached to it had pulled it out of shape. The enormous yet fragile puzzle was then pieced together and returned to its original position. Jacques Chirac, then mayor of Paris, awarded M. Dhulster the National Order of Merit for the realization of this building.

Before you leave the vaulted window, look to your left on the ground. Here is a well that once stood outside this church window in a tiny alley. Not only is its border in perfect condition but the well still has water in it, beautifully limpid. Dhulster let himself down this deep well and, as usual, made another discovery. Some of the stones move on pivots; that means there is still another buried cellar, farther down.

Be sure to see the stone spiral staircase down to the basement and the beautifully finished wooden one from the ground floor to the first.

Directly across the street at **no. 57** is a well-run restaurant, **La Rôtisserie Galande**. The chef worked for nine years with the celebrated Jacques Manière, of Dodin Bouffant. They use two huge rotisseries, one for meats and one for fish. We had slices of rare roast beef and roasted potatoes smothered in garlicky green beans. Plain but delicious and reasonably priced.

Outside on the wall of **no. 42** find the sculptured stone rectangle depicting Saint Julien and his wife rowing their charge across the river (see page 26). It is the oldest standard in Paris and mentioned as early as 1380.

At the corner to the right, at **no. 4 Rue Dante**, is the **Librairie Gourmande**. This is one of the two cookbook stores in Paris. The proprietor, Mme Geneviève Baudon, was a bookseller, *bouquiniste,* on the Seine for over thirty years with her husband. When she reached three thousand books, she had to make a decision: open a bookstore or a restaurant. Now in her bookstore, she advises some of the best chefs in France and sells to "foodies," collectors, and people like the rest of us. The walls, tables, and even the floor are covered with books old and new; the valuable ones are in a glass case at the back of the store. A picture of her dear friend Julia Child hangs on the wall next to her desk.

Continue down the Rue Galande with the Rue Dante on your right. At **nos. 29 and 31** you can see fine examples of medieval gabled roofs. Notice the room tucked in between the sloping gabled roof and the straight wall of the house next door. The restoration of these buildings, like most restorations here, took place about thirty years ago under the careful surveillance of the Monuments Historiques, a group that watches over all historic renovations in Paris. Claude Frémin, the architect, has hopes of restoring the gabled rooftops to the entire street.

Rue de l'Hôtel Colbert

Across the Rue Lagrange on the **Rue de l'Hôtel Colbert** is the **Hippopotamus**, where at all hours of the day you can get grilled steak or hamburger—without the roll.

On the other corner, be sure to look at where the plaster has been neatly chipped away to show you the original stones underneath. Walk down a bit, past the first two windows, and you will come to a rounded one, probably once an entrance. If you have the good fortune to find the curtain pulled back, look in and you will see an extraordinary blend of old and new—a huge stone fireplace to the left, a modern sunken kitchen to the back, a spiral staircase to the right. A few steps farther, and you can enter the apartment building (remember that you might have to press a button in order to be admitted and again to leave) and look through an iron grille to an interior garden. Tall French windows look out on to a raised grassy section dotted with trees.

At **no. 12**, a sixteenth-century house, is the restaurant **Les Bouchons**, once used by the homeless as *un asile de nuit*, shelter, where they slept *à la corde*, on the rope. A rope was stretched across the room and for a sou men (where were the women?) could stand and rest their arms and heads on it. At dawn, the rope was dropped, and all the men, brutally awakened, fell to the floor. Notice the wooden doors, beams, and stone spiral staircase. François Clerc serves excellent southwestern cuisine, ranging from reasonable to fairly expensive. Wine is sold at the store price. Reserve.

The **Hôtel Colbert, no. 7**, is a superb recent copy from a seventeenth-century plan found in the archives of the Ecole des Beaux Arts. This is an elegant but personal small hotel and a lovely place to stay. A *salon de thé* decorated with large, upholstered chairs is perfect for relaxing after a long day of Pariswalking. The rooms have all been redone, and they are now air-conditioned. An apartment for four under the eaves with a skylit view of Notre-Dame and the rooftops of Paris just might fulfill your most romantic dreams.

Look across the street at the corner building. Above the street sign on the wall, **no. 8**, you will find an old name of the street cut into the stone, Rue des Rats, the "street of rats." An old resident assures us the name was fitting, that rats abounded just a short time ago. The name of the street was originally the Rue d'Arras (arrah) because a college from the diocese of Arras was founded here in 1320. A poet rhymed it with *rats*, and it wasn't long before the new name took hold and was inscribed as such when street names were cut in stone. In 1829 the inhabitants of the street petitioned for something more elegant, and the city authorities took the name from an important *hôtel* (that is, a grand private residence) that once stood on the street. Why that house was called the Hôtel le Colbert no one knows, for Colbert never lived there. In any event, the original building was demolished when the Rue Lagrange was cut through in 1887.

The wall into which this street sign has been carved is the side of the Amphithéâtre Winslow, part of the old Faculty of Medicine. Look up at the round decorated window, called a bull's-eye, *oeil-de-boeuf,* which you will soon see inside. The entry is just around the corner to the left on the Rue de la Bûcherie.

When you get there, notice the ironwork on a 1909 grille inside the courtyard on the right-hand wall. Enter the building, which is now a center to advise government employees about city benefits, from vacations to jobs. Take a comfortable seat to the left and read the history.

The Faculty of Medicine was created by King Philippe VI in 1331. Before this, in the Middle Ages, only monks had studied medicine, necessarily limiting medical care to men. (Given the ignorance of the medical profession, the women were lucky to be neglected.) In 1131, however, an ordinance forbade men of the church to study medicine, a prohibition confirmed in 1163 by the Council of Tours and thereafter enforced by excommunication.

Thus, there were no trained doctors in France until 1220, when several small schools were opened; they subsequently merged into this Faculty of Medicine more than a hundred years later. At first, classes were held with the other schools on the Rue du Fouarre, and exams were given in the masters' houses. It was not until 1472 that the present buildings were started. They were subsequently enlarged on several occasions, and they flourished until the Revolution, when the Faculty of Medicine, like all the other schools, was abolished. In 1808 the buildings passed into private hands, and in the next century knew a wide variety of uses: as a laundry, an inn, an apartment building, even a brothel. In 1909 the structures were finally rescued and restored and classified by the city as historic monuments.

In Jacques Hillairet's *Dictionnaire Historique des Rues de Paris*, there is a marvelous description of the kind of medicine that was taught by this school in the fourteenth and fifteenth centuries:

> The prescribed remedies were, for a long time, limited to a choice of three: laxatives, enemas, and bleeding. It was in this tradition that Charles Bouvard, Louis XIII's doctor, administered to the king in one year 47 bleedings, 212 enemas, and 215 purgatives, total: 474 treatments, after which the doctor was ennobled. Richelieu submitted in the same year to 54 bleedings and 202 purgations. As to Ambroise Paré, he bled 27 times in four days a 28-year-old young man, that is, a bloodletting every 4 hours for 4 days, and in 1609 Le Moyne took 225 pints of blood in 15 months from a young girl.

There were, however, other treatments. A treatise on medicine that appeared in 1539 affirms that the blood of a hare cures gallstones; the droppings of mice, bladder stones; the excrement of dogs, sore throats; boiled wood louse, scrofula. It is also written that lung of fox washed in wine cures asthma; earthworms washed in white wine, jaundice;

kittens, finely chopped with a goose and salt, gout; the excrement of a red-headed man, weak eyes. The wax from your ears applied to the nostrils promotes sleep. Montaigne wrote that a man's saliva will kill a serpent. In 1540 André Fournier, professor at the School of Medicine, gave this recipe to make hair grow again: boil three hundred slugs, skim off the grease, add three tablespoons of olive oil and one tablespoon of honey, and anoint your skull with the mixture. One of his colleagues in this same period recommended the following remedy to get rid of fleas: take the heads of many red herrings, tie them with a string, place this in the mattress, and the fleas will flee.

From the reception room, enter the room to your left, where people are being helped, and turn left again into the rotunda, the Amphithéâtre Winslow, built in 1744. The floor of the amphitheater is inlaid with rosewood in a pattern representing the sun. The balconies are embellished with wrought iron and friezes of roosters and pelicans, supported by eight Doric columns. It is said that this room was used for medical demonstrations. We wonder what one could see from the balconies.

Rue de la Bûcherie

Turn right into the **Rue de la Bûcherie** to **Galerie Urubamba** at **no. 4**, which was formerly a kosher butcher shop. Find the marble slabs that served as counters and the meat hooks above the window. Today, the shop has a fascinating collection of Native North and South American arts, including fabulous feathered headdresses and silver-and-turquoise jewelry.

Rue Frédéric-Sauton

You are now at the intersection of the Rue de la Bûcherie and the **Rue Frédéric-Sauton** (on the right) and the **Rue du Haut Pavé** (on the left, or river, side). This apartment building on the left-hand side, between the Rue de la Bûcherie and the *quai*, shows the kind of reclamation and restoration that is taking place throughout the area—beautiful work for a privileged few. It costs a lot of money to buy land in the heart of old Paris, relocate tenants, then gut the buildings and redo the interiors from scratch. But then, people are prepared to pay a great deal to live across the river from Notre-Dame.

Rouvray, at **no. 3 Rue Frédéric-Sauton**, was one of the first shops to brighten up this once dark and dreary street. It is run by an American, Diane de Obaldia, who is a connoisseur of American patchwork quilts, and is the center for this art in Europe. Next door, where women gather and quilt, Rouvray offers classes, equipment, and books for instruction.

In **no. 2 Rue du Haut Pavé**, don't miss **Tapisseries de la Bûcherie**, the showroom for exquisite tapestry and embroidered creations. Mme Dominique Sarl has written a book on medieval tapestry, recognized by its field of "the thousand flowers." She gives courses and lectures here, as well as at Cluny and the Louvre and all over France. She hopes to make this corner a center of embroidery and tapestry. If you have a conversation with Madame, ask to see, from her window, the historic courtyard next door.

Impasse Maubert

Next door is the entrance to the **Impasse Maubert**. There is a private house on the right, in a small garden. It was on this same spot that one of the first "colleges" in Paris stood. In 1206 a college of Constantinople, conveniently close to Place Maubert and the Rue du Fouarre, was created for Greek students.

Return to the Rue Frédéric-Sauton, now barred to the automobile. **Jeanne et Jérémy** at **no. 4** sells collectors teddy bears and dolls that are absolutely fascinating. Each character is signed and numbered. The expressions and clothing are so singular and appealing, you feel you'd like to meet them. Dolls are made in a series of eight, each dressed differently. Well worth the price tags that begin at $200.

The **Tortue Electrique** at **no. 7** is a toy shop specializing in antique and unusual toys. The mock turtle in the store is its mascot. The book collection contains contemporary works on the theme of games, as well as iconography and documentation related to the concept of play. This is a grown-up toy shop. Tortue Electrique (electric turtle) is the name of an early game.

This new building replaced a jumble of old buildings around a large courtyard. One section used to house a famous Czech puppet theater that played wonderful fairy tales with the help of a devoted audience.

At the back of the courtyard of **no. 19**, a long subterranean passageway leads to no. 16 on the street behind, **Rue Maître-Albert**. If you can get access to it, you will see prison cells on either side.

Across the street, on the corner, **Chieng Mai** serves very good Thai food and fragrant tea. The service is quick and the atmosphere pleasant.

At **no. 25 Frédéric Sauton** was once a Michelin one-star restaurant, **Dodin-Bouffant**. This is the second great loss of an elegant restaurant in the area.

Down a few steps at **no. 29** is a large Vietnamese grocery store, **Thanh Binh**. In front, women sell piles of fresh herbs and packages of meat from cardboard cartons. Inside, the shop is tightly packed with a bewildering assortment of exotic foods, fruits, and ready-to-eat rice and meat steamed in banana leaves, tapioca in grape leaves, and shrimp muffins. Language can be a problem here.

You are now in the **Place Maubert**, where there is a large open market every Tuesday. In the thirteenth century the square was famous for its outdoor classes; the philosopher Albertus Magnus lectured here on Aristotle. Diane

Johnson has written a delicious novel, *Le Divorce,* about a Californian married to a Frenchman who walks out on her. Thereupon follows the ins and outs of French-American relations. The events take place on these few streets near Place Maubert. If you read it, you will be walking familiar territory—always a delight.

If you are energetic enough at this point, visit one or more of the spectacular monuments in the area, such as Notre-Dame, La Sainte-Chapelle on the Ile de la Cité, the Sorbonne, or the Cluny Museum, all within easy walking distance.

Walk · 2

La Huchette

Voici la Rue de la Huchette, mais
prends bien garde à ta Pochette.

This is the Rue de la Huchette, but
better watch out for your wallet.

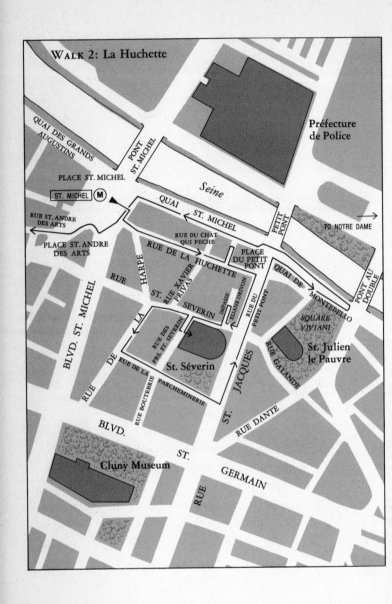

WALK 2: La Huchette

QUAI DES GRANDS AUGUSTINS

PONT ST. MICHEL

Préfecture de Police

PLACE ST. MICHEL

ST. MICHEL Ⓜ

Seine

RUE ST. ANDRE DES ARTS

QUAI ST. MICHEL

PETIT PONT

TO NOTRE DAME

PLACE ST. ANDRE DES ARTS

RUE DU CHAT QUI PECHE

RUE DE LA HUCHETTE

PLACE DU PETIT PONT

RUE

LA HARPE

RUE ST. XAVIER PRIVAS

ST. SÉVERIN

IMPASSE

ELIANE DREVON

RUE DU PETIT PONT

QUAI DE MONTEBELLO

PONT AU DOUBLE

BLVD. ST. MICHEL

RUE

DE

RUE DES PRS. ST. SÉVERIN

St. Séverin

ST. JACQUES

SQUARE VIVIANI

RUE GALANDE

St. Julien le Pauvre

RUE DE LA PARCHEMINERIE

RUE BOUTEBRIE

RUE DANTE

BLVD.

Cluny Museum

ST.

GERMAIN

RUE

Starting Point: Place Saint-Michel, 5th arrondissement
Métro: Saint-Michel, RER
Buses: 21, 24, 27, 38, 47, 58, 63, 70, 81, 86 (all close to
    the Place Saint-Michel)

When you leave the Boulevard Saint-Michel and turn left
into the **Rue de la Huchette** to the point where the street
narrows, imagine yourself back in the crowded and dirty
Middle Ages. This neighborhood of tangled streets and
narrow houses looks in many ways the same as it did hundreds of years ago. Aside from the contour of the land,
which then sloped down to the water's edge instead of rising to the level of the present embankments of the Seine,
this quarter is the same maze it was in the twelfth century,
although the houses date from the seventeenth.

Baron Georges Haussmann, Napoléon III's famous city
planner, cut wide swaths of boulevards (Saint-Germain,
Saint-Michel, Saint-Jacques) all around this neighborhood
but was stopped from touching the interior. He did, however, widen the western entrance to Huchette, which is
why the houses from Saint-Michel to the Hôtel Mont Blanc
are nineteenth-century.

Just before you enter the old Rue de la Huchette you
will see, to the left, the **Hôtel du Mont Blanc**. The hotel
has had its ups and downs, going from country-style inn to

badly run-down. Now it is on the upswing again and half of the ground floor has been converted into a French restaurant. The hotel is reasonable and all the rooms have been redone and include direct-dial phones and double windows.

It was in one of the back rooms of this hotel that Elliot Paul started his nostalgic, intimate account of life in the Rue de la Huchette, *The Last Time I Saw Paris*. The title is taken from the song of the same name, which recalled the happiness and sweetness of Paris before the German occupation.

To the right of the door, against the wall that juts out and narrows the street, you will see a plaque commemorating an event from World War II. Before the Allies entered Paris, street fighting broke out all over this area and barricades were erected at each end of Huchette. Just across the Seine, Parisians liberated the Prefecture of Police from Nazi control and used the spot as a vantage point for shots at the enemy. One of the tragedies of the fighting on the Rue de la Huchette was recorded on this tablet: "Here fell Jean Albert Vouillard, dead in the course of duty, killed by the Gestapo the 17th of May, 1944, at 20 hours. Rainbow." "Rainbow" was the name of his cell of resistance fighters. The bullets that were sprayed into the wall have been plastered over.

The irony here is that the width of the street at the top is the unfinished work of Haussmann. His intention was to widen all these narrow pathways so that revolutionaries would be unable to barricade the streets as they did in the Revolution. At the end of the German occupation during the Second World War, however, it was the resistance fighters' ability to do this that permitted them to defend Paris against the Germans at this spot.

Across the street at **no. 23** you will find the smallest theater in Paris. It used to perform only Ionesco—*The Bald Soprano* and *The Lesson*—the same plays since the mid-fifties. A third and avant-garde play—one that changes and is *not* one of Ionesco's—has been added to the repertoire.

World War II commemorative plaque on the Rue de la Huchette

The plays are performed at 7, 8, and 9 P.M. You can buy tickets for one, two, or three of the performances. The theater holds eighty-five persons, seated straight across the room, no aisle. If you visit after three in the afternoon, try the door to the box office, then smile at the lady who sells the tickets, open the inside door, accustom your eyes to the dark, and get a glimpse of this tiny theater. At one point the son of the founder wanted to turn this into yet another restaurant (!) but he fortunately was stopped by the government. Attend a performance if you can; Ionesco's French is easy to understand, and the plays are pure fun. The intermission is almost as good as the play; this street is really a night street. Turn to the right for some Tunisian delights before going back to see the rest of the play.

In the fourteenth and fifteenth centuries Huchette was called the Rue des Rôtisseurs, the street of roasters. Whole sheep and oxen were turned on spits over open wood fires, and beggars held up their bread to soak up the smoke and smell. A papal delegate called it "verily stupendous."

Today Greek and Tunisian restaurants have returned the street to its old activity, and the roasting goes on. Starting at 11 A.M., the lambs and pigs turn and crackle on spits, a sight that takes some getting used to. The *schwarma*, lamb on a spit, and the stacks of kebabs, ready for the grill, wait for your order.

Xavier-Privas

You are now at the crossing of **Xavier-Privas** and Huchette. Xavier Privas was a singer from Montmartre who was famous in the 1920s, and although that is not particularly interesting, the previous names for the street are. At first this part, from Huchette to Saint-Séverin (to your right), was known as Sac à Lie, "bag of lees." Lees are the dregs of wine, which, when dried, were used to prepare and clean leather hides and parchment. That was in the days when streets were known by their activities. Since few people could read, written street names were not displayed until 1729. With time and the disappearance of the sacks of lees, the street name changed from Sac à Lie to Squalie. It was finally engraved into **no. 19** up the street as "Zacharie" in the seventeenth century, and so it remained for almost three hundred years.

The part of the street that runs from Huchette to the *quai* used to run down, not up, to the Seine and was filled with the life and business of fishing scows, which were moored at the bottom of the street. Owing to many unpleasant incidents and the general filth, the street was gated in during the first half of the seventeenth century. Recently, when the Paris sanitation men went on strike, it rivaled its medieval reputation. You will notice that there are no entry doors on this small section of the street between Huchette and the river. No one's territory, so everyone dumped. One morning the pile reached over six feet, and the army was forced to come down and shovel away the mountain of rubbish.

As for incidents, the street has not lost its old vigor. At any and all hours of the night one can hear shouts and screams and songs. One night when militants were trying to mount a demonstration, the riot police ploughed up this street, six abreast and eight deep, driving young and old before them like chaff in the wind.

Each morning, however, the pedestrian walkways (no cars) take on the most picturesque and old-fashioned appearance. The shop and innkeepers are outside in their white aprons washing their windows and their walks; the residents stop and talk or hurry about with their baskets of bread and meat (which, however, they now are forced to buy five blocks away at the Place Maubert). Huchette once boasted a butcher, a baker, and even a candle-maker; in fact, Xavier-Privas from the Rue de la Huchette to the *quai* was once called the "street of three candle-makers."

Look across Huchette at **no. 14**, a five-windows-wide seventeenth-century building. The ironwork of the balconies is handwrought, made to order for the owner. He had his initials, D. C., laced into the decoration except for two windows, on the first floor, which say *Y* very clearly. There is still another *Y* to be found. You can see it on the stone space between the two windows—a framed circle with a graceful *Y* incised in its center. What is it all about? Shoppers 250 years ago understood. The letter *Y* (called a Greek i in French, *i grec,* pronounced ē-grek) advertised the wares of the shop below. This shop was a *mercerie*, a sewing shop, famous for its needles and sewing materials. There was also an important article of clothing sold here—a garter that tied a man's breeches to his leggings. The tie was a *lie* (as in the word "liaison"), and breeches were *gregues*. One of La Fontaine's rabbits has a pair; in a moment of danger he *"tire ses gregues"* (hitches up his breeches) and runs away. When you put the tie and the breeches together (the *lies* and the *gregues*) you hear *l'i grec*. Now look once more at the incised *Y* on the wall between the windows—it looks like a garter. There are more of these amusing plays on words, called *calembours* (rebuses) left in Paris, one close by on Saint Séverin. Among the best

Rue Saint-Séverin

of them was a sign with six circles, *Os*, which when spoken (*seezō*) sounded like *ciseaux*, scissors. It represented a scissors and knife shop on the Rue Dragon.

Rue du Chat qui Pêche

Look down the alley to the left at one of the most nondescript but oft-described streets in Paris, the **Rue du Chat qui Pêche**, the street of the fishing cat. It took its name from a sign that hung above a shop, no doubt a fish shop, though no source actually says it was. Before the street took its present name, it was called the Rue des Etuves, the

street of steam baths. There were half a dozen such streets and alleys in the Paris of the late thirteenth century, and some twenty-six bathing establishments. Every morning the crier was out on the street calling to prospective clients: *"Li bains sont chaut, c'est sanz mentir!"* (The baths are hot— no fooling!) They were hot in more ways than one. Many of them provided mixed bathing and supplementary services. As one preacher warned his flock: "Ladies, do not go to the baths, and don't do you-know-what there." The combination of clerical disfavor and public harassment reduced the number of these establishments to two by the early seventeenth century. The result was a malodorous population. Those who could afford to doused themselves with perfume; the others, well, people's noses must have been tougher then.

This narrowest street in Paris was, contrary to what you might expect, wider in the sixteenth century. The six-foot-wide alley with its gutter of water (and urine) running down its middle looks and sometimes smells like a medieval street. Walk up the alley away from Huchette. The alley suddenly widens, brightens, and then opens on to the Seine and, to the right, to a surprise view of Notre-Dame. In the sixteenth century this street, like Xavier-Privas, tumbled down into the Seine. It too was gated in at night, though no sign of the gate can be seen in the stone.

Return to the Rue de la Huchette. **No. 12**, on the corner of Huchette and Chat qui Pêche, was built at a later date than its neighbor and is the reason why Chat qui Pêche is narrower today than it once was. **No. 10** next door is the "corner" house where Bonaparte lived in his poorer days in a room at the back, facing the Seine. He was reputedly dying of hunger when Paul Barras, later important in the Directory (1795–1799), gave him a chance to show his mettle. Bonaparte began his rise to glory when, with a "whiff of grapeshot," he dispersed the Paris mob in front of the church of Saint-Roch. Jacques Hillairet, in his superb dictionary of the streets of Paris, summarizes Bonaparte's career in a change of address: "From this point on, fortune smiled on him. When he resided once again on the banks of the Seine, it was, in 1800, at the Tuileries."

Notice the absence on Huchette of wide doorways (*portes cochères*) that were built to allow a horse and carriage and later an automobile to enter a courtyard. Huchette was never a luxury street. The doors are narrow, and the halls lead back deep inside to reach the one staircase that serves both front and back of the house. Long and narrow buildings were common in the seventeenth century because street-front property was so costly. Open any of the doors, and if a restaurant kitchen hasn't filled the space, you will have a long, dark walk to the courtyard and stairs.

At **no. 5**, the **Caveau de la Huchette**, dedicated to the jazz of the 1920s, calls itself "the celebrated cabaret of jazz where one dances." It is open every night from 10:15 P.M. to 2 A.M., Saturday until 4 A.M. Friends of ours spent a night of nostalgia there dancing the lindy to tremendous applause from the young connoisseurs who frequent the club. This is a good place for singles. Although the French dance style is different from ours, you'll have fun. There is a low cover charge, but no drinks minimum.

The building that houses the Caveau dates from the sixteenth century and was connected by secret passageways to the Petit Châtelet, then a prison at the Petit Pont. A publicity flyer put out by the proprietors states that the Templars, a Catholic religious order, used the cellar as a secret meeting place in the late thirteenth century. Their riches were so great King Philippe IV felt the need to suppress them in order to relieve them of their wealth. It was the curse laid by the Templars on the king and his descendants that Maurice Druon took as the theme of his series of historical novels, *Les Rois Maudits,* the accursed kings.

In 1772 the Freemasons met here in secret. Then, during the Revolution, these cellars and subcellars served as tribunal, prison, and place of execution. The process was swift. A deep well in the lowest level is said to have washed away all traces of this summary "justice."

During World War II secret resistance cells found their natural home here, while outspoken patriots filled the cafés. Jacques Yonnet, in his strange and haunting book, *Enchantement sur Paris,* describes the street as one of the ignition points of the occupied city. Perhaps "Rainbow" met here.

There is also a story of the discovery of a two-thousand-year-old bracelet during excavations in the Caveau. A huge treasure, including a five-hundred-pound gold cross, is supposedly buried under these buildings, hidden during the French Revolution.

No. 4 is a large seventeenth-century building, originally with three *portes cochères*, that was redecorated in the eighteenth century. Typical of this kind of face-lifting was the placing of masks on the façade. Here, fortunately, in a black rectangle, someone has preserved an old sign reading *"a la Hure d'Or,"* at the golden boar snout, dated 1729. Look above the awning for the sign. Today, a club called **Le Prestige** has found a home here. The restaurant on the corner changes hands almost every year.

Leave the narrow Rue de la Huchette and enter the **Rue du Petit Pont**, which becomes **Rue Saint-Jacques**. To the left is the *quai*, the Petit Pont, and Notre-Dame. To the right is a long avenue that stretches south toward Orléans and, for the pilgrims who went on France's most popular pilgrimage of the Middle Ages, to Santiago de Compostela in Spain. The building on the south corner of the Rue du Petit Pont and the Rue de la Huchette looks like a seventeenth-century structure but was actually built from scratch in 1979.

Face the Seine and cross the street to the north corner. Where the street is renamed Place du Petit Pont, close to the ground you will find a plaque commemorating bravery in World War II. It tells of two anonymous civilians and one soldier, Jean Dussarps, who were killed defending the little fort on the street. Below that, honor is paid to Béatrice Briant, who was the leader of a group of voluntary fighters against the Germans.

Walk south around the corner to **no. 6 Rue du Petit Pont**, where an old and elegant grocery finally closed after holding out for more than fifty years. The shelves of the bookstore now at this address, the Librairie Saint-Nicolas, date from the grocery.

Rue Saint-Séverin

Walk away from the Seine, down the Rue du Petit Pont, and right again into the **Rue Saint-Séverin**. Countless nineteenth-century descriptions of this street and its neighbors all sound the same theme:

And you wonder, remembering that these streets were full of cut-throat alleys, just how any Parisian managed to reach even middle age. I never pass here without seeing some long-lost villain lying in wait ready to pounce out on some unsteady wayfarer.

All these streets, as I say, are picturesque and dirty.

Between Cluny and the river is a network of very old, squalid, and very interesting streets.

To some degree the same comments can still be made. If you happen to walk here in the early morning when the crowd has gone home (whenever that may be) and the rubbish remains, you would be tempted to use the same adjectives. Half of the food from the restaurants seems to have landed in the gutter. But at 7:30 the street cleaners arrive, and a new day begins.

The street was widened in 1678. If you look at the massive Gothic church on the left, it is not difficult to see why the houses on the Rue Saint-Jacques were chosen for removal. The houses on the side of the church date from the late seventeenth century.

The **Latin Mandarin** at **no. 4** is a small restaurant with a minute kitchen in the back. The restaurant may once have been a hall or a courtyard. It was started fifteen years ago by a tiny lady, Mme Duc, who ran the restaurant with the help of her ten children. Her husband worked elsewhere, as an accountant. Vietnamese women often run small restaurants and food shops, but you rarely see Vietnamese men in the neighborhood; they work elsewhere. On the other hand, you rarely see North African or Greek women; the men run the restaurants. The present owner is a close friend of Mme Duc and he offers the same fare with some new dishes of his own.

Impasse Salembière, now **Impasse Eliane Drivon**, is a

closed alleyway. Once it was an open street, notorious for its piles of rubbish and sleeping *clochards*, who found it a haven. Now that the doors are locked at night, the alley is immaculate. Take a few steps back and see how the walls of the buildings almost touch each other up above, typical of many medieval streets to protect the pedestrian from the rain. Look at the old street name cut in stone above the street sign: "Rue [blank] Séverin," and the number 10 for the section of the city. The stationery store that used to be at no. 6 has sold out to yet another restaurant and moved into the narrow hall of no. 8; the presses were moved to the courtyard.

Notice a very low, narrow seventeenth-century door to **no. 12**. Press the top button of the keypad to the right. Push open this small, heavily carved door to a centuries-old entry that boasts rafters in the ceiling, exposed building stones on the walls, a wrought-iron gate too heavy to budge, and an iron stair rail followed by a odd hand-carved wooden one.

Turn left now and look to the entrance of the **church of Saint-Séverin**. In the sixth century, when everyone else lived on the Ile de la Cité, a hermit named Séverin found a patch of dry ground in the swampland across the river and settled there. The site was ideal for a hermit—separated from society but close enough to receive visitors. Contrary to popular belief, the main aim of a hermit was not to cut himself off from humanity, but to induce it to beat a path to his solitary door. Séverin must have received many, for at his death his reputation as a good man was so widespread that an oratory was built in his memory and called Saint-Séverin. From that early date onward, several churches have been built and destroyed on this site—one by fire, one by a Viking invasion—but all have been named for the hermit Saint Séverin.

After you have looked at the massive exterior, partly cleaned, enter the church, take a seat in one of the back rows, and take in the whole of the structure. The present church represents a combination of styles that stretches across the centuries from the thirteenth to the twentieth. There was never enough money to complete the building at any one time, so the work went on and on, and still does. Before the nineteenth century, architects and builders felt no compulsion to preserve or restore original forms. No age or style was sacred and all construction was "of the day." As a result, the church has a parade of arches that tells the story of Gothic architecture from its primitive beginnings to its last flamboyant manifestations.

Look up the right-hand aisle. The three pillars enclosing two arches closest to the entrance are early thirteenth-century Gothic and are among the few remains of the previous church, which was destroyed by fire. The two arches between them, though broken (or pointed), are almost round, as in the earlier Romanesque style. The pillars are short, cut by capitals halfway up their length. On the wall above the arches and above the columns is a simple cloverleaf pattern, sculpted in stone. Look now at the next four arches, done two centuries later. The columns are tall and straight, and the arches meet at a tighter angle. The goal of Gothic architecture was to reach higher and higher into open space up to God. Notice the arcs that radiate outward from the stone trefoils on the wall above these arches. The small semicircles turn on themselves to make new ones, and the effect is that of a flame, from which we get the term "flamboyant." All of this is still controlled, however, in contrast to the late flamboyant pillars behind the altar.

But look first at the pillars and arches surrounding the altar. Study the stonework carefully, and you will notice that the basic structure of the arches is the same as that of the fifteenth-century ones just described. Why, then, do they look so different? It's a seventeenth-century story.

The famous and capricious cousin of Louis XIV known as la Grande Mademoiselle got into a dispute with the curé of Saint-Sulpice, her neighborhood church, and decided to change parishes. To show her pleasure with the one and annoyance with the other, she bestowed her gifts and her idea of fashion on the church of Saint-Séverin. The priest dared not, or at least did not, refuse. In the spirit of the Renaissance, la Grande Mademoiselle wrapped the pillars in red marble and rounded off the archways with the same red marble. There is more of the same stone in the shape of an altar now in a side chapel on the left. (Formerly it was placed in the center to match its surroundings.) The lady was busy elsewhere as well. If you look at the bottoms of the early flamboyant pillars of the fifteenth century (numbers 4–7, counting from the entrance), you can see the remains of fluting, which was added to the simple pillars. The pillars are now being restored to their original shape, and by the time you visit, there may be no trace of these alterations. Almost every time we visited, we found further work in progress.

Now let us go to the flamboyant pillars behind the altar. The effect is astonishing and marvelous. This spot is often called the Palm Grove; the pillars do look like trees spiraling up into palms overhead. The central twisted pillar is the prime example of French flamboyant Gothic. The spirals begin at the bottom and palm out above into so complex a network that it is almost impossible to trace their path. The grove has been called "a sanctuary of serenity," but we find this particular pillar anything but calm. It is known as "Dante's pillar"; Dante is reputed to have leaned against it often. The fact that he lived two centuries before the pillar was built did not stop the nineteenth-century chroniclers of old Paris from linking it to him!

Now, as you face the entrance, follow the outside aisle behind Dante's pillar around to the left (back toward the entrance) until you come upon a stout pillar capped by the figure of a magnificent broad-shouldered man holding up the arch and reading out a message. Half of this pillar was built in the fourteenth century and the other half in the fifteenth. It would have been simple to complete the pillar as it was begun, but here is proof that emulation of the past or any idea of unity of style was totally absent from the thinking of the time. And so it stands, fourteenth and fifteenth centuries both embodied in one pillar.

Continue up this side aisle toward the entrance and on the wall to your left you will find one of the best collections of votive tablets in Paris—if they are still there. This was the parish church for the Latin Quarter, and grateful students covered the walls with votive tablets that gave thanks to God for success in exams. The sexton told us "they" planned to remove them because gratitude was no longer *à la mode*.

Cross over to the other side aisle (on the left side walking away from the entrance), and in the first chapel you will find a red porphyry marble altar. Professor Raoul Gaduyer, a venerable theologian-sociologist who knew every stone in this church, spent hours explaining and telling us stories. At the red altar, however, he hesitated, smiled, then hesitated again. We waited patiently for the smile to reappear and the story to begin. This large porphyry altar was another of the gifts of la Grande Mademoiselle. But the antiheroine of this story was Louis's mistress, Mme de Montespan. During her long liaison with the king she was concerned about his attentions to other, younger women. In her anxiety and despair she finally contrived to get the priest (Heaven help him!) of Saint-Séverin to say a black mass on the red altar to ensure Louis's fidelity. The tender hearts of two unfortunate turtledoves served as the unholy instruments of her black magic. Bad enough, but her magical exploits continued (and here we are discussing only her black masses, not her poisoning of some of Louis's other mistresses).

Another mass was said elsewhere in Paris with the same thought in mind—Louis and his love. That time the red altar was supplanted by a smaller and softer one, the naked body of Madame de Montespan. But the chalice would not stand upright, because of either her curves or her trembling. The solution was to place it securely between her thighs. All of this, as you can imagine, was done in great secrecy. Private records were kept, however, and these have recently turned up in the archives of the Prefecture of Police.

Continue down this side aisle to the chapel where the modern windows begin. The sixteenth-century painting on the wall to the right of the windows was uncovered in 1968, when the modern stained-glass windows were installed. The painting is a Last Judgment. The words on the right call up all saintly souls, men and women, to Heaven. On the left (sinister) side, however, are those damned to eternal Hell—they are all of them women, beaten on their way by devils, all of them men. An interesting testimony to the artist-priest's view of the roles of the two sexes. Look at the nonrepresentational stained-glass windows. During World War II the fifteenth-century windows were shattered, and temporary ones took their place. In 1966, enough money was finally raised to commission an artist, Jean Bazaine, to make new ones. Bazaine is a fine colorist in abstract art who also did the mosaic at the UNESCO building in Paris. He drew his inspiration from the Bible, using quotations about fire, earth, and water. The bold primary colors of the windows set in solid shapes, one next to the other, create a striking contrast to the quiet strength of the stone.

This is a marrying church. Come any Saturday morning and you will be sure to see a wedding. Outside, go to your left and look at the freshly cleaned cloisters and garden.

Across Rue Saint-Séverin at **no. 22** is one of the narrowest houses in Paris. It is eight feet (two windows) wide. This was the house of the abbé Prévost, an eighteenth-century minister who wrote voluminously, though only one original manuscript remains, that of *Manon Lescaut*. We are convinced that the inspiration for his book came from his proximity to Saint-Séverin and a shocking practice the church then indulged in. Each year an award was given to the five most virtuous maidens in the parish. It was not enough, however, to praise the good. To warn against immorality, the church placed the most scandalous and unvirtuous women of the parish in cages and exposed

The letters ST (for Saint) have been scraped away from the stone sign above the modern sign

them outdoors to the scorn and not-so-tender mercies of the passersby. It was the Last Judgment—the blessed and the damned—translated from life to art.

In 1763 Abbé Prévost, then living in a suburb of Paris, succumbed to a stroke of apoplexy. An autopsy seemed in order, but when the good doctor used his scalpel on the corpse, it rose up and called out. The abbé was not dead after all! A few minutes later, the abbé obligingly passed away, not of apoplexy, but of the doctor's deep cut.

The corner house, **no. 24**, is a lovely rounded building, and on the corner above the blue street sign you can still see the street name cut into the stone, as you saw earlier. It says "Rue" on one line and on the next line "Severin." The "Saint" was scraped out here as elsewhere during the Revolution, when the passionately anticlerical populace ravaged all things religious. Look for evidence of this on other streets named after saints. The number 18 cut into the stone refers to the old divisions of Paris.

Look through the window down the long narrow hall of **no. 30** at the plaster-and-wood construction of the walls. In the seventeenth century, walls were built of timber framing with a gravelly mixture filling the spaces between. This mixture was held together by pieces of wood and rags, just as clay bricks are held together by straw. This filler was usually covered over with white plaster, with timbers exposed, but the heavy incidence of fire in these oil-lit interiors led King Henri IV to decree that any wall with exposed timbers had to be completely plastered over. A white clay, which was found just below ground not far from here, in Paris, was quarried and used widely in the area at Notre-Dame, Saint-Julien-le-Pauvre, and Saint-Séverin. "Plaster of paris" has since become the generic term for any white plaster. Many walls were so weighted down with their coat of plaster, however, that they buckled and even collapsed.

Above the first floor at **no. 13** there is a fourteenth-century *enseigne*, a standard, for what was once an inn; it depicts a swan whose neck is wrapped around a cross. This is another rebus, like the Y on the Rue de la Huchette. A swan in French is *cygne*, a homonym for *signe*, meaning "sign." Combining the *cygne* with the cross yields the "sign of the cross," the standard symbol for lodgings.

No. 34 is the most elegant building of this street and was a stylish private home in the seventeenth century. One sure sign is the presence of a large coach entrance for the carriages of the proprietor. The other residents of the

The sign of the cross, a fourteenth-century standard for an inn

quarter obviously were not expected to own coaches, or if they did, were expected to keep them elsewhere. The Ministry of Cultural Affairs has classified as monuments the entrance doors, the courtyard, and the iron stair rail. The wide and graceful courtyard is decorated with eighteenth-century *mascarons* (mask decorations) just above the first floor. One is missing, however, as a result of fire. Look through the keyhole if the door is locked.

Rue de la Harpe

Turn left into the **Rue de la Harpe**. This was one of the great streets of Paris from Roman days until the middle of the last century. It ran parallel to the Rue Saint-Jacques and wound its serpentine way from the river down toward the South of France. This long street, which was the principal north–south thoroughfare of its day, was amputated by two thirds when Haussmann laid out a new, wide, straight north–south route across the Left Bank, the Boulevard Saint-Michel, which took over much of the old right-of-way.

From the earliest times at least fourteen different names for the Rue de la Harpe have been recorded, several of them used concurrently. To some the street was known by a standard or an inn or a school, to others by the people who lived there. It was the street of Reginald the Guitarist or Reginald the Harper, the street of Old Jewry, the street of the Old Buckler, the street of new Saint-Michel, and so on.

A standard of King David playing a harp finally won out and gave the street its present name. The standard is said to have identified the house of Reginald the Harper but may bear some relation to the fact that in the eleventh and twelfth centuries there were Jewish schools on the Rue de la Harpe between Huchette and Saint-Séverin.

The first recorded synagogue in Paris, tenth-century, stood on the corner of the Rue de la Harpe and Rue Monsieur le Prince, approximately four blocks south. Nothing at all is known about it, except that it was just inside the wall of King Philippe Auguste, which encircled and protected Paris. When the Jews were expelled from Paris and their synagogue confiscated in 1182, Philippe Auguste gave their houses to twenty-four drapers and eighteen furriers.

The Rue de la Harpe has been the heart of the Latin Quarter for centuries. Roger de Beauvoir in *Paris Chez Soi*, published in 1855, describes it as it was in the early sixteenth century when Latin, though losing ground to French, was still spoken. To paraphrase his description:

> There was a time when a mass of strange costumes could be seen milling around the greasy, dirty street. There was first of all the *mire*, the first doctor of early times, who sold his drugs and unguents in the street, escorted by a child with a monkey that was bled by the "practitioner" on request [for what we can't imagine]. Then followed the hanging sleeves and furs of a professor as grave as Erasmus, the flowing cloaks of the students mixed in with the jackets of the men-at-arms, the pointed hats of the Jews, and later on the wig of Dr. Diafoirus. . . . How many little working girls, the girlfriends of the students, did these black, filthy houses not shelter? Girls singing like canaries in their cages, the frightful cages of the seventh floor of the Rue de la Harpe. The whole anthill of the schools . . . begins every morning to move its thousand legs from the bottom of the Rue de la Harpe—the medical student who goes off, nose to the wind, hand in pocket, looking at his colored anatomical plates; the high school student buying a cake; the law student ogling a shop girl; the tutor taking the rich man's son to his exam for the baccalaureate. The point is that rents were reasonable; even so, no chance that a Chinese, a Turk, an Arab, or even an Englishman would lodge there. It is a special people that enlivens this quarter; a people with

ink on its fingers and in its lips; an undisciplined,
haughty, noisy people, the people of the schools, the
drinking joints, the furnished rooms; the Rue de la
Harpe with its thousand side streets is the "heart of
the students."

Today it is not the "heart of the students" but the heart of
the tourists. As you have noticed, the Arabs and the Vietnamese, if not the Chinese, the Greeks, and the Turks,
have found their way to this quarter and have changed the
business of the street from one of student housing and
small food shops and workshops to one of restaurants,
cafés, boutiques, jazz clubs, and hotels. The street must be
seen at night, and Saturday night is the best night of all.

The "frightful cages of the seventh floor" are now
restored as studios (one room and a cubby of a kitchen and
bath) renting for large sums, and are snapped up before the
rental signs are put up.

No. 33 is a narrow, one-window house called La Petite
Bouclerie. Remember the street was once called the street
of the Old Buckler. The name is written inside a sculpted
stone frame inside the door.

Look up at **nos. 35**, **45**, and **47**. You will see elegant eighteenth-century houses with impressive doorways,
rounded stone window-frames, and sculpted façades. The
old coach entrances are now filled in, the courtyards occupied by restaurants; but up above, the ceilings are twelve
feet high and the rooms are large and bright. The cellars,
once filled with mud from Seine floods or used as wine cellars, are fast giving way to restaurants and movie houses.

Look in the courtyard of **no. 35**, past the entry on the
right. You'll see a staircase with a classified (historically recognized) iron railing and a wall of beige building stones.

This wide street, closed to traffic, is a pleasant place to
walk despite some poor-quality clothing stores. In pleasant
enough weather musicians and singers vie for the corner of
Rue de la Harpe and Rue de la Huchette, one block north.
Enormous crowds gather and often richly fill the empty hat

in appreciation of good music or just the pleasure of the spectacle. We once heard a violinist who really was first class, probably on holiday from a symphony orchestra.

Rue de la Parcheminerie

Turn left into the **Rue de la Parcheminerie**. In the Middle Ages this street was the "bookshop" of the Rue de la Harpe. Before 1530 it was called Rue des Escrivains, the street of writers; then it was renamed for the parchment the writers wrote upon. The first parchment paper was thick and rough and lent itself poorly to handwriting. It was only in 1380 that the experts developed a grain so tight they were able to write the whole Bible in one small volume. The scribes who worked here were privileged souls, exempt from taxes and held in high esteem, though their morals were infamous. This street has been cleaned up and widened, and so transformed from its former dark-alley appearance to a quiet and pleasant residential street.

The odd luxury of the street is **no. 29**. It was built for a gentleman named Claude Dubuisson in 1750. One of its beautiful doors was removed when the building served as a wine depot. Each pair of the tall, curved, graceful windows, all three stories of them, opened onto a large room. Today these rooms have been divided into apartments; the previous occupant, who was there during the restoration of the splendid façade, explained to us that the architects had made space to squeeze in the necessary bathrooms in the thickness of the wall.

The second door of no. 29 now opens to **The Abbey Bookshop**, competition for Shakespeare and Company. The Abbey Bookshop, opened in 1989, offers a large and carefully chosen selection of books in English, especially Canadian books. The owner, Brian Spence—Canadian, intelligent, informed, and charming—claims that in this busy and crowded part of the Latin Quarter, his bookstore is a quiet refuge for the poet, the scholar, or the pilgrim.

Join the Canadian Club of Paris for a small fee and attend book discussions, artists' shows, and wonderful outings, one of which was a hike to Vaux-le-Vicomte.

If you are outrageous or "abnormal" you might get into **Charly's Bar** across the street. The guard at the door gives you the once-over to see if you fit with the 150 swarming, sweating, swaying, and drugged mass that jam this cellar bar. This new breed of "stay-outs" go to the first bar from 11:30 P.M. to 5 or 6 A.M. They push on to the second at 7 A.M. and leave at noon. Then they stagger here. The doors close at 9 P.M. The warning on leaving says, "Be quiet! The neighbors are not 'cool.' " If you can't get in, ask to take a peek—show them *Pariswalks*.

The recently built **Hôtel Parc Saint-Séverin** at **no. 22** benefits from a sunny, open site in this neighborhood of crowded, twisted streets. No. 70 is the penthouse suite, with a circular terrace that spans views from Notre-Dame to Montmartre.

In 1935 plans were drawn up that called for a complete modernization of the area, a transformation of these winding, narrow streets into neat, airy thoroughfares flanked by modern apartment buildings. But then the campaign to save old Paris took over; the Ministry of Cultural Affairs classified every possible treasure and forbade the destruction of most of the buildings, though they could be restored. Alterations were usually permitted in the interior, hence the opportunity for profitable conversion to new commercial uses and to luxury apartments. And so the restoration goes on at a galloping pace, but always far behind the rise in demand.

The medieval name of the **Rue Boutebrie** (on your right) connects it to the Rue de la Parcheminerie. It was the street of illuminators, Rue des Enlumineurs, when the other was the street of writers. This was the book center of Paris, and Paris was the intellectual center of the world. Follow the continuation of Parcheminerie to the Rue Saint-Jacques and turn left.

Rue Saint-Jacques

Cross the **Rue Saint-Jacques** to the store side—the better to see the back of Saint-Séverin, which was smothered by shops until the street was widened a hundred years ago. The stores on this street change with time and style, but many of their names—the Cloister, the Pilgrim, Tentations—still tell the history of past centuries.

To the left of **31 Rue Saint Jacques** and to the right of **no. 27**, on the right corner of the wall that juts out, there is a plaque that tells of the death of a soldier, a policeman who was killed at the barricade in 1944. On the adjoining wall, high up, is an etching by Salvador Dali of a strange sundial. The garland-decorated door at **no. 21** leads to a courtyard with an arched doorway with a wooden frieze. Also at no. 21, **Tentations**, a friendly, lived-in kind of restaurant, serves light meals and desserts.

Look into the hole-in-the-wall café, **Polly Magoo**, at **no. 11**. Most of the patrons here seem to be permanently settled behind their backgammon boards and chessboards, surrounded by timers, kibitzers, smoke, and drinks. Players come from everywhere, as they did in certain cafés in the early 1900s. France's second-best backgammon player and the world champion have played here. The owners of the Polly Magoo also own the Caveau de la Bollée at 24 Rue de l'Hirondelle, where even more serious chess players go at it all night.

Métamorphoses, **no. 15**, is true to its name: it changes its wares. It was originally an eccentric 1900s store. Today, Suzanne Sauvanaud (a poet as well) sells strictly jewelry— 80 percent is old pieces and the rest is a collection of mainly Deco reproductions made by the same companies that made the jewelry in the 1920s and using original molds. Her stock may be more expensive than others in Paris (still very reasonable), but the quality and selection are superior. The store and front window are crammed with treasures, so take your time.

Quai Saint-Michel

Cross the street to the corner of Place du Petit Pont and the **Quai de Montebello**, and walk right, toward the Pont au Double. You will pass in front of the famous bookstalls of Paris and be across the street from Shakespeare and Company (Walk 1). The booksellers, *bouquinistes,* represent one of the oldest trades in Paris, and one that has changed very little. The men and women who are lucky enough to get a spot on the parapet to hang their metal boxes consider themselves a special breed. They love the outdoors and the freedom to open and close at will. When the *quai* is quiet, they sit and read, or sleep, or knit, or smoke, or play chess with their neighbors. Story has it that they are never sick and live to very old age. Most of them have a specialty, but many buy whatever looks saleable.

The real fear of the *bouquinistes* is the automobile. The noise is deafening, the air polluted, and the traffic so dense and steady that they see themselves under siege. Even worse are the huge and huger tourist buses that park themselves directly in front of their stalls. Although plans to transform the *quai* into an expressway have been abandoned, the fear is always there.

We found the stalls between the Petit Pont and the Pont au Double more interesting than those near the Pont Saint-Michel. Some stalls down, opposite La Bûcherie, M. Lanoizelée has a serious stand. He collects first editions, many of which have inscriptions from the author on the flyleaf.

One of the best of the stalls is **no. 103**, at the corner of the Pont au Double, where M. Leleu sells old and beautiful leather-bound books, many from the eighteenth century. He has a private collection of more than fifty thousand volumes. If you are especially interested he might invite you to his home to do some serious buying. Leleu also restores old manuscripts. One day he showed us a medieval Arab manuscript bound in crumbling leather and clasped in bronze fittings that he hoped to revive in about a month. We must warn you that he is not always pleasant; he says so himself. His books mean too much to him, and he is exasperated by the careless handling—as well as the occasional rip-off—from passersby.

On the west corner of the Petit Pont, **stall no. 1**, opposite 9 Quai Saint-Michel, is the stall of Véronique Le Goff, who has followed M. Korb as the president of the *bouquinistes'* union. Participants pay a yearly fee of $50. The union offers an annual literary prize that is celebrated with a fine repast and copies of the speeches in their journal, *Bouquinistes des Quais de Paris*. They also help each other out in bad times.

Many of the bookstalls offer the usual fare of pages torn from old books, reproductions of Daumier prints, and modern paintings of children with large liquid eyes. But many have a specialty worth a close look.

Go back to the corner of the Petit Pont and the Quai de Montebello. Diagonally across the street you will see the usual souvenir and poster shops that fill the **Quai Saint-Michel**, but tucked in between are serious galleries and entrances to choice apartments that look out on the Seine and the bustle of the *quai*. A gallery of fine engravings has moved out to make way for a *métro* elevator for the physically handicapped. We once lived in 13 Quai Saint-Michel and the building quaked during the underground drilling.

No. 15 is home to an elegant hotel, **Les Rives de Notre Dame**. We were impressed by the beauty of the décor. We visited the wonderful sitting room with its glass roof sheltering wooden vaulting, Provençal fabric–covered couches, and caged birds singing. This is a four-star hotel with only ten rooms, so reserve early.

Sartoni-Cerveau at no. 15 begins a row of serious collectors' stores. M. Sartoni-Cerveau's shelves are packed with antique books and etchings. The major topics of his collection are travel, maps, landscapes, and decoration. His motto is "The love of books unites us."

The cupboards on the walls of the **Galeries Michel, no. 17**, are filled with original seventeenth-, eighteenth-, and nineteenth-century prints. M. Michel, whose father ran the gallery before him, is both informative and friendly. Now, his daughter works there as well. The labels on his cases cover any subject you might think of—circus, interiors, romantic, mountains—as well as individual artists. Michel will be glad to give you a chair and a standing wooden frame to rest a folder in and leave you on your own. Prices range from numbers with one zero to numbers with many. Most of his business is done with collectors by mail, despite his location on this very busy street of tourists. Ask to see the back room, which is a small museum of fine etchings.

Gibert Jeune: there are three of these, two on the *quai* and one around the corner on the Place Saint-Michel. They are offshoots, though now separate, of the older firm of Gibert, chief bookseller to generations of students at the Sorbonne and the Lycée Louis le Grand farther up the Boul Mich.

Gibert Jeune, like every other Paris enterprise that can get away with it, sets up displays of merchandise on the pavement outside to catch the fancy of the passersby. These take up a good half of the pavement, and although they create a minor pedestrian traffic jam, it's fun. Take your time walking through the crush during morning and evening rush hours. At those hours parking is not tolerated on that side of the *quai*, and cars tear along in the outside lane a foot or two from the pavement.

The first Gibert Jeune offers art books, guidebooks, books for collectors (about dolls, playing cards, trains, buttons, pipes, anything) at remainder prices. An example of their offerings was a large book, illustrated in color: *Delacroix* by René Huyghe, reduced 50 percent.

The second Gibert Jeune has perhaps the largest selection of schoolbooks in Paris; they range from beginning readers in the back of the store to Keynes on economics in the front. When secondary school starts in the fall, lines stretch around the corner, and students wait for hours with their lists of books in hand. The shop closes at five, the line at three.

The third, and the largest, is on the Place Saint-Michel. Turn the corner and you will see a book and stationery shop literally in the street. Every morning and evening the stands are carried in and out. The ground floor has all kinds of stationery and office equipment. Enjoy yourself buying new kinds of pads and pencils and paper clips.

It is certainly time to sit down at the corner café, **Le Départ,** for espresso, fresh lemonade, hot chocolate, or beer. If you like lemonade with bubbles, ask for a *siphon*, or seltzer bottle, with your *citron pressé*. Le Départ is a choice spot for people-watching.

You are now back where you started, but there are a few more remarks we would like to make. The *métro*, with its easy map of instructions, will take you anywhere faster than a taxi. This particular entrance is one of the seventeen remaining in Paris that were built around 1900 by Hector Guimard, the architect of the period. Go to see the façade and interior of one of his prize-winning houses at no. 14 Rue La Fontaine in the sixteenth arrondissement. Sometimes the art of the period, Art Nouveau, is called Style Métro because these subway entrances typify the imaginative floral spiraling that marked the style so clearly. Note the curved squares on the sides of the *métro* entrance. We watched painters one day, as we sat at the café, preparing to put on three layers of paint to get the exact soft green coloring they wanted.

An Art Nouveau show at the Museum of Modern Art in Paris in 1960 appropriately used a *métro* entrance as the passageway into the exhibit. The appreciation of 1900s *métro* entrances soared, but the Museum of Modern Art in New York managed to buy one before Paris realized their future worth. The entrance in the Place Saint-Michel is

Art Nouveau metro railings designed by
Hector Guimard

missing its curved arch. It has been replaced by a straight
pole, typical of the Art Deco of the 1930s, which holds up
the rectangular nameplate.

Look across the street at the very high large fountain
that marks this central outdoor lounge and meeting place.
On a Saturday after school began, we—myself and Alison's
daughter Elana, who was spending a semester with us
and attending the Ecole Active Bilingue J.M. (excellent
school)—were on the hunt for a special history book.
What we found were at least a thousand students staking
out territory on the place to hawk their secondhand
schoolbooks. It was fun pushing through the shouting and
the bustling and hustling.

The fountain was built between 1858 and 1860 by
Davioud to hide the back wall of an apartment building
that ruined the view down the boulevard. That accounts
for the unnatural height of this fountain/monument. Four
red marble columns surround a bronze statue of Saint
Michel, by Duret. With outspread wings, he stares down at
a demon in the water below. The work was not appreciated. Read the following.

In this execrable monument
one sees neither talent nor taste
The devil is worth nothing at all
Saint Michel isn't worth the devil.

If you look down the boulevard, you will see how jammed it is with people and pavement vendors. The Cluny Museum is three blocks south, away from the *quai*, and the Sorbonne, five. The Rue Saint-André-des-Arts to your right is a busy, funky street that leads to the Saint-Germain-des-Prés area.

Walk · 3

Saint-Germain-des-Prés

> In my last letter, I told you that the guillotine is taking care of some dozens of rebels every day, and that about the same number are shot. Now I want to inform you that several hundreds *are to be shot every day* so that we will soon be rid of those scoundrels who seem to defy the Republic even at the moment of their execution. . . .
>
> —From a loyal republican to his section

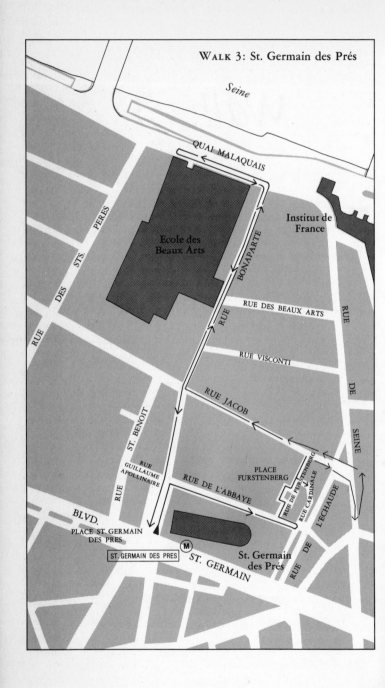

WALK 3: St. Germain des Prés

Seine

QUAI MALAQUAIS

Institut de France

Ecole des Beaux Arts

RUE DES STS. PERES

RUE BONAPARTE

RUE DES BEAUX ARTS

RUE VISCONTI

RUE JACOB

RUE DE SEINE

ST. BENOIT

RUE GUILLAUME APOLLINAIRE

RUE DE L'ABBAYE

PLACE FURSTENBERG

RUE DE FURSTENBERG

RUE CARDINALE

RUE DE L'ECHAUDE

BLVD.
PLACE ST. GERMAIN
DES PRES

ST. GERMAIN DES PRES

ST. GERMAIN

St. Germain des Prés

RUE DE

Starting Point: Place Saint-Germain-des-Prés, 6th arrondis-
    sement
Métro: Saint-Germain-des-Prés
Buses: 48, 63, 70, 86, 87, 96

As you take in the busy and curious scene of Saint-Germain-
des-Prés, wander over to the hollyhock-filled garden on the
side of the church at the corner of Rue de l'Abbaye and the
Place Saint-Germain. We suggest you begin this walk by
taking a seat in the garden and reading a bit about its illustrious abbey and the bloody events of the French Revolution that took place on and around this spot.

In Roman and Merovingian times, up to the early
eighth century, this area consisted of open fields (prés)
stretching westward away from Paris, and there was a
temple to the Egyptian goddess Isis on the site where the
church of Saint-Germain now stands. The modern suburb
of Issy-les-Moulineaux took its name from this ancient
temple.

In 542, Childebert, son of the first Christian king,
Clovis, went on a crusade in Spain to punish the Visigoths,
who, though Christian, were guilty of heresy. The inhabitants did not defend themselves in any way, and Childebert laid siege to their key city, Saragossa. The Visigoths,
despairing of their fate, paraded around the walls of the city

in hair shirts, carrying sacred gold relics and the alleged tunic of Saint Vincent. The men chanted psalms; the women, with hair unkempt, sobbed hysterically, as if in mourning. Childebert was fascinated by this procession, and, when he saw the relics they carried, offered to lift his siege in exchange for these treasures. He returned triumphantly to Paris with the sacred tunic and the objects of gold. There is evidence, however, that the Bishop Germain (later Saint Germain) of Paris, as well as the chronicler of this tale, Gregory of Tours, considered Childebert a fool to have settled for so little. They felt his father, Clovis, would have done better.

In any event, the bishop took the opportunity to get Childebert to build a church to house the sainted relics on the location of the former temple of Isis. There, a magnificent basilica with marble columns and gilded rafters was built in two years. The outside was covered with gilded copper and gold mosaic radiant in the sunshine. The church was called Saint-Germain-le-Doré, Saint Germain the golden.

Three hundred years later, Norsemen, drawn by the glitter of what looked like pure gold, descended on Paris and ransacked the church four times in forty years, between 845 and 885. They were disappointed each time, for the true gold relics that Childebert had brought back from Spain, along with the tunic of Saint Vincent, lay safely somewhere in the country. In the meantime, the devastated church was left a ruin for more than a century. Then, in the beginning of the eleventh century, it was rebuilt. The central bell tower dates from this reconstruction and today is the oldest church structure in Paris.

What decided the fate of this area for many centuries was the establishment of an abbey, with rights to the land and its revenue over an enormous area stretching from the Seine all the way to what are now the suburbs of Paris. The abbey also received exclusive jurisdiction in all religious and legal matters within its territory. The fortified walls that enclosed the abbey proper formed a square between the present Boulevard Saint-Germain and Rues Jacob, Saint-Benoît, and de l'Echaudé. The size and riches of the abbey of Saint-Germain rivaled those of the city of Paris.

The bishop's abbey was his palace, his clerics were his court, and the peasants who lived outside the walls (bakers, butchers, prison guards) were his servitors. This imitation of courtly life did not go unnoticed by the king, who kept a close watch on the rival power just outside his city walls.

The most interesting tales come to us from the thirteenth century and concern the perennial conflict between the monks and the students of the Latin Quarter nearby. The students used to come to talk and sport on the fields that stretched along the Seine north of the abbey. They made noise, trespassed on areas the clerics would have closed to them, and troubled the peace of the local residents—as students are usually accused of doing. In return, the residents of the abbey harassed the students at every opportunity. From time to time this hostility broke into violent conflict.

The worst of these confrontations took place in 1278, when the abbé Gerard built some houses along a path that the students customarily used in going from the Latin Quarter to the playing fields. The students saw this as a provocative impediment to their passage and proceeded to dismantle these structures. The abbé rang the tocsin, summoning monks, vassals, and serfs to defend the rights of the abbey. Chroniclers tell us that an armed company fell on the students with swords, pikes, and clubs, shouting, "Kill! Kill!" The students took a terrific beating. Two were killed, one blinded, several badly wounded. Prisoners were paraded bareheaded through the marketplace and thrust into the abbey's dungeons, on the site of the present Hôtel Madison at no. 143 Boulevard Saint-Germain.

However great the provocation offered by students, the abbé was felt to have overreacted. The students appealed to the papal legate and the king, and, surprisingly, got a quick and sympathetic response: perhaps this was because both

the church and the crown had come to feel that the abbey was too rich, powerful, and arrogant for anyone's good. The leader of the abbey forces was exiled; the chapter was compelled to build and endow two new churches in memory of the slain students; the parents of the victims were granted substantial indemnities. And the students were confirmed in their legal use of their sporting meadow, the Pré aux Clercs, so called because the term *clerc* denoted all men of instruction, whether or not they were members of the clergy. The students were overjoyed at this victory and in the following years continued to exercise whatever rights of destruction they felt appropriate.

Three centuries later, Henri II, plagued by student uprisings, decided to dampen their ardor and sent Parliament orders to pursue persons guilty of acts of violence. Its action culminated on October 6, 1557, with the burning at the stake of a student named Croquoison, who received the bleak mercy of being strangled before being burned on the Pré aux Clercs. This seems to have been the last major incident in the student-monk war, although their mutual animosity produced incidents well into the eighteenth century.

In the spring of that same year, the people of the *quartier*, as well as those who came streaming from all over Paris, had been treated to a more dramatic execution at the stake. Two Huguenots, who had been captured at a secret religious meeting two weeks earlier and had refused under torture to abjure their faith, were brought into the square that is now Place Saint-Germain, in front of the church, and asked one last time to renounce their heresy in order that they might be strangled before being burned. If not, their lying venomous tongues were to be ripped from their mouths. They refused. After the executioner had done the terrible deed (to the roaring approval of the crowd), the heretics were bound and hoisted onto the stakes, which were placed high above the wood in such a manner that the lower halves of the bodies would be reduced to ashes while the top halves were still intact.

Less gruesome stories are told about the fairgrounds that were a central feature of the abbey's power. Every year for a month after Easter, a great fair was held in an area that stretched from the Boulevard Saint-Germain to the Luxembourg Gardens. This was one of the great medieval fairs, drawing people from all over France as well as Spain, England, Burgundy, Flanders, and the Holy Roman Empire. Here were hundreds of stalls selling every kind of product and service available then; troupes of performers, dancing bears, and minstrels; the most impressive swirl of colors, smells, and noises a commoner would ever see. This fair served as a gathering point for students as well as courtesans and men of state. The rest of the year the area was far from deserted. There was always some activity, and it seems to have been the place to find whomever it was you sought in Paris. In addition to attracting courtiers, merchants, and students, the fairgrounds were frequented by a group of Italian ruffians, called, ironically, *braves,* because they hung out in groups of five or six. They were available, at the right price, for carrying out whatever vengeance one might seek, as the following story illustrates.

In the court of Henri III there was a nobleman whose mistress dumped him rather rudely. Having given her large sums of money in happier days, he wished to collect his "loans." His former lady, believing that in love, money loaned is money given, refused to comply and sought vengeance. One night, the nobleman was returning home after a walk through the Saint-Germain fairgrounds. On the *champ crotté* (the dunged field of the cattle market), which was understandably solitary, a band of braves jumped him and held him by the nose, which the leader began to cut off with a knife. The victim's screams aborted the full operation, and the nobleman was left watching his assailants flee as his nose dangled by a thread. The nose was sewn back on, but, in the testimony of a contemporary, slightly off-center. The story had unpleasant results for some of the actors; one does not lightly cut off a nobleman's nose. One brave was hanged, and the lady and her friends had to buy their way out of trouble, no doubt with the hapless victim's money.

Henri III too appreciated the promenade, where he would stroll in the company of his *mignons* (literally "cuties," the name given to his favorite young men, with their curly hair, powdered faces, and makeup). They rapidly became the butt of student jokes. Returning one day from Chartres, the king had several students imprisoned for following his suite with long pieces of curled paper and shouting out loud in the middle of the fair, *"A la fraise on connaît le veau"* (You can tell the calf by its birthmark—a French proverb that meant in this context, "You can tell the faggot by his curls").

The monastery reached the end of its twelve-hundred-year history when the forces of the French Revolution moved in and took over. They replaced intermittent violence with the organized violence of the Terror. They filled the abbey's jail until it was overflowing with prisoners (aristocrats, clergy, and common people), and then set up tribunals to thin out the crowd. These tribunals made use of "guest houses," which stood on the corner of the Rue de l'Abbaye and Rue Bonaparte, just outside the entrance to this garden. These houses had extra rooms called *chambres à donner*, which meant rooms that could be given to guests of the abbey. These rooms, which once provided shelter and comfort, were turned into tribunals of condemnation—swift and deadly. The stories about the trials held there are hard to believe.

One concerns Mlle de Sombreuil, a carefully brought-up young lady who rarely left her house unaccompanied. One day, however, she left, alone, on a terrible mission. Her father, a prisoner, was scheduled for one of the infamous swift trials in which no one was found innocent. When she appeared at the tribunal, she begged for her father's life. The guards found the situation amusing and offered to make a deal. If she would drink the still-steaming blood of the latest victim, they would spare her father. She did, and her father lived, for a few days.

During September 2 and 3, 1792, these tribunals carried out the ostensibly judicial massacre of more than two hundred victims. Each defendant was dressed in his best clothes, because he had been told when arrested that he was being sent away. The questioning that followed demanded simply a yes or a no; either answer proved the defendant guilty. After this mock trial, the prisoners were led out of the tribunal into the courtyard of the abbey and were there hacked and stabbed to death by two rows of hired citizens, in many cases local inhabitants.

One hundred and sixty-eight men and women, including several of Louis XVI's ministers, his father confessor, and surely many "irrelevant" people, were executed in this fashion on September 3 alone, because Judge Maillard (nicknamed "the Slugger") insisted on having them killed at once. The executioners, however, were soon to rue their zealous slaughter when they learned that as a prize for the day's work they could claim the victims' clothes. These were so badly cut up that they were worth little. The massacre continued with the slaughter of the king's personal Swiss guard. Late in the afternoon, another judge came onto the scene, and, drinking to the nation, shouted to the executioners (whose arms still dripped with blood): "People, you slaughter your enemies, you do your duty!" On September 4 the slaughter was followed by a long auction of personal effects while the pile of corpses lay in this garden, alongside the church.

In all, the number of citizens killed in Paris during the month of September 1792 is estimated at 1,614. Many victims were burned at the door of the prison, and even at the door of the church, but the largest number were massacred in front of the tribunal, at the corner of the Rue Bonaparte and Boulevard Saint-Germain.

After the Revolution, Paris was very different from what it had been. The church of Saint-Germain was reconsecrated, but simply, as the parish church it is today, and the abbey served, as it still does, the social needs of its parishioners. The neighborhood today is an intellectual center of Paris in which the church of Saint-Germain-des-Prés simply happens to be found.

Now it is time to look at the garden itself, the **Square Laurent-Prache**. This quiet spot, in the midst of a confusion of cars and people, is a flowered and shady retreat in summer and a startlingly bare sculpture garden in winter. The first piece of sculpture you see is most unexpected; it is the strange and powerful bronze head of a woman, dedicated to Guillaume Apollinaire, sculpted by his loyal friend Pablo Picasso. The bust sits on a four-foot-high white stone pedestal; it is dated 1959, although Apollinaire died years before, in 1918, at the age of thirty-eight. Picasso and Apollinaire, the artist and poet, were favorites of the arty café world and were courted by all the would-be artists and hangers-on who spent their days drinking and talking together.

One of these admirers, an employee of the Louvre Museum, wishing to show his appreciation and respect for the two, presented each of them with a statuette. Picasso and Apollinaire thanked him, put the objects away, and thought no more about it. Several months later the guards at the museum, shocked out of their negligence by an important theft, realized that other objects were missing as well. It wasn't long before they found the culprit, and he led them directly to his friends, pleading that he had simply given Picasso and Apollinaire the statues as gifts. Because he was not a French citizen, Picasso was let off with a few sharp words and warnings; but the case was different for Apollinaire. The officials not only entangled him in the ever present web of French papers and procedures but also questioned him so harshly that the poet was driven to ask why in the world they didn't accuse him of stealing the Mona Lisa. That did it. The Mona Lisa had just been stolen, and Guillaume Apollinaire was put in prison. The situation could have been merely ludicrous, but for very special reasons this experience became tragic.

Apollinaire was born in Rome of Polish parents named Kostrowitzki, but he turned from this background to a love

Pablo Picasso's head of a woman, dedicated to Guillaume Apollinaire

of France that led him to change his name and his allegiance and to fight valiantly in the First World War for his new country. To be accused of stealing the nation's treasures and imprisoned was too great a blow. He died soon after, a disappointed and unhappy man. It is, therefore, particularly suitable that tribute was finally paid him by placing this statue here, among medieval remnants (you will find on the grass a gargoyle whose spout—which was in the shape of a dog's head—has been broken off and stolen by "lovers" of Gothic architecture) and archways, the treasures of France.

These treasures are fragments from the thirteenth-century chapel of the Virgin, which stood within the walls of the abbey, diagonally down the street at the present **no. 6 bis Rue de l'Abbaye**. The chapel, begun in 1245, took ten years to build and was the work of Pierre de Montreuil. The city is planning to remove the sculpture and fragments for repair. The neighbors are concerned they will never be returned. The remains that you see on the two walls of the garden, pieced together stone by stone, make clear how delicate this masterpiece of thirteenth-century flamboyant Gothic must have been.

The chapel was partly destroyed in 1794, when the refectory and library next to it exploded and burned. It was completely dismantled in 1800, when the street was cut through. Additional remains of the chapel decorate the garden of the Cluny Museum.

If you have not been in the church yet, you may wish to go now, or you may enter later, when the walk ends back here. This is one of the few churches that have kept their original interior painting. The vaulting is sky blue sprinkled with stars. Each gilt pillar is decorated differently. Today we are accustomed to plain stone, but originally churches were very colorful. For example, the entire façade of Notre-Dame and the interior were brightly painted and gilded in the Middle Ages. Saint-Germain's modern clear glass doors keep concert music in and street noise out.

The entrance to the garden Laurent-Prache was actually the site of the Revolutionary tribunal. It was here that the incredibly bloody hacking to death of 168 persons took place. This street was cut through in 1800, and shortly after was given the whitewashing name of Rue de la Paix, the street of peace, but finally took the name of its earlier history, Rue de l'Abbaye. The Place de la Concorde on the Right Bank, the site of most of the guillotine murders and crowd madness of the French Revolution, has somehow managed to keep its name, despite its violent past.

Rue de l'Abbaye

Originally, **no. 18 Rue de l'Abbaye** was the site of the well-known bookstore **Librairie Le Divan**, owned by Gallimard, one of the most distinguished publishing houses in Paris. This corner spot, stuffed with books on tables and shelves, was an announcement of all the publishing houses and bookstores dotting the streets behind: Seuil, Hachette, Gallimard. The city, which owns the property, increased the rent so high that Gallimard made the momentous decision to move. And they did—to the far reaches of the fifteenth arrondissement.

Why was the rent suddenly so high? Who could afford it? Christian Dior. And who is moving into the famous American Drugstore? Armani. And who bought half of Arthus Bertrand? Louis Vuitton. Cartier was the first to move in. What happened was a takeover by the big names from the Right Bank's Rue Saint-Honoré.

Mr. Brenner of **La Hune**, whose store you will soon visit, says these big names are bringing the showcases of high luxury here, more for advertising than actual sales. Mr. Brenner and the group he represents feel this intrusion will take over and destroy the soul and the spirit of Saint-Germain. They feel the oldies—Hemingway, Natalie Clifford Barney, Camus, Sartre—would have put up a fight. They want everyone to sign their petitions. They want to preserve their bookstores, galleries, and artisans. They want to save the neighborhood's soul.

A meeting was held April 22, 1997, at the Café Flore to inaugurate the organization and make their case known. Juliette Greco, a longtime resident and famous actress and singer, with the help of actors Jean-Paul Belmondo and Catherine Deneuve, and singer Charles Aznavour, pleaded their case with the minister of culture, Philippe Douste-Blazy.

Saint-Germain is the heart of Parisian culture, the soul of learning, and the meeting place of intellectuals. The books sold at Le Divan were the source of debate and dis-

The front and back of the doorknob of La Hune at no. 14 Rue de l'Abbaye

cussion that animates the cafés on the boulevard. Concerned members of the neighborhood have started the organization SOS, Saint-Germain-des-Prés, Save Our Souls, with headquarters at La Hune. The petition reads, "The undersigned ask the public officials and legislators to do everything they can to maintain the cultural affairs which mark Saint-Germain as *the genius of the place*."

Before you enter La Hune, **no. 16** is the spot where the refectory of the abbey stood. Unfortunately, the door is usually locked; but try it anyway. The refectory was built by Pierre de Montreuil in 1239. Nearly five hundred years later, in 1714, a library was built over the refectory. During the Revolution the refectory served as a magazine for powder, which exploded on the night of August 19, 1794. The refectory collapsed and fire broke out, completely destroying it and the library above. Fortunately, most of the manuscripts were saved, including the original *Pensées* by Blaise Pascal, written on little bits of paper.

It was thought that no trace of the refectory remained. But a few years ago the government was in the midst of putting up moderately priced housing on this spot when the workers uncovered a marvelous windowed wall that had been the outside wall of the refectory. Its two and a half flamboyant windows, tall and graceful and intact, had been covered by plaster and totally forgotten for almost two hundred years.

The wall is preserved on the right-hand side of the entrance hall to the apartments. Some of the stones below are part of the old wall as well. The monks' cells in the *cave* are now filled in with brick walls and serve as storage rooms for the tenants. Niches for holy statues dot the walls.

Now visit **La Hune** (crow's nest), a fine and refined gallery, whose exhibitions and *vernissages*, openings, are always wonderful. Notice the bronze door handle in the shape of a man's face. When you leave the gallery, look at the back of the man's head on the handle. The artist is Igor Mitoraj.

Past La Hune, enter **no. 14** and walk to the back of the courtyard. To the right you will find a neat, small white stucco house. We saw it years ago when the place was in ruins and overgrown with bushes.

The door of **no. 12** can be opened by pushing the button at the bottom of the keypad. To leave, push the button on the wall to your left.

The building was a small rectangular cloister, thirteenth century, plainer than the larger one across the street. The bays have been filled in and rebuilt, but the shape remains the same. If you look all around, you will see the perfect symmetry of the four sides.

In **no. 13** are the remains of the abbey's larger cloister (built in the thirteenth century, restored in the seventeenth), in which the priests could walk. Remember that the Rue de l'Abbaye did not exist at that time and these cloisters were in fields surrounding the church. Note the three floors built above the arches of the cloister. Curtainlike vines drape the walls, green in summer, red in the fall.

No. 10 Rue de l'Abbaye houses an interesting shop, the Library of Museums. Here you can buy books, catalogs, and posters that are printed for the Louvre. They also have a gift catalog (free) of all the museum reproductions and exhibit a number of the jewelry and sculpture items that are for sale in the Louvre gift shop.

Nos. 11, **9**, **7**, and **5** have recently been restored. **Rubelli** at no. 11 shows decorator fabrics in an ultramodern setting. Between nos. 9 and 7, there is a parish office whose garden offers a fine view of the church. No. 7 has a hook for a pulley on its gabled top window.

Look into the glass door of **no. 8**, a *grand standing* apartment house (built in 1963), at a variously marbled, tiled, and flowered entry. Notice the spectacular wood sculpture shaped like a series of abstract totem poles. In the courtyard is a carefully tended (and that is unusual) walled garden with pool.

Nos. 1–5 are the remains of the palace built in 1586 for Cardinal Charles I of Bourbon, the abbot at Saint-Germain. The unusual style is marked by a sharply slanted slate roof and open pediment and particularly by the use of both brick and stone for the façade. The few remaining examples of this style are the houses on the Place des Vosges (see Walk 5) built under Henri IV, and the apartment houses that form the prow of the Ile de la Cité, facing the famous statue of Henri IV. Brick is, in general, rarely used in Paris. When you spot some turn-of-the-century brick apartment houses here and there, you will probably agree that stone suits Paris better.

Until recently these buildings were hidden by a temporary wall that also hid a gallery, a garage, and a social services center. Now two thirds is owned by the Institut Catholique and one third is still the social services office for this parish. Go in the door with names and door bells at **no. 5** to see the restored stone staircase and, through the metal grille, the lovely garden. The main staircase at **no. 3** originally served as the grand entrance to the abbey from the Rue de Furstenberg, behind you.

No. 6 bis is another of the many decorating shops in this area. These wallpaper and fabric shops often work with their neighbor **Manuel Canovas** at **no. 6**. Canovas was the first to move here. He also has showrooms at 7 and 5 Place Furstenberg. Note the Art Nouveau floral motif of the building.

For a light bite, pack a vegetarian lunch at the very busy **Guenmai**.

No. 2 is an old building with odd triangular windows on the right side of the house that follow the line of its staircase. A Greek restaurant, Au Vieux Paris, was opened by M. Nico on December 6, 1941, during the German occupation. When M. Nico could get limited meat supplies, he would call his best customers and serve it to them concealed beneath puréed potatoes. The building has been scaffolded and unused for years. Surprising in this coveted neighborhood.

Rue de Furstenberg

Retrace your steps to the **Rue de Furstenberg**. When Egon de Furstenberg was abbot of Saint-Germain-des-Prés in the last decades of the seventeenth century, he opened a new entrance to the palace, one that led into the Rue Colombier, street of doves, now the Rue Jacob. This entrance descended from the grand staircase of the abbey into the Rue de Furstenberg.

The square in the middle of this short street, with

its four pawlonia empress trees, and old-fashioned light globes, is a picturesque spot. Benches were removed because it became too much of a hangout. Although the trees are named after Anna Pavlova, daughter of Czar Paul I of Russia, they are Chinese (some sources say Japanese) in origin. They are admired in the spring for their perfumed mauve blossoms and large leaves. The two smaller ones are recent replacements. Symmetrical houses were built next to each other on either side of the square; **nos. 6** and **8**, still standing, and recognizable by their low doorways and brick-and-stone painted façades, were stables of the abbey.

This is the spot filmmakers choose in Paris for romance. Remember that Martin Scorsese filmed the final scene in *The Age of Innocence* in this square with Newland Archer sitting on a bench looking up, but never going up to the apartment of Mme Olenska to finally join the woman he loves. Edith Wharton did not put Newland in the Place Furstenberg, but in the more formal setting of the Place des Invalides, perhaps more fitting for his controlled rather than romantic response.

Walk through the stable archway of **no. 6**, across the courtyard to the center door, to the **Delacroix Museum**, home of the painter for the last six years of his life, 1857 to 1863. This is an exciting small museum, with changing exhibitions, fine drawings, and small sketches of Eugène Delacroix's completed masterpieces. Through the museum windows look to see a small cream-colored building with a pebbled garden. This was the infirmary of the abbey, where the invalids were kept, more as protection for the healthy than care for the sick.

After the museum, go outside and downstairs to Delacroix's atelier. It is a beautiful room with a huge skylight, high ceilings, and oak floors. It was here that Delacroix created his last works, which were exhibited at the Salon of 1859.

In the street once more, walking left toward the Rue Jacob, you will notice at the point where the street narrows

A stone torch on the pillar of no. 4 Place Furstenberg

a sculpted stone torch on the pillar of **no. 4**. It is the remains of the decoration of the Court of Honor, a place where ceremonies were performed when the palace on the Rue de l'Abbaye was Furstenberg's private domicile. The house was sold to the government in 1797 and taken down. Only this pillar, an entry, remains.

Directly across the street is an ultrachic Canovas retail store of items made with superb fabrics and available at lowered prices. Pillars from the abbey are carefully enclosed in glass, preserving traces of polychrome decorations.

As you head out to the Rue Jacob look to your right, down the small, picturesque **Rue Cardinale**. The street once lay within the boundaries of the Abbaye Saint-Germain and was named for the abbot, Guillaume de Furstenberg. It was originally the abbey's open-air tennis court but became a street in 1701. The house at the elbow of the street, **no. 3**, has an attractive terrace with wrought-iron grillwork, a sagging roof, and flowers (sometimes) that evoke a lost picture of this city's past. The last time we were here, a photography gallery had just opened. A few steps to the right of this house at **no. 5** is **Cipango**, selling creative jewelry made only from natural stones. Half the store is an atelier where the jewelry is made. Open afternoons only, except on Saturday.

There are interesting shops on your way to the Rue Jacob: choice seventeenth- and eighteenth-century antiques at **Yveline**, and at **no. 1**, **Aux Armes de Furstenberg,** a fine antique shop, almost an institution, specializing in scientific instruments, globes, and military objects. One more decorating shop at no. 1 has replaced a serious bookshop. Spot the exposed stone and beam inside.

We are going to turn right on Jacob; visit the Rue de Seine, packed with galeries and sights to see; and then return to visit the Rue Jacob.

In front of you and across the street, **no. 6** houses a curious shop, the **Huilerie Artisinale**, the kind that defies the chain stores. L'Huilerie resembles a perfume store with its many bottles of different oils. You can sniff and taste.

The young people here are members of a family that has been pressing oils in Bourgogne since 1878. They sell to fine restaurants and to you.

No. 1, **La Bonne Renommé**, at the corner on the right, lives up to its name. Its "good fame" is based on the ingenuity of these costume-like garments and accessories. If you wear one, anyone in the know knows what it is—without the logo. The phrase *la bonne renommé* comes from the maxim *La bonne renommée vaut mieux qu'une ceinture d'orée*—"Good reputation is worth more than a gold belt." (It rhymes in French.)

Rue de Seine

Turn right onto the **Rue de Seine*** to the attractive **Paris Art Gallery**, **no. 50**, (also at no. 1 Rue Jacob). There is a permanent collection of nature paintings by artist Saint Alban of Giverny, whose work "makes one sing of France" à la Monet. In addition, there are excellent sculptures, colorful posters, and nice people.

The **Hôtel de Seine**, **no. 52** in this central location, is a good choice. It is up-to-date, with telephones, color TV, individual safes, and reasonable prices.

No. 54 is an important, recently restored building, twelve windows wide. Note the stone pillars on the second floor, the mansard roof, and the tiny balcony.

Così at **no. 54**, sells a good, quick, inexpensive lunch of focaccia with original toppings. Open every day from lunch to midnight.

At the corner, **no. 56**, look up at the gable (*pignon*) roof in this 1744 building. Odd, because these pointed roofs facing the street were outlawed in the early 1500s. The rain gathered between the rooflines, instead of falling on the

---

*Note: The Rue de Seine is lined with well-known galleries (as are Jacob and Bonaparte). We cannot describe them all in detail, so if you are an art aficionado be sure to allow plenty of time to explore.

street below, causing serious water damage. There are only about thirty left in Paris.

In front of you is the wonderful **Buci food market**, one of the best in Paris. Find the old street name incised in stone at the corner of 75 Rue de Seine, "Rue de Seine" and "Rue de Bussy 16." The "16" refers to the sectioning of Paris before the city was divided into its twenty arrondissements.

Return to right side of the Rue de Seine. On this street **nos. 73**, **71**, **65**, and **63** are "old houses." Train your eyes to recognize differences with the other buildings.

The ironwork at **no. 73** is classified. The **Galerie de Buci** has exceptional paintings and sculpture. **No. 73, Art O'Leary's** pub, is a quiet dark spot off this busy street where you can sit indefinitely. We think husbands sit here while their wives shop.

La Table d'Italie at **no. 69**, a famous Italian deli, also sells terrific pasta dishes to eat in the little park next to the church of Saint-Germain.

No. 63, once the home of poet Adam Mickiewicz, the national poet of Poland, is beautifully restored with lovely wrought-iron balconies. **No. 57** with its four *mascarons*, three women on the second floor and a man on the third, is typical of eighteenth-century decoration. Find the man in the medallion above. The three-windows-wide balconied façade is classified.

Jacqueline Subra at **no. 51** collects quality estate jewelry and antiques. If you go through the first courtyard, through a building, and to the second courtyard, you will find a small garden with bushes and flowers set out in a pattern—a rarity in Paris.

At the back of the courtyard of **no. 49** is a charming shop called, appropriately, **Au Fond de la Cour**. Here you will find a tremendous collection of colorful majolica, serving dishes of all kinds (we have never seen so many variations of an asparagus plate), and furniture designed for greenhouses.

A "sliced lady" representing all the arts

Now we come to a watering place with dash. Sit outside a 1900s café at **La Palette**, **no. 43**, a lively hangout for actors, artists, and cinema people. It is off the beaten track of the boulevard, the café food is good, and the service is informal. Walk past the tables on the Rue Jacques Calot to find an amazing statue by Arman that is almost symbolic of the café and the neighborhood. The statue of a woman is sliced in vertical layers to show her many talents. Walk all around her and find all the signs of artistic creation: a pile of books, a painter's palette, brushes, a violin, and more.

A remnant of the French Revolution sits directly across the street at **no. 34**. The building is a *Temple d'Amitié*, a temple of friendship. These temples were built during the Revolution to replace churches. The words *A l'Amitié* (to friendship) are inscribed on it. This neighborhood was rich in such Revolutionary clubs, but very few remain.

At the corner (and officially at **no. 40 Rue de l'Echaudé**) is an ornate apartment building dating from 1910. It is interesting to compare the curves and lush decorations on this façade with the more sober seventeenth- and eighteenth-century buildings in the neighborhood.

Retrace your steps, stopping in galleries, to the garden on the corner of Seine and Jacob. This Japanese-type garden with stones, fountain, and grasses is lovely amid all the buildings and stores. There is often a bird perched on the highest stone.

Rue Jacob

Return to the **Rue Jacob** opposite the Place Furstenberg to visit this famous street. Streets in Paris are often named after famous people, important places, or interesting signs, but rarely do they get the name of a Biblical patriarch like Jacob. The name was given in memory of a vow taken by Marguerite de Valois, whose colorful life has left its mark on the history of this area and is worth recalling in some detail. Marguerite, known as "*chère* Margot," was the daughter of Henri II and Catherine de Médicis. She was the sister of two kings and the wife of Henri de Navarre, later Henri IV. In addition to having this noble background, she was beautiful and learned. Her memoirs are among the best written by nobility, but when the French refer to *chère* Margot with a knowing smile, they are thinking less of what she wrote than what she left out.

As one historian put it, "She knew love at eleven," and thanks to this early start was able to collect a long list of lovers in the course of her career. She had, of course, good teachers: her brother Henri III and his flamboyant *mignons*, as well as her cousin and husband, Henri, who is recorded as having had fifty-six mistresses.

Margot was married in 1572 at the age of nineteen to the Protestant Henri de Navarre (who was second in line for the throne) very much against her Catholic convictions and the will of the Pope. This mattered little compared to the determination of her brother Charles IX.

It took more than marriage to slow Margot down. She had her establishment; her husband his. All went well until one day in 1583 when Margot's brother Henri, now Henri III, denounced his sister's debauchery before the entire court. The actual cause of his anger was that Margot openly parodied him and his court of homosexuals.

This denunciation made it harder for Henri de Navarre to put up with her scandalous behavior, and finally, in 1587, under social pressure, her husband put her away in the Château d'Usson in Auvergne, where she managed to seduce her jailer. She made the best of her exile—eighteen years of a small court—writing memoirs and adding to her list of conquests. Nevertheless, she missed Paris and swore to raise an altar to Jacob if ever she was allowed to return. Jacob had also suffered exile, had worked and waited fourteen years for Rachel, and had finally been able to go back home, where he had given thanks to God for his safe return by building an altar.

The happy day came in 1605. By this time Henri de Navarre, now Henri IV, had long since divorced Margot and married Marie de Médicis. The king installed Margot in the château of the Archbishops (an ironic touch) of Sens, located on the Right Bank of the Seine at the entrance to the Marais quarter. (See Walk 7 for the Hôtel de Sens.)

Margot was then fifty-two, fat, bald, but as insatiable as ever. Her weight was so great she ordered the doorways widened. Her hair was so thin she snipped the locks of her blond valets for her wigs. Jean Duché, in his *Histoire de France Racontée à Juliette*, claims she wore around her ample waist amulets containing pieces of the hearts of her dead lovers.

Her lover of the moment was the twenty-year-old Count of Vermond, but finding him perhaps too old, Margot brought in the eighteen-year-old son of a carpenter from Usson. The Hôtel de Sens became a place of revelry. Vermond couldn't stand it. He lay in wait for his rival and shot him in the head right in front of Margot, who was returning from her religious devotion in a nearby church. Margot was enraged. She had Vermond pursued and arrested, and when he was brought before her, she cried out, "Kill the wretch. Here, here are my garters. Strangle him!" They cut off his head instead, while Margot looked on.

But all this blood and gore depressed her, and two days later she decided to leave the Hôtel de Sens and inhabit a house she was then building on the Pré aux Clercs, at what is now nos. 2–10 Rue de Seine. She remembered her vow and built the convent of Petits Augustins (now no. 14 Rue Bonaparte) in the back of the garden of her château. There she installed fourteen Augustinian friars, who took turns every two hours singing praises to Jacob with words and music written by Margot. Five years later she chased them out, claiming they sang badly. The name of the street is all that remains of Margot's celebrated gesture of thanksgiving.

This street is what we call one of the hidden streets of Paris. The unknowing eye sees shop after shop below five-story apartment buildings that show little decoration and little difference from one to the other. Not so. There are gardens, courtyards, staircases, even ceilings to discover on the Rue Jacob.

The building at **no. 5** is the spot where one of the towers of the surrounding walls of the abbey stood. It was twenty feet in diameter and stood next to the dovecote (hence the old name of the street, Rue Colombier) of the abbey.

Enter the **courtyard of no. 12** and go through the archway. At the back you'll find a small garden and to your right an Indian art gallery, **Mohanjeet,** which continues to attract a steady clientele.

Contrast the renovated house at the back of the courtyard with the untouched building at the left. Note the stone steps of the staircase, the old railing, and the rafters.

No. 12 is an antique shop that has replaced an old bookshop that was once the meeting place for lovers of Paris. The Huysmans Society met here every Saturday from three to six. Joris-Karl Huysmans is the famous nineteenth-century writer who described Paris in a manner so poetic, so unbelievably full of love, that his books today are collectors' treasures and are sold at auction for very high prices. Huysmans could write about the garbage smells of Paris in a way that would make you mourn the passing of the open garbage truck.

No. 7 dates from 1640 and was called the Hôtel Saint-Paul. Racine lived here with his uncle in 1656, when he was seventeen years old. Pierre Frey, another big decorating name, has moved in, replacing an art gallery.

Richard Wagner lived at **no. 14** for six months in 1841–1842.

A new building for this street, **no. 18**, built in 1928, is a nice example of Art Deco architecture, not often found here.

In the seventeenth century, **nos. 9**, **11**, and **13**, built next to the old abbey wall, were all one house, belonging to a member of Parliament, M. Chabenat de la Malmaison. Later, the building was the Hôtel de la Gabelle, the main office for the collection of the salt tax. **No. 9** is now an expensive art gallery.

No. 11 is **Le Petit Atelier**. This was once a studio where children seven to sixteen years old learned English through play-acting, mime, and music "in the language of Shakespeare." Today it is a theater workshop offering six-week seminars that result in a performance. If the group is not too busy, ask if you can go upstairs to see their ceiling. There are hundreds of rafters in Paris but none like these remarkably well preserved and painted ones. They date from the end of the fifteenth century; the painting, however, was done later. Various trades of the City of Paris are pictured in the medallions in the center. Part of this building was owned by an antique dealer, who had never uncovered what was certainly the most valuable treasure his store had ever seen. The entire ceiling had been hidden (and preserved) by plaster. Very skillful restoration has saved most of it. Imagine the beauty of this room when it was two floors high and the fireplace on the side wall was huge enough to reach this height.

When you reach the entry to **nos. 11** and **13**, stand back and look. The tall, rounded doorways are topped by the typical eighteenth-century mask decorations called *mascarons*. These two must have been done either at different times or by different people. One of the nicest pieces of iron sculpture, a flamboyant *S* projecting tridents, to ensure privacy, is attached to the wall above the two doorways.

If you can enter no. 11 (push the release button and the door might unlatch), turn left through the entrance before the courtyard, go up a few steps, and you will find an imposing, wide stone staircase. What is truly impressive is that the banisters and railing were cut in stone by hand—a tremendous task, in comparison to the already difficult one of turning a banister in wood. This Louis XIII style is often used for wooden staircases, as is the case on the upper floors of this building. In summer this wide stair-

Mascaron at no. 13 Rue Jacob

Mascaron at no. 11 Rue Jacob

well is a cool, quiet spot; in winter, when it gets dark early, turn the *minuterie* light on until you have seen it all. Please be discreet and polite if you meet residents.

On the other side of no. 13 is an antique store, **Galerie 13 Rue Jacob**, that specializes in period furniture and particularly in games: chess, backgammon, game tables, ivory counters, and more.

Much has been said and written about **no. 20**, but today little can be seen. A little Temple of Friendship, like the one on Rue de Seine, is hidden in the courtyard behind an iron door. If you try to look in, the concierge will peer out her curtain and call a huge dog who will bark loud and long, but safely behind a high wall. The garden and the temple are owned by Michel Debré, former right-hand man to de Gaulle and then to Pompidou.

Natalie Clifford Barney, a very French-American woman, lived here. She was called in her youth the Amazon or the Sappho of 1900. She was beautiful, intelligent, and at the forefront of a literary movement that championed women's independence. In her second-floor apartment she received a procession of the greatest writers and artists of the twentieth century: Hemingway, Joyce, T. S. Eliot, Colette, Rilke, Apollinaire, Anatole France, Max Jacob, Anna de Noailles, and many others. She was a legend to the people, a lesbian in her personal life, and catholic in her hospitality. Her generosity was legendary; she once hosted a boat trip around Greece for fifty friends. She did as much for the artistic life of the quarter as did the well-known cafés on the Boulevard Saint-Germain.

As you leave the courtyard notice the classified wrought-iron banisters and gate and the consoles of phoenixes in the entry hall.

Comoglio's, no. 15, now a fabric and antique store, used to sell odd objects to theaters for scenery. The back-yard was piled high with screens, statues, and curiosities. That is part of the old Paris that is disappearing—which is, of course, inevitable.

Nos. 17 and **26** are two bookshops that indicate the range of specialized bookshops in Paris. One is agricultural and horticultural; the other, specializing in maritime books and overseas editions, shows maps and prints in the window as well. Look also at the old houses above the shops.

Hôtel Millisime, no. 15, decorated in warm Provençal fabrics and colors, is one of several charming, not overly expensive hotels in this neighborhood. They serve breakfast in their beautifully restored vaulted cellars. These hotels are always popular, and you must book far in advance for reservations in the spring and summer.

Within the interstices of **no. 19**, down hallways,

through doors, past offices of the publishing house Editions du Seuil, there is a private house and garden with a view of the back of the Delacroix Museum. Prudhomme, an active pamphleteer against the ancien régime, lived back here. He was an editor of the *Revue de Paris*, a revolutionary journal, and it was in the quiet of this garden that he wrote the incendiary articles that led to numerous arrests.

No. 21, the **Hôtel des Maronniers**, with its courtyard of chestnut trees that can be seen in winter through glass walls, is one of the many attractive medium-priced hotels on this street.

Atelier d'Anaïs, at **no. 23**, is a fine old-fashioned needlepoint and knitting shop. The ladies are skilled, capable of drawing your design for you or supplying their own. They send you on your way either with marked canvas, needles, wool, and samples of each stitch already begun on your canvas, or with their lush wool and a knitting pattern. The store was named after their aunt Anaïs, not Anaïs Nin.

At **no. 25**, the **Hôtel des Deux Continents**, another favorite of the Rue Jacob. For high season reserve two months in advance.

No. 28 is a shop selling rare stones and minerals. Claude Boullé specializes in stone slices that look like seascapes or the countryside. The stones come from Tuscany. Not expensive and full of wonder.

There are no old houses or antique staircases in the back of the courtyard of **no. 30**, but you will find a collection of young artisans who restore paintings as well as and probably better than their predecessors hundreds of years before them at **Restoration-Depretz**.

The first time we visited these talented artisans they were barefoot and hirsute, seemingly antiestablishment. The following year they wore jackets and shoes, but the ambience remained the same. They move within one another's work areas, talking and joking all the while. This easy atmosphere is the setting for the highest degree of delicate, technical, and artistic work. They were gone when we visited again, but a resident says they will return. An old bookbinder from another era next door is also gone.

Twenty years ago the Editions du Seuil, an important French publishing house, took over the lovely private home and front garden of **no. 27**. Ingres, the champion of classical painting, lived here more than 150 years ago.

No. 29 replaces a traditional hotel with a whole new look for this Saint-Germain neighborhood. **La Villa** is a high-fashion, Memphis-decorated hotel. It is rated as a four-star hotel (more luxurious than most in this area), and the furniture and colors have all been carefully chosen to make a "statement." Try their bar and popular jazz club at night.

Across the street on the corner to the right, **Mme Castaing** was an Art Deco institution. She would, for example, buy a dress at Chanel and improve on it by removing the sleeves. She bought only the most curious and interesting objects, mainly from the nineteenth century. Her son has taken over and continues the style. Room after room is filled with strange furniture from the colonies or from England. Elephants' feet serve as ashtrays, goats' legs hold up tables, and palms and rubber plants flourish everywhere.

Rue Bonaparte

Despite too many cars in the road and too many people on the street, the **Rue Bonaparte** is still a favorite of visitors and Parisians. The shops are rich with the art of today and yesterday; nobility of all ranks lived on this street, and although the colorful history of the street is less obvious, it is nevertheless there to see and imagine.

Seven hundred years ago there was no street here at all, simply open fields that belonged to the abbey. You will recall the stories of the university students battling violently with the priests of the abbey over the use of these lands. These conflicts were settled only in 1368, when the monks built a wall and moat around themselves for privacy and safekeeping. At that time they also dug a canal, sixty-five feet wide and twenty-five feet deep, which ran from the Seine down the present Rue Bonaparte to the corner where you are now standing, Rue Jacob and Rue Bonaparte.

Here is where this arm of the river, La Petite Seine, emptied its waters into the moat of the abbey. Boats sailed up and down, bringing in and taking away goods. But the canal's most important function was to provide a natural division between the field frequented by the students, which was a small piece of land that covered the area between what are now the Rues Jacob and Visconti up to the Rue Bonaparte (called the Petit Pré aux Clercs), and the larger field on the other side of the canal favored by the priests (called the Grand Pré aux Clercs).

For almost two hundred years the little Seine character-ized the *quartier*, and when it was eventually filled in in 1540, it gave its name to the paved road that took its place, Rue de la Petite Seine.

In 1606, when the famous Margot received a gift from her ex-husband, Henri IV, of a piece of land on the Rue de Seine, she built the beautiful château whose walled gardens and walks cut through the Rue de la Petite Seine, closing it off from the river itself. But Margot was generous with her new domain and allowed her meadows and gardens and shaded walks to go on giving pleasure to the simple folk of the neighborhood.

Marie de Médicis, who was Margot's successor as wife to Henri IV and whose money no doubt paid for Margot's château, was jealous of the latter's reputation for generosity and her popularity with the people. And so Marie tried to outdo her by building the Cours de la Reine, the queen's way, a wide and beautiful road on the Right Bank of the Seine, parallel to the Champs-Elysées. These two ladies, Marie and Margot, spent more time outfoxing each other than Henri spent thinking about either of them; his con-stant love was Gabrielle d'Estrées.

Margot's gardens and the convent of Petits Augustins, which she had built farther up the street, lasted until 1628, thirteen years after her death. At that time her property was divided among many, and the street was once again opened, this time named the Rue des Petits Augustins. Look across the street to see this old name cut in stone on the corner.

The name Bonaparte was not given until the year 1852. Why is there no Rue Napoléon in Paris? Was he too formidable a hero? Perhaps the idea of the republican Bonaparte is more acceptable.

And now for the street, to find what is new and what remains of the old. Your route will turn right at the corner of Bonaparte and Jacob, continue up the right side to the top, and then cross to the other side and back down the street to return to the Place Saint-Germain.

Today, as part of the upscaling of the neighborhood, an elegant real estate office at **no. 18** has replaced **Bulloz**, now in the courtyard. Few establishments in the old-fashioned style of Bulloz still exist in Paris or anywhere. The moment you enter the uncluttered, quiet premises and are greeted by the gentle ladies who serve you, you realize that although their type of photographic service is greatly in demand today, they remain unaffected by the passing of time. Here you can have a picture of yourself, or a landscape, or a document, or a painting, or anything blown up to any size you specify. Their work is excellent as well as dependable. Pictures come in black and white or in color, and there are thousands to choose from if you like the idea but don't have one of your own to develop.

The door to the courtyard of **no. 21** on the left gives you an idea of the grand houses that surrounded the abbey in the sixteenth century. The garden of Queen Margot's palace on the Rue de Seine extended all the way to the other side of this street just a few yards up from here. The grand house before you now was built in 1760, around the courtyard of an earlier one, for Prévost de Saint Cyr, and was lived in during the Consulate (1799–1804) by the

Princess de Rohan-Rochefort, who was secretly married to the Duke of Enghien. After the Revolution these houses changed their tenants and their appearance, as the neighborhood turned popular. Today it is once again a street of high rents, coveted apartments, and very special shops and galleries. It is also one of the most heavily trafficked streets in Paris.

This large courtyard is picturesque, with its thick ivy, ornamental ironwork on the balcony windows, and large iron hook for a pulley on the dormer, or mansard, above to the left.

If you wish to buy a fancy gown starting at $1,000 and rising quickly, visit **Vicky Tiel** in the courtyard. Elizabeth Taylor has been a customer here and is an old friend. It was through Vicky's husband, who was Richard Burton's makeup artist, that the initial contact was made. Some other customers here include Farrah Fawcett and Ivana Trump.

We were told that D'Artagnan's stables were here, but then again we were also told that about the Rue Saint-Gilles on the other side of town. Continue up the street to the corner of Rue Visconti.

The façade, the door, and the courtyard of **no. 19** are classified.

The **Librairie du Cygne** at **no. 17** specializes in books on the history of art. Their window display usually consists of books relating to a scholarly theme.

You are now at the intersection of the Rue Bonaparte and the Rue des Beaux Arts. If you wish to take the time to see a beautifully appointed hotel, called simply **L'Hôtel**, walk a few steps down to the right. Wander in under the atrium and walk to the back of the reception rooms, where there are bowers of plants and perhaps still a parrot flying free. Oscar Wilde is memorialized; he had a room here.

On the corner of Bonaparte and Beaux Arts is the **Restaurant des Beaux Arts**. This is a local hangout with typical food like herring filets or steak-frites and crème caramel for dessert.

Art galleries abound here and the twentieth century seems to be king. **No. 7** sells Deco furniture and **no. 5** sells Deco and Nouveau *objets* of high quality. Most of these galleries don't open until eleven or eleven-thirty and then close at lunch for an hour at one. **No. 5**, like no. 21, is typical of the eighteenth century, presenting an impressive wall and entry on the street and apartments that look down on the beautiful courtyard. Note the plaque on the outside wall: "Here, formerly 5, Rue des Petits Augustins, was born Edouard Manet, 1832–1885."

The **Galerie Damien** sells exquisite sculptures and figurines of the Art Deco period.

If you have walked to the end of the street, you've reached the **Quai Malaquais**; to the right is the **Institut de France**, home of the French Academy, where the renowned dictionary writers and protectors of the purity of the French language work. Election to the Académie Française is open to only forty "immortals," who choose their own colleagues. The ceremony of admission calls for an ornate dress uniform with sword. These swords are much too expensive for most academicians to buy themselves, so friends usually contribute to the cause. Later you can visit Arthus Bertrand, which makes these swords. Across the *quai* there is a romantic footbridge over the Seine to the Louvre.

The little low house across the street, **no. 4 Rue Bonaparte**, with dormer windows and with hook and wheel for loading above one of them, was built in 1620. Cross the street to look up at it. This site was originally a hospital run by the Brothers of Charity until Queen Margot forced them out in order to build her neighborhood estate. The **Paris American Art** is a huge art supply store serving the Ecole des Beaux Arts, the school of fine arts down the street.

There are two modern art galleries at **no. 6**. Look up at the roof garden on top of the building and the small corner room that leads into it. This building was redesigned and restored in the eighteenth century.

At **no. 8**, **Félix Marcilhac** has collected some beautiful pieces of Art Deco and Art Nouveau. They are few but extremely fine.

Librairie E. Rossignol, also at no. 8, is an antique bookshop passed from father to son since 1906. The family moved here in 1940 when they were dispossessed by the Germans. They publish a yearly catalogue and maintain special-interest files in order to notify customers of relevant acquisitions.

At **no. 10**, **La Porte Etroite** is exactly that, a narrow door, the title of a book by André Gide. This bookshop was probably a hallway. Also at no. 10, **Jacques de Vos** buys, sells, and appraises art of the period 1910–1950.

At **no. 12**, **M. Roux-Devillas** spends his days surrounded by memories of the past. He specializes in old books, old documents (autographs), and old scientific instruments. The collection ranges from sundials and eighteenth-century dental tools to treaties signed by kings. One home inventory of the wife of a French lieutenant general in Martinique in 1791 divided her possessions into three sections: furnishings, silver, and slaves. All the slaves were identified and described in the same way: name, job, age, and price. There was Jurançon who took care of the boats, thirty-two years old, and worth 3,300 francs; Caroline, no duties, five years old, worth 500 francs; and Lucille, who was too old and incapacitated to do or be worth anything at all, but was listed simply to note her existence, *"laissée pour memoiré."* Documents of this kind form the basis of historical research on slavery today. This is one of the few shops that offer valuable historical items at reasonable rates.

The **Ecole des Beaux Arts** is at **no. 14**. This site is a mini-stage for the history of Paris. The first record of inhabitants dates from 1603 when Marie de Médicis, Henri IV's Italian wife, brought five priests from Florence and built for them, here, a charity hospital. These priests were also surgeons and pharmacists. Clearly Marie de Médicis felt she needed more than serving ladies to accompany her to her new country and established, in effect, for her use as well as that of others, an Italian hospital and an Italian pharmacy. The Brothers of Charity Hospital moved three years later to the corner of the Rue des Saints-Pères and the Rue Jacob, where it became a large and important hospital, lasting until 1937, when it was taken down.

After the removal of the original hospital, the eccentric Margot built her promised altar to Jacob here. Although the continual singing of litanies by the monks was stopped after five years, the convent remained until the Revolution, at which time it was forced to close down. It was left abandoned, but not for long.

During the French Revolution it was the sworn duty of each citizen to remove every symbol of religion and royalty he could find. (See Walk 2, page 49 for the altering of street signs.) A young painter and critic, Alexandre Lenoir, was quick to see the threat to all the art treasures and manuscripts in Paris. After eloquent and anguished pleading, he received permission to take or buy all the treasures he could find, to store the books and manuscripts in two other convents, and to store the art treasures in this one. There followed frenzied years of snatching books from fire, saving statues of precious metal from the mint, and rescuing kings from their coffins at Saint-Denis. A bayonet pierced Lenoir when he threw himself upon Richelieu's tomb in the church of the Sorbonne to save it from the mob in 1839.

He was unable to save the row of statues under the first balcony of Notre-Dame (the one in The *Hunchback of Notre-Dame* that the beggars climbed to save Esmeralda from the hands of the Hunchback). These statues, meant to represent the kings of the Bible but done in the anachronistic style of Merovingian kings, were thought to be kings of France and were pulled down. They were presumed lost until a few years ago, when they were found buried in the basement of an apartment house in the seventeenth arrondissement. They are now in the Cluny Museum. But Lenoir got whatever he could, however he could, and gathered it in, until this old convent became an amazing storehouse.

When the Terror was over, Lenoir could stand back and look at the most eloquent creations of eighteen centuries of French art. He was inspired to make this cave of Ali Baba into a museum of French monuments. In 1795 that became a reality. Chroniclers describe the display of treasures as the most beautiful and impressive ever gathered in one place. It lasted through the Directory, through the Consulate, and through the Empire. Napoléon, in his zeal to preserve the glory of France, showered gifts and privileges on it. Perhaps that is the real reason for the present name of the street. But Louis XVIII made the irresponsible decision (one of many) to close the museum and disperse its contents. He allowed each locality to reclaim its old art treasures.

Although the collection was dispersed, it has reappeared in the sixteenth arrondissement at the Place du Trocadéro as the Museum of French Monuments, with copies (magnificently done) of religious art from throughout France. The monastery here was then turned into a school of fine arts, the Ecole des Beaux Arts, familiarly called just the Beaux Arts.

Enter the courtyard. On the right, high in a niche, should be a statue of Alexandre Lenoir. He was missing on our last visit, but we hope he was gone only for cleaning and restoration. The classified and odd remains of château doors and pieces of sculpture that decorate the courtyard have been taken from châteaux. The classical building at the back, just cleaned, was put up in 1858 and was the original building of the school. Go through the main door to see the neoclassical frescoes, the lecture rooms, and the students' work in progress.

When you are back in the courtyard facing the street, enter the middle of the wing to your left and go into the delightful Cour du Mûrier, the court of the mulberry tree, which was a cloister of the convent. The pedestals in each cloister bay are capped by pieces of Roman sculpture (mostly legless and armless) made by students who had won the Grand Prix de Rome. This coveted prize allowed the winner to go to Rome to study the antique and Renaissance masters in the Villa Médicis. Critics claimed, however, that as long as the best talent got such training, French art was likely to remain "classical."

It turns out, however, that the students at Beaux Arts were among the most disruptive in the revolt of 1968, and they destroyed and damaged a good deal of the school. At that time the school granted all sorts of student demands, including one to separate the faculties for painting, architecture, sculpture, and so on, in order to improve the level of teaching, which the students felt was too general. The administration, cleverly, has continued this idea of division to such a degree that it has weakened the communal role of the students. Classes are held all over Paris, painters never see sculptors, and even the famous costume ball of the Beaux Arts has not been held since the uprising. Political interest has waned, although there was a poster inviting everyone to a Saturday evening demonstration denouncing imperialism.

We were sitting on a stone ledge in the big courtyard on the Quai Malaquais, wondering where the spirit of art students had gone, when we were suddenly doused with cold water from a balcony above. Amid gales of laughter, we were told how lucky we were it hadn't been ink or paint.

Return to the Rue Bonaparte, where, at **no. 20**, **Boulakia** exhibits twentieth-century art. This building is one that marks this area as Henri IV's. Of all his women, Gabrielle d'Estrées was the one he loved most, and in the back of this courtyard is a house in which their son, César de Vendôme, once abbé of Saint-Germain, lived. He was born illegitimate in 1594, recognized the following year, and would have been king had Louis XIII not been born.

If it is unlocked, go into the courtyard of **no. 28** to look at the elegant open staircase with its fountain and thick, flowering vines. Look at the modern art in the **Galerie Jacob**.

This next section of Rue Bonaparte (between Rue Jacob and Rue de l'Abbaye) seems to belong to **Nobilis**, an important interior decorating firm. They occupy **nos. 29, 31, 38,** and **40**. At no. 29 they sell finished goods made from their own fabrics, including very nice traveling bags and lap rugs. Very chic and expensive.

At **no. 25**, **Simrane** sells high-quality very attractive cotton cloths, napkins, and place mats made in India but in French style. Note the antique jewelry and silver at **no. 27**.

The **Hôtel Saint-Germain-des-Prés** at **no. 36** has one of the most charming lobbies in Paris. The back wall is a sheet of glass sandwiching a beautiful display of flowers growing in a hothouse against the stone wall of the building. The building is eighteenth-century, and although the décor reflects this, every room provides all the modern amenities at reasonable prices. August Comte lived here between 1818 and 1822.

Fabrice at **no. 33** specializes in jewelry and accessories that are always unique and avant-garde.

To the right is the small street, **Guillaume Apollinaire,** named for the artist whose statue sits across the street in the garden of the church. The restaurants with historic names, **Le Bonaparte** and **Le Clocher**, are pleasant spots when the cars are not too close.

At the end of the street is the famous restaurant **Le Petit Zinc**, which has moved here from the Buci Market. The interior is an authentic Art Nouveau setting. The decorations were brought here from other buildings, but the tiles, wrought-iron railings, bar, and furniture seem to have been made for the room. Moderately priced.

Continue on the Rue Bonaparte on the opposite side of the street from the church of Saint-Germain to the very proper and dignified **Arthus Bertrand**. It is now cut to one-half its size by the coming of **Louis Vuitton**, the expensive leather goods store (that means a small over-the-shoulder alligator pouch costs $3,000).

Enter Arthus Bertrand, a 150-year-old firm that specializes in museum reproductions of jewelry and honorary medals. They reproduce the Louvre's artifacts, but in sterling silver or 18-carat gold. This is a serious shop; the merchandise is exhibited in cases and you must sit at the table and have trays brought to you for inspection as the saleswoman consults a separate price list. They engage 180 employees to make their jewelry. Arthus Bertrand is especially famous for military medals and decorations. They supply 80 percent of the medals for the African nations and the individually designed academician's swords for the Institut de France. The latter range in price from $10,000 to $20,000. Claire Chretien told us how much she personally enjoys designing the swords for the academicians.

Notice the fountain in front of **no. 24**. (See Walk 4, page 154.)

You now come to a wide pavement once used in the summer months for late-night plays, pantomimes, and acts by sword swallowers, fire-eaters, and chain breakers. A stage was set up here and crowds gathered to watch, as in medieval times. The hat was passed for contributions. As another part of the "refinement" of the area, Les Deux Magots has extended the restaurant into this spot behind a row of hedges. The square is now quiet in the evening.

Take a table at the famous café **Les Deux Magots**, or its rival, the **Café de Flore**.

You are now in the heart of what was, and to some extent still is, the artistic and literary center of Paris. Before the First World War, Picasso and Apollinaire were already installed at the Flore, in the back, although they were also habitués of the even more popular cafés of Montparnasse: the Dôme, the Rotonde, and the Closerie des Lilas. How many cafés can one frequent? When did they work, and where did they work?

The "lost generation" of expatriates after the First World

Anytime at Les Deux Magots

War, some of whom drank themselves into oblivion, frequented both Saint-Germain and Montparnasse. One distinction, however, between the two areas seems to have been that writers favored Saint-Germain-des-Prés; artists, Montparnasse. Reread Hemingway's *A Moveable Feast* and *The Sun Also Rises* for the feel of these days gone by.

Les Deux Magots was the birthplace of surrealism, the Café de Flore the home of the existentialists. Simone de Beauvoir and Jean-Paul Sartre had their regular table at the latter, drawing young intellectuals like a magnet. Albert Camus came, but not often, because Sartre was supposedly jealous of Camus; at any rate the two did not get on.

Today café life is still fascinating. The talk is at once stereotyped and unbelievable. It is about ex-husbands and weekend houses or business deals concerning art, films, and books. Most of the publishing houses have offices in this quarter, so a constant stream of intellectuals will be around for lunch or a drink. Tourists come to look at everyone else; the French come to be looked at. It is still true that many of these people know one another, and the neighborhood keeps the character of a small town.

These cafés got their odd names the same way so many other places and streets in Paris did. A small statue of Flora (goddess of flowers and mother of spring) used to stand at the door of the Café de Flore. Visit the interesting room on the second floor of the Flore decorated, as the French say, "in the English style."

Les Deux Magots was the name of a novelty shop that planned to move to this spot from the Rue de Buci in 1873, but before that actually happened, a bar opened, used their name, and has been here ever since. The *deux magots* are the two wooden statues, inside the café on the central pillar, of Chinese dignitaries (most often portrayed in porcelain) that were to be the standard of the novelty shop.

In 1984 the Deux Magots was sold at auction. M. Mathivat, who has operated the café for the last thirty years, bought it. "I bought it for sentimental reasons," he said. "Don't worry. It will always remain what it has been. I don't want to start a fast-food joint." The auction was carried out in the Chambre des Notaires tradition. After the bidding was finished, the auctioneer lit two candles. As they burned, those with a possible change of heart had the opportunity to come in with a higher bid. Under the law M. Mathivat was not the true owner until ten days later. A bid of ten percent more than his could still have been accepted.

Before his death, our late friend Georges Perec (author of *La Vie: mode d'emploi*), had, as have others like him, ceased to come to Saint-Germain any more. But the small cafés off the beaten path are still frequented. Cafés are not only an important part of people's lives, about which they write, but are also the places where literature is made.

Behind the Flore on Rue Saint-Benoît are several restaurants that have outside tables in the warm weather. In particular **La Grosse Horloge**, with a huge clock as its standard, is worth trying. They serve classic French food, very tasty, the kind you wish you could make at home. **No. 26**, **Boutique du Café Flore** offers fun kitchen souvenirs.

Le Drugstore, which was across the street from the Flore and the Deux Magots at **149 Boulevard Saint-Germain**, was an American institution that became famously popular overnight. The French loved the hamburgers, which they ate with a knife and fork, and they hung out there until closing time at two in the morning. **Armani** has now moved in.

In an effort to placate the SOS movement and to keep the genius of the area, Armani has paid for the new windows in the church of Saint-Germain-des-Prés. Their clothes prices are still prohibitive, but the café fits into the general ambience of the neighborhood.

Across the Boulevard Saint-Germain visit **Arts et Bijoux, no. 147**, an old-timer in the neighborhood. In addition to elegant estate jewelry, there are sculptures of rabbits, cats, and other animals by the son of the owners, Marc Poncini, a well-known *animalier*. These are objects you want to take home with you.

There are two famous restaurants nearby. **Brasserie Lipp, no. 151 Boulevard Saint-Germain**, is a restaurant that has done what we would have considered the impossible. The French, as you know, consider themselves the arbiters of fine taste, and the food they might least copy would be German-style food. The namesake of the restaurant, Lippmann, was an Alsatian who was desperately unhappy about the separation of his homeland from France. Alsatian food and drink are, however, typically German— frankfurters and sauerkraut, along with light and dark beer. The amazing fact is that this dish caught on; it appears today on almost every Parisian menu. *Choucroute alsacienne* is sold fresh in every charcuterie, in cans in every grocery, and it is now the raison d'être of countless restaurants in Paris, including Bofinger, described in Walk 7.

In the early 1900s Lipp was *the* after-theater place to dine, as the Plaza Athénée was fifty years later. The lovely ladies shown in engravings, picking up their long dresses as they step from horse-drawn hacks, were no doubt going to dine at Lipp. By 1924 the area had become so much the quarter of editors (two steps to Grasset, four to Gallimard, and six to Hachette) and their prize-winning writers that Lipp was forced to enlarge, not like the Deux Magots, which could extend its stomach onto the pavement, but by turning and twisting into the recesses behind the restaurant. In the 1960s Lipp was the eating place for politicians as well as writers. François Mitterrand, then president of France, used to dine here.

Vagenende, no. 142, is a joy to behold. Here is 1900 in all its fantasy and variety. You will see many a floral door on the Boulevard Saint-Germain, but they are a product of the 1970s. This restaurant and the even more fantastic restaurant of the Gare de Lyon (which was shown in the films *Travels with My Aunt* and *Murder on the Orient Express*) are the real thing, built when the creation of Art Nouveau was at its height.

Although you have walked and talked and looked for a good two hours, these few streets are only a sample of what the neighborhood has to offer. It is no doubt time, however, to sit down at a café or restaurant and restore yourself. *Bon appétit!*

Walk · 4

Mouffetard

De par le roi, défense à Dieu
De faire miracle en ce lieu.

By order of the king, God is
   forbidden
To perform miracles in this place.

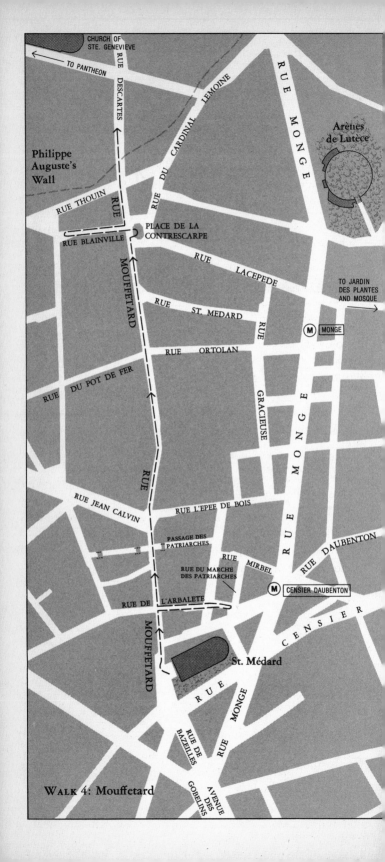

CHURCH OF
STE. GENEVIEVE

TO PANTHEON

RUE DESCARTES

RUE DU CARDINAL LEMOINE

RUE MONGE

Arènes
de Lutèce

Philippe
Auguste's
Wall

RUE THOUIN

RUE

RUE BLAINVILLE

MOUFFETARD

PLACE DE LA
CONTRESCARPE

RUE LACEPEDE

RUE ST. MEDARD

RUE

MONGE

TO JARDIN
DES PLANTES
AND MOSQUE

RUE ORTOLAN

RUE DU POT DE FER

GRACIEUSE

RUE

RUE JEAN CALVIN

RUE L'EPEE DE BOIS

RUE MONGE

RUE DAUBENTON

PASSAGE DES
PATRIARCHES

RUE MIRBEL

RUE DU MARCHE
DES PATRIARCHES

CENSIER DAUBENTON

RUE DE L'ARBALETE

MOUFFETARD

St. Médard

CENSIER

RUE

RUE MONGE

RUE DE BAZEILLES

AVENUE DES GOBELINS

WALK 4: Mouffetard

Starting Point: Eglise Saint Médard, 5th arrondissement
Métro: Censier Daubenton
Bus: 47

Rue Mouffetard

The **Rue Mouffetard** is different from our other walks because, although it is one of the liveliest streets in Paris and has a fascinating history, many of the events that happened here have left no traces. We recommend that you read this walk beforehand so that you won't be trying to read while being jostled by the crowds. This will also allow you to spend your time discovering the pleasures of the *marché* for yourself. Bring shopping bags.

You can do your advance reading in the garden of the church of Saint-Médard before you venture into the market. After you have left this garden, you will be unable to find a place to sit other than cafés, curbs, and the public library (when open) at no. 74.

There are two good times of the day to come and visit this neighborhood: the best is between nine and noon, particularly on a Saturday or Sunday, when you can see the most colorful outdoor food market in Paris (closed Mondays); the second is at night, when all the restaurants and cafés are open and the youth of Paris (and the tourists) are out to eat and people-watch.

In ancient times the Rue Mouffetard was important as the main Roman road to the southeast, Lyons, and Italy, but it owes its real development to the Bièvre River. This river flowed across the base of the hill where the street ends today (originally the road continued to the Porte d'Italie). Its banks offered excellent land for settlement, and in the twelfth century the area, called the Bourg Saint-Marcel, was a village where wealthy Parisians had farms and country houses. The list of residents of the mid-fourteenth century reads like the social register. In a huge area (currently delineated by three streets—Mouffetard, Lacépède, and Geoffroy-Saint-Hilaire—and the Bièvre River) there were only two roads, Mouffetard and Daubenton and, apart from the church, only seven estates. These were owned by bishops, lords, the president of the courts, and Charles V's architect.

Nevertheless, the dominance of the upper class was not long-lasting, again because of the Bièvre. The river ran with sweet water, which encouraged cultivation, and was famous for its freshwater shrimp, described by Madame de Maintenon as "the best that could be imagined." The river, however, was soon discovered to contain properties efficacious in skinning and tanning hides. Rabelais offers his own bawdy explanation for this phenomenon in *Pantagruel*, book 2, chapter 22. In this story Panurge takes revenge on the finest lady in town, who had scorned his love. He kills a bitch in heat and carefully prepares "that part [about which] the Greek necromancers knew." The following day is a feast day, and, finding the woman in her best clothes in the church,

> Panurge deftly sprinkled the drug that he was carrying on to various parts of her, chiefly on the pleats of her sleeves and her dress. . . . All the dogs in the church ran up to the lady, attracted by the smell of the drug he had sprinkled on her. Small and great,

big and little, all came, lifting their legs, smelling her and pissing all over her. It was the most dreadful thing in the world.

. . . She ran to hide, with the dogs after her and all the chambermaids laughing. But once she was inside and the door closed behind her, all the dogs ran up from two miles around and pissed so hard against the gate of the house that they made a stream with their urine big enough to swim in. And it is this stream which now passes by Saint Victor, in which Mme Gobelin dyes her scarlet, thanks to the specific virtue of those piss-hounds, as our master Dung-powder once proclaimed in a public sermon.

In the sixteenth and seventeenth centuries, the population of the Bourg Saint-Marcel became working class—tanners, slaughterers, skinners, dyers, and similar craftsmen. They named their bridge the Pont aux Tripes ("tripe bridge"). The famous Gobelins' wool factory is the only survivor from this period. It was because of the Flemish tapestry weavers at the Gobelins' that the second characteristic of the neighborhood developed. The Flemish were great beer drinkers, a tradition they would not leave behind, and soon cafés and cabarets proliferated to serve them. The successors to these establishments are still here.

Industry, together with the rotting animal wastes, rapidly polluted the Bièvre. By the nineteenth century, this neighborhood was the commercial and shopping center of the Left Bank, but the fumes from the Bièvre were more noxious than ever. There is a theory that the name of the Rue Mouffetard comes from these sewerlike qualities of the river: the French for "skunk" or "bad smell" is *mouffette*. There is another less amusing explanation that claims that in the Roman times the hill was called *mons cetardus*, perhaps named after a now forgotten Roman, which became *mont cetard*, then *montfetard*, and finally *Mouffetard*. In 1828 a portion of the river was covered; in 1840–1848 studies were done to try to save the Bièvre; in 1910 the only possible solution finally came to pass: the river became part of the underground sewer system. Even now, in the summer, at certain corners, a foul odor still seems to emanate from the pavement under your feet.

The door to the **church of Saint-Médard** faces the market on the Rue Mouffetard. Architecturally, this church is not particularly notable, though some of the events connected with it are. The first church on this spot is thought to have been built in the seventh or eighth century, in dedication to Saint Médard, but there is no evidence to support this theory. The first positive proof of the existence of this church is in a papal bull of Pope Alexander III. It dates from 1163, when the pope came to Paris to consecrate the choir of Saint-Germain-des-Prés and to lay the first stone for Notre-Dame. This bull mentions, under the rights and lands of the Abbey Sainte-Geneviève, the Bourg Saint Marcel and a church, Saint-Médard, on the left bank of the Bièvre. There are no physical traces of this church except for the bell tower, since renovated, which was originally separate from the body of the then much smaller church. The actual building is from several periods. The nave and the façade, in flamboyant Gothic, are from the middle fifteenth century. The money for their construction probably came from a donation from the sister of Reilhac, the lawyer of Charles VII. She wanted the priests to say 261 low masses a year for her brother, who was buried there. In 1736, three hundred years later, the priests continued their prayers, but had cut them down to sixteen; today they are reduced to zero.

During the years 1560–1586 the choir was enlarged and chapels rebuilt in the style of the Renaissance, like the windows of the nave. This time the money came from fines imposed on Protestants after a religious battle. The money ran out, however, when it came to the vaulted ceiling, which had to be completed in wood. It remains wood to this day, a refreshing change from stone vaulting. In 1665 the side aisles were added, although the vaulting, which had served as buttressing for the church, is earlier (sixteenth century). At this point the church was considered complete and Saint-Médard became a parish.

In 1784 the church was again redone to fit the existing fashions. The columns were fluted in the neoclassical style and the apsidal Chapel of the Virgin, behind the choir, was built. The walls are covered with votive tablets that give thanks for miraculous recoveries, exams passed, and life in general. During the Revolution, the church was made into a Temple of Labor—a citizens' meeting place—and the standard still hangs over the choir. In 1901 the *petit charnier*, a small roomlike enclosure for common graves located behind the church, was condemned and transformed into the catechism chapel. In this and other chapels there are some interesting paintings: note *The Merchants Being Chased from the Temple* by Matoire and the *Multiplication of the Bread* by Restout. In the last left-hand chapel (as you stand with your back to the entrance) is a painting of Sainte Geneviève that was at one time thought to be by Watteau.

The cemetery of Saint-Médard was once outside the church. Originally, it included the area in front of the church, where the square now is, and the entire south side back to what is now the Rue Censier. At the beginning of each winter, before the ground froze, a large ditch was dug to serve as a common grave for all who died during the winter. It was closed in the spring, and several smaller ones were dug to take the fewer summer dead. (In primitive conditions on the margin of subsistence, the winter months were always far more deadly than the summer, if only because the poor could not get enough food to keep warm and sustain resistance to disease.) The combination of the Bièvre and the rotting corpses must have been overwhelming.

The church buried about three hundred people a year in this fashion. After nine years they would reuse a large ditch and after three or four, the smaller ones. When the

Rue Censier was opened in 1913, a layer of bones twenty-four inches thick was uncovered ten feet down. A coin found among the bones dates from the 1590s.

In 1765 a law was passed forbidding any burials within the limits of the city. The people of the neighborhood had no desire to be buried at Sainte-Catherine, which was, far away, so with the complicity of the old beadles, who had the cemetery keys in their safekeeping, they continued to be buried at Saint-Médard in secrecy. This went on through the Revolution, until the police, in 1795, became indignant about this *"manie de perpetuer l'ancien régime,"* nonsense of perpetuating the old regime.

The most famous corpse of Saint-Médard was a young Jansenist, François Pâris. (Jansenists were so called after Cornelis Jansen [1585–1638], bishop of Ypres, who held doctrines the main body of the Catholic church found heretical.) Pâris was a novice with a great reputation for humility. He preferred to spend his life performing menial tasks, such as knitting socks for the poor, and he died at the age of thirty-six on May 1, 1727, at the height of the Jansenist persecution, exhausted from a life of extreme abstinence and self-punishment. Pâris was buried with the poor in the *charnier*, having insisted before he died that he was not worthy of the cemetery.

The Jansenists declared him a saint, and a black marble stone was laid over his tomb. The grave became a gathering place for his admirers, and before long the word spread that the site was holy and capable of miraculous cures. This was the beginning of an unbelievable history of hysteria that lasted thirty-five years.

Young girls, fanatics, began coming to the *charnier* to eat the dirt of the novice priest's grave. There they would fall into religious ecstasies or convulsions and have to be restrained. At first there were eight to ten girls, but after two years the number had risen to eight hundred. The girls' activities escalated from day to day, changing from mere convulsions to atrocities.

They would ask to be beaten while crying out, "Oh!

How good that is. Oh! How good that makes me feel, brother. I beg of you, continue if you can!" They wanted to have their tongues pierced, twenty-five-pound weights placed upon their chests, their bodies raked with iron combs, or their breasts, thighs, and stomachs trampled on until they fainted. Pain was voluptuous, and it had no bounds. They had their breasts crushed or were hung head down. Some girls had themselves tortured in this way more than twenty times.

On January 27, 1732, the government, in desperation, had the cemetery walled, locked, and guarded. The next day at Saint-Médard, on the locked gate, the following rhyme appeared:

> *De par le roi, défense à Dieu*
> *De faire miracle en ce lieu.*

> *In the name of the king, it is forbidden to God*
> *To make a miracle in this place.*

The girls had to move their activities to private houses; the tomb of the novice priest was no longer necessary. In fact, in March 1733 another law was vainly passed, forbidding all those seized by convulsions to turn their affliction into a public spectacle or to arrange meetings for this purpose in private houses. Some girls were imprisoned, but this only made the others more impassioned and caused some of the most unusual scenes to occur. The girls borrowed an idea from ancient Miletus and began strangling themselves; they also swallowed live coals and leather-bound editions of the New Testament. Sister Rosalie, we are told, lived for forty days on air sipped from a spoon, and one girl had herself nailed to a board and was thus crucified.

In direct association with the ecstatics were the *mélangistes*, who pretended to distinguish between useless, indecent acts and true religious ecstasy. The *secouristes* were those who gave aid to the convulsive girls. They gave "small aid" and "big aid." Small aid consisted of helping to prevent falls and other accidents and helping to defend the girls' modesty by rearranging their often disordered clothing. Big or "murderous" aid entailed inflicting all the forms of martyrdom that the girls begged for.

Not everyone was so helpful. In a convent near Saint-Médard the nuns would meow ecstatically in unison for several hours every day at the same time. It was a disturbance, and the neighbors were up in arms. The nuns were told if one more noise was heard from their convent, the Garde Française, which was posted at their gate, would come in and whip them. There was complete silence.

The activities of this Jansenist cult continued for thirty-five years, until August 1762, when the Jesuit society that had, with the help of the government, persecuted them for so long was disbanded and expelled from the country. As for the girls, French historian J. Dulaure delicately points out, if a girl is brought up by people who believe in possession of the soul by the devil, and the girl herself believes this, she is bound to become very anxious at a certain age about new and unavowable emotions that seem to be tormenting her. She finds it easy to believe she has become possessed. Dulaure also offers another explanation: if a girl has been reared by very devout people and is herself religious, her own devotions and abstinences may continue increasing until she reaches a point of religious ecstasy. In her case it is love that has taken a wrong turn. Dulaure alludes only in passing to the explanation that we today might find most plausible, namely, that this was a search for a form of sexual release that would be acceptable in the religious and social milieu of the day.

In 1807 Pâris's tomb was opened in order to give certain eminent Jansenist families relics of this saint; the rest of his bones lie under what are now the unmarked stones of the Chapel of the Virgin.

Saint-Médard has also played a small role in literature. Fans of Victor Hugo's *Les Misérables* will remember, perhaps, that it was here that Jean Valjean accidentally encountered Javert. There was always a beggar by Saint-Médard, posted under the street lamp, to whom Jean gave a few sous. One evening the beggar lifted his head briefly to look at Jean under the light. Jean shivered with fear, for he was certain that he had seen the face of his enemy, Javert, and not the old beggar.

Today, the *marché* stretches out from the Carrefour des Gobelins, which is not on our walk, to the Rue de l'Epée de Bois and spreads right and left almost a block on each side street. The scholars tell us there has been a street market in this area since 1350, and it is this that shapes the character of the street.

The origins of the market, however, are a bit disquieting. We are told that, in the fourteenth century, on the Ile de la Cité under the shadow of Notre-Dame, there was a butcher who sold the finest pâté in Paris. One day, however, his unusual source of ingredients was discovered: the meat used in his excellent pâtés was human flesh. The butcher and his friend the barber had been abducting students who lived under the auspices of the church, away from their families, and were killing them behind the barbershop. Some readers may remember the play *Sweeney Todd*, which told a similar story.

These poor youths, living anonymously among the crowds of students, were not missed until the day the barber picked out a young man who owned a dog. When his master did not return from the barber's, the dog put up such a howl that the youth's friends came to investigate and caught the barber and the butcher in their bloody work. Judgment was swift: the two men were suspended in cages in front of Notre-Dame and publicly burned.

The clerics of the cathedral, however, were in a more ambiguous position. The well-fed priests had long enjoyed this pâté, but to eat human flesh, even unknowingly, is the sin of anthropophagy, and is punishable by excommunication. Several of the priests of Notre-Dame, therefore, had to be exiled from their cathedral.

They banded together in their exclusion and decided to make a pilgrimage to the Pope in Avignon to plead their cause and beg forgiveness. They set out barefoot one morning on the road to the southeast. They arrived twenty minutes later at what is now the Carrefour des Gobelins (then just outside the city limits). There they decided that their feet hurt enough and that they should stop at that very spot and become mendicants.

They lived from their begging until later in that same year when Jean de Meulan, the new bishop of Paris, came to visit his property and farms on the hill of Mouffetard. During his visit he was attacked by thieves and would have been killed if not for the aid of the mendicant priests. In appreciation, Jean de Meulan gave the priests absolution and allowed them to open a market on his property to sell *"toutes merchandises et objets dont on n'aurait pas à rechercher l'origine"* (all goods and objects of unquestionable origin).

There are official records from 1654 of a vegetable market held every Wednesday and Friday in the courtyard of the Maison du Patriarche, then owned by the family of Maréchal Biron. An ordinance of September 20, 1828, authorized the clearing of this site, and the architect Châtillon was given a commission to build a covered market in place of the house. It was inaugurated on June 1, 1831. At that time the market sold primarily old clothes and ironwork, with only a small section for food.

The actual building was later used as a garage, then for a long time as a public bathhouse (there was one on the Rue de Lacépède), and today it is a gymnasium with a paved square in front, suitable for Rollerblading.

The street market we see today is devoted almost exclusively to food. It is an especially important *marché*, because unlike the peripatetic markets assembled from temporary stalls that are set up in a given street one or two mornings a week, Mouffetard consists almost entirely of permanent shops that set out their goods daily, covering the pavement. The street is reserved for pedestrians.

The stores on Mouffetard resemble their medieval predecessors. In the Middle Ages, each shop had a large, horizontally split shutter that was opened for selling. The top half was a shade to protect against the sun and the rain, and the bottom was used as a table on which to make and display the goods. All workers, from the shoemaker to the butcher, were required to work in public to ensure honesty and quality. Hanging out past the shutters was the shopkeeper's standard with a symbol representing the shop's name and business. The room behind was used for storage, workshop, or living, or all three.

Although the shutters are gone, and the displays are richer today, the room behind is still used to store the crates of vegetables and fruits. Butchers and fishmongers often extend their shops into that area.

The array at the *marché*, particularly on Sunday mornings, is dazzling. The fresh vegetables and fruits are architecturally mounded into shining pyramids or laid out in cupped rows. The bursting tomatoes are redder than elsewhere, the tender white peaches more fragrant, and the orange carrots look more crunchy and sweet. Bring your own shopping bag or cart.

The square in front of the church hosts several stands selling vegetables, flowers, and Mediterranean delicacies. These market sellers start work daily at 4 A.M., when they first buy their goods from the central market, Les Halles in Rungis, and then come to Paris to set up and begin selling from nine until seven in the evening with only Monday off. The merchants bemoan the rise in popularity of prepared foods sold in supermarkets, but one has only to look at the arrays of splendid vegetables, flowers, cheeses, and glistening olives to understand that the supermarket can never replace the specialty shop. Food out in the open is more appealing and tempting than food in a supermarket.

Take the time to walk around, comparing quality, variety, and price. If you are lucky enough to be staying in

Paris for some time, become Parisian. Choose the best bakery in your neighborhood and try more than the famous baguette. Taste *charcuteries* that you have been brought up to think are unswallowable. Experiment with cheese. Contrary to popular belief, the smell of a cheese does not necessarily indicate how strong it is. Chaume, a mild, creamy, sinful cheese, reeks. On the other hand, Poisse is strong enough to make you cry. Most cheese stores these days will give you a taste if you are a serious buyer. Avoid the supermarket versions. The *crémerie* sells the unpasteurized, purer version.

The Mouffetard market fulfills every food need imaginable, a reputation this street has long had. August Vitu wrote about Mouffetard in the late nineteenth century:

> There is an average of two shops in each building, and all of them are dedicated to the daily subsistence of a very large, very crowded population with little time to spare and a large appetite to satisfy. On the ground floor of the 142 houses on the Rue Mouffetard there are 52 wine merchants, plus 9 wine merchants who also cater food and roast meat—yours or their own—16 grocers, 8 butchers, 6 bakers, 6 dairies, 5 delicatessens, 5 pastry shops, 4 lemonade stands, 3 tripe butchers, 2 café-bars, 1 horse-meat butcher, 3 coal sellers, 1 coffee shop. This, which could feed an entire city, was complemented by fish, fresh vegetables, fruits, and flowers sold from outdoor rolling carts. The housekeeping of the Rue Mouffetard is kept up by three stove and pottery shops, one bottle shop, two glaziers, two brushmen and shoe repair and tool shops, one lighting shop, one wallpaper and business supply shop. Between the butchers and delicatessens with their reddish tinge and the pastrymen and bakers with their crusty tidbits are six linen and sewing shops; eight shoemakers for men, women, and children; four umbrella

shops; three hatmakers for men, three for the women; and four gift shops spilling their wares out into the street, closely followed by a launderer–stain remover. While five barbers are caring for the heads hatted by the hatters, two watch and jewelry shops represent luxury, two wash-it-yourself-by-hand laundries represent cleanliness, teamed with a bathtub and bathroom fixtures salesman. The health of the body is watched by a doctor, two pharmacists, two *herboristeries*, two dentists to whom are attached three midwives in case of need. There is an office for job placement, one post office, one barracks of the Garde Républicaine (once the Garde Française) to guarantee security. For intellectual culture one finds on the street one kindergarten and one reading room. Even art has its representative in the person of a photographer.

There are fewer shops now, and certain trades—lemonade stands, hatters, coal merchants, brush shops, and sewing shops (*merceries*)—have all but vanished. Today they have been replaced with too many clothing shops and Greek restaurants. What hasn't changed is the animation and dedication to good eating and the beauty of food. A line of thirty people at the bakery and flowers peeking out of shopping bags attest to that.

An aspect of the street Vitu didn't see in his day is the construction and renovation that is so common now. Whole blocks of eighteenth-century buildings were condemned; one was torn down for senior citizen housing. Asked about the destruction, any old-timer will shake his head and mourn the changes in the neighborhood: "It's just not the same, the atmosphere has changed." Although we were frustrated several times searching for vanished historical sites, for us, having come from the New World, the atmosphere and age are still palpable and exciting.

The oldest standard on the Rue Mouffetard

Rue Mouffetard

As you walk up the **Rue Mouffetard**, take your time to look at the buildings and courtyards. The houses are almost all from the seventeenth century and are generally very plain, with simple mansard windows and undecorated façades. They were built for ordinary people of modest means. **No. 134** (to the left of no. 132; the number is not clearly marked), however, is very different. Its façade was extravagantly decorated by an Italian artist, Aldeari, a friend of the family who owned the house, in the 1930s. On the second floor are panels of painted wood depicting country people at their tasks. (There are other panels similar to this on the bakery on the corner of the Passage des Patriarches and the Rue Mouffetard.) Above on the stucco is an unusual scene showing wild game and birds intertwined with a floral pattern. Even the seventeenth-century mansard windows have been decorated.

The shop below, **Fachetti,** is, appropriately, that of a butcher and charcuterie. Seven to eight people work full-time in the basement kitchen to produce the offerings of pâtés, sausages, cured meats, and savories enveloped in golden crusts. Even if you don't need any food, go in and sniff the perfumed air—you'll soon change your mind.

Next door at **no. 130** is **Occitane**. This store is part of a deservedly popular chain. Find wonderful, hard-milled soaps from natural ingredients such as seaweed, honey, almond, and floral extracts. They are artisan made and are inexpensive. This is one of the few good buys in Paris and is a perfect gift for everyone you left at home. The store also sells dried lavender labeled with the year of the harvest and makes up gift baskets to order. Sample cheeses across the street at **no. 131**.

No. 122 is decorated with the oldest original standard on the street: **A la Bonne Source** (at the good spring). Look above the doorway and notice the bas relief of two boys, dressed in the style of Henri IV's reign, drawing water from a well. In 1592 this shop was owned by M. du Puy (the name means "of the well"), who sold wine and used the name of the shop as an implicit seal of approval. This type of pun as well as the link to the shop owner's name was typical of the play on words of medieval standards and necessary in a time of illiteracy and no street numbers.

Standards go back to the thirteenth century and beyond, when noblemen marked their houses with their coats of arms. If you were not a nobleman, you might distinguish your residence by placing a statuette of your favorite saint in a niche above the door. That way you got a little holy protection besides. **Nos. 44** and **45** of the Rue Mouffetard still have niches in their façades, although the statues are long gone.

The first commercial standards were put up by taverns and hotels so that a foreigner could find a place to eat and sleep in a strange city. These standards generally represented a bundle of straw, which gives a good idea of the character of the sleeping accommodation. Even today there is hardly a city in France without a hotel called the Lion d'Or, the "golden lion," or, in rebus form, *le lit [où] on dort,* "the bed [where] one sleeps."

In the thirteenth century, the commercial standard was soon understood to be a smart way to advertise; by the fifteenth, it had become a serious problem. The standards were made from sheets of iron, cut and painted, and hung on long poles to extend into the street past the large shop shutters. Like signs today, they were hung out as far as possible and made as large as possible to attract the most attention. Although Mouffetard had always been the same width that it is today, the combination of the shutters and an open sewer running down the center of the unpaved street, the whole overhung with huge groaning and clanking signs that blocked the sun, made for a dark and cluttered street.

A *parfumerie* had a standard of a glove, each finger of which could have held a three-year-old child. A dentist hung a molar that was the size of an armchair. These standards were constantly threatening to fall; one man was reputedly killed when the dentist's tooth fell on his head. For reasons of safety rather than aesthetics, the government tried to pass legislation to limit the size of signs. In 1667 they said the signs could be no more than thirty-two inches wide and had to be hung at least fifteen feet above the ground, so that horsemen might ride safely in the streets. It was not until 1761 that standards were banned altogether, to be replaced by wall decorations like those at A la Bonne Source. A few of these decorations and old names still remain. Visit the Hôtel Carnavalet, the Museum of the History of Paris, in the Marais (Walk 6) for an exhibit of standards.

Not all signs designated the trade of the shop below so clearly as A la Bonne Source. Since literacy was rare, the names were more often simply visual recognition or mnemonic devices. Actually this decorated house had previously been called The Bat, which leaves us wondering. Among several old unrevealing names are The Bottle Tennis Court, The Small Hole, and The Cage. Other names were clearer. The Tree of Life was a surgeon's house; The Red Shop, a butcher shop (the surgeon might have used that one too); The Reaper, a bakery (another possibility for the surgeon). One common name whose symbolism was clear in the Middle Ages was the Salamander. Salamanders were at that time believed to be impervious to fire, and therefore salamander was the old name for asbestos, the "wood that wouldn't burn." Bakers often took this name to symbolize their clay baking ovens, and the word is still in use today for the ceramic room heaters commonly found in Europe.

Many of the names were religious, some specifically so: The Golden Cross, The White Cross, The Red Cross, The Name of Jesus, The Fat Mother of God (which was not vulgar but, rather, complimentary in the hungry Middle Ages). Some names were only vaguely religious in that they used the number three and thus invoked the Trinity. The number three was extremely popular: The Three Catfish, The Three Goddesses, The Three Pruning Knives, The

Three Torches, The Three Panes (this was a bakery and not a glazier's), The Three Nuns' Coifs, The Three Doves, The Three Fish, The Three Pigeons. These were only a few of the names used on the Rue Mouffetard, for each shop had as many as its changing ownership required. Today, with the return of the small boutique, interesting names are again common.

On your right, a little farther up the hill, is the **Rue de L'Arbalète**, which leads to the **Rue des Patriarches**. It was here that the **Maison du Patriarche** once stood. This estate occupied the land between the Rues Daubenton, Mouffetard, L'Epée de Bois, and Gracieuse. The house was set back from the street and was approached from an alley located where you are now. The first owner was Jean de Meulan, the Bishop of Paris who pardoned the mendicant priests. The property passed through several hands before Simon de Cramault, Archbishop of Rheims and Patriarch of Alexandria, bought it. It was then that the estate received the name Maison du Patriarche. This was changed gradually to Maison des Patriarches, when Simon de Cramault was mistakenly associated with the Patriarch of Jerusalem, Guillaume de Chanac, and it was assumed that they had lived on the same property.

The fate of Simon de Cramault is disputed by historians. Some say that he was evicted from his house for not paying a tax to the Abbey Sainte-Geneviève. Others say, more logically, that he was forced to abandon the house when Jean Sans Peur, Duke of Burgundy, pillaged the entire village on his way to Paris, followed by the Armagnacs, who occupied it, and finally the English, who devastated it. Whatever the reasons, Cramault did not have enough money to run the estate and in 1443 abandoned it to Thibault Canaye, a hotel owner on the Rue de la Harpe and husband of the wealthy wool factory heiress, Mathurine Gobelin.

The house remained in this family until, in the sixteenth century, Jean Canaye, a great-great-grandson and militant Calvinist, rented it to a friend who opened the house to the Huguenots. The Huguenots turned the house into a Protestant temple, one of the two that had been allowed in the villages outside Paris. The Catholics of the Bourg Saint-Marcel were not at all pleased to see the Huguenots installed right beside their church, and on Saturday, December 27, 1561, religious violence broke out here. It was the holiday of Saint John the Evangelist, and two thousand Protestants had gathered to hear Jean Malo, the former priest of Saint-André-des-Arts, give a special sermon. The congregation was unable to hear the sermon, however, because the sexton of Saint-Médard (only two hundred feet away) insisted on repeatedly ringing the bells for vespers. Malo sent four men to the church to ask the priest for quiet, but that was a serious mistake, for they fell into an ambush. When they arrived at the church doors, one man was snatched inside and beaten by parishioners. He was never seen alive again. The other three helplessly faced a locked-up church front, while stones and slates rained on them from above.

The three men returned to the Maison des Patriarches ready for blood. The Huguenots quickly armed themselves and stormed the church of Saint-Médard. They killed and wounded parishioners, broke all the religious statues and windows, profaned the altar and sacked the sacristy, throwing holy wafers to the wind. The Catholics, in retaliation, set fire to the temple and then called for government support. Constable Anne de Montmorency, head of the royal army, authorized the Catholics to raze one section of the house and to execute four of the Protestant offenders. The Catholics turned the execution into a public spectacle. Near the portals of Saint Médard the prisoners had both hands cut off and their tongues pierced. Then they were gently strangled so as not to expire entirely and finally burned to death. As a final measure the Catholics confiscated all their goods to pay for the repairs to the church. There were only six buildings, a garden, and some dependencies left to the

Maison des Patriarches when it passed into the hands of Maréchal Biron, who authorized the construction of the *marché* on the site of the house.

Today the *place* is clean and open and children Rollerblade and ride skateboards in the piazza. A new gymnasium stands on the site of the Maison des Patriarches, replacing a public bath.

Notice the small green fountain consisting of a base and four women holding a crown from which a stream of water flows down. In 1842, a British gentleman named Wallace visited Paris and was unable to obtain a glass of water from a local restaurant. On his return to England, he purchased over one hundred of these water fountains and had them distributed all over Paris, where they became a main source of drinking water. Drinking cups were suspended from the hooks below the women's feet. Still in love with Paris, Wallace offered his collection of paintings to the city, which turned him down. His paintings became the famous Wallace collection in London.

After World War II, most of the authentic fountains were stolen and modern copies were made. The originals had four different women, but the copies all have the same face, the same eyes and lips. This is an original. Other differences are the positioning of the feet, the ruffles on the bodices of the dresses, the way the folds of the dress fall. Look for other Wallace fountains as you walk around the city.

Return to the Rue Mouffetard. The **Brasserie, no. 116**, is decorated with designs of grapes and masquerons and the windows are hung with lace. Stop for a quick lunch.

On the corner of the Rue Mouffetard to your right are two superb bakeries. The first is **Les Panetons** (a *paneton* is a cloth-lined basket in which bread can rise), which sells much more than the standard baguette. Here you find a varied array of breads of different shapes and different grains. White bread is no longer de rigueur and new breads are on the rise (pun intended). The second bakery, **Le Moule a Gâteau, no. 113**, is also not a traditional bakery.

The Three Mushrooms at no. 80 Rue Mouffetard

Here you won't find éclairs and napoleons. Instead, pastry cream has given way to fruit-based mousses, flourless chocolate cakes, fruit tarts on almond crusts, and the ever-present American brownie. Don't wait to stop in here. By noon they are almost all sold out.

Across the street there used to be a store that sold coal and wood. This was home base for some of the last of the *bougnats*, coal deliverers. A highly respected, old yellow-toothed woman, Mme Courtine, owned this business. When we first spoke to her, she sat wrapped in layers of black, dunking her croissant in her coffee, and told us that the business was started in 1903 by her husband's father. When she married in 1923, she came to work here. She said that, at that time, the street was very *charbonnier* (coalish): there were thirteen coal dealers. People bought their coal in the summer when there was time to sort it and wash it and the price was lower. They stored it in the basement, or in a bathtub if they had one. Now no one buys coal in the summer because, Mme Courtine said, they can't leave it anywhere since it will be stolen. She planned to retire to the country, but never did. She died still working at the age of ninety.

According to her, the street had changed. It used to be a street of workers. It was "proper." Now it is "a cabaret." Once a street of food, ranging from the best quality to medium quality, it is now a "bazaar"; everyone is a foreigner or a student. Work once went on from 6 A.M. to 10 P.M. every day; today shops close at noon on Sunday and stay closed until Tuesday. Her final comments to us were to the effect that her heart bleeds for her old *quartier* and that the *"fameux mazout"* (famous—or infamous—oil) had ruined not only her but the whole world as well.

Today, the twentieth century has moved in and brought tastier options to the street. **No. 112** is **Jeff de Bruges**, home of our favorite gift to bring home from Paris. The proprietor stacks colorfully wrapped chocolate squares and ties them with a ribbon. The chocolates come in traditional flavors and also some less common ones, such as

tea. Nearby at **no. 114** is **Chocolatier Nicolsen**, which, in addition to chocolate, sells Berthillon, *the* French ice cream. There is serious wine tasting and buying at **Le Repaire de Bacchus**. A flourishing flower stand ends the block and ends the food section of Mouffetard.

As you walk up the street, look at the buildings on the left. They are mostly new, **nos. 100** and **98**, for example. The old ones that were replaced were certainly decrepit, but these are well on the way to fitting in.

No. 85 hides a treasure deep within. Press the main button and go down the long dark hallway until you come back outside, and look to your right. There is a garden and a charming stone house that has been restored. Notice the wooden lintels and the old glass in the windows. Here the country atmosphere that is all but lost from Rue Mouffetard still exists.

The doorway of **no. 81** is unusual for this street. It is all that is left of a former chapel built in the beginning of the seventeenth century. Try **Le Jardin de la Mouff** at no.75, with a pleasant garden in the rear.

The **Théâtre de la Mouff**, **no. 73**, finally has a new home. It spent many years struggling to exist in a rundown building across the street. Today it is in an interior court-yard in the midst of a new apartment complex. A bowling alley is beneath the theater.

Above the entrance to **no. 69** is a curious decoration in the form of a tree. The sign is carved from an old masthead taken from a sunken ship. There were two identical stan-dards carved from the wood, and both advertised a restau-rant named **Au Vieux Chêne** (at the old oak tree). The second once stood on the Right Bank, but the building there has been demolished. Wood from sunken ships is said to have a strange power, and mastheads that have been refashioned are supposedly even more potent. Legend has it, however, that the two restaurants bearing these trees were cursed, particularly this one. Every seven years there was supposedly an unexpected argument at Au Vieux Chêne, and someone would die a violent death, right in

The proprietor of an 1890s shoe store for workers

front of the other diners. The first restaurant owner was forced to sell the property, because he could not cope with its macabre reputation. A second owner also fell victim to the curse and eventually sold out to a discotheque owner, who sold out to a restaurant, then a night club, followed by a pub, and now . . .

No. 64 is a true working-class shoe shop. Here you can find real peasant *sabots*, wooden shoes that farmers and laborers wear to this day. They also sell woolen slipper *sabot* linings, rubber boots, and plain espadrilles. This shop has no pretensions. It was started in 1890 and the wooden boxes with brass handles which you see on the wall were made for shoes. They are still in use. George, at age sixty-five, is one of the oldest merchants on the street. His father came from Armenia and opened the store in 1928. Notice the horseshoe sign above.

No. 62 is a beautifully restored seventeenth-century building, but you will probably only be able to peer through the grille. The apartment entrance and the stone hallway have beamed ceilings. On your right is an excellent example of a Louis XIII staircase with its solid, rounded oak balustrades. The first diagonal section is a reproduction; the sections above are original. At the end of the hall is a small stone courtyard; to the left is a stone balcony with plants. This is a perfect example of the restoration and upgrading of old neighborhoods in Paris. And no change is so expensive as the kind of controlled renovation-plus-preservation that is required in Paris.

Aesthetically this is progress, but socially it means dislocation of residents. These fine houses, on their medieval foundations, must be repaired and restored, and the high rents that follow limit occupancy to the well-to-do. The municipal government has tried to help by renovating some buildings for the tenants, who are placed in temporary housing while the work proceeds and are then allowed to return at subsidized rents. But there are limits to the city purse, and most of this work is being done by private investors. The result for now is a widening of the social range: many of the poorer residents are still there, but they have rich company. In a strange way, this is a return to the social arrangements of long ago, when Paris buildings were microcosms of the larger society and these old neighborhoods in the center housed the rich as well as the poor.

No. 61 was once a convent devoted to poor and sick women. The nuns of the convent of Notre-Dame-de-la-Miséricorde bought this property, which stretched back to Rue Gracieuse, in 1653. By the beginning of the eighteenth century, however, the buildings were falling into ruins. In 1717 help came from an unexpected source. Mme de Maintenon, between her marriage to the poet Paul Scarron and her secret marriage to Louis XIV, had lived in a similar convent on the Rue des Minimes. She was always grateful for the hospitality she had received, and so now, as an all-powerful marquise, she arranged for all the convent's expenses to be paid by the royal treasury. She ordered the lieutenant general of the police, Marc-René d'Argenson, to supervise the reconstruction. The convent's problems were not, however, at an end. D'Argenson did not have the morals a man in his position was expected to have, and when he came to supervise the work he had just separated from his latest mistress. During his brief inspection d'Argenson fell madly in love with a young and innocent novice; he tried to seduce her with promises of money. When the mother superior heard of the scheme, she took steps to make it impossible for the novice to leave. D'Argenson was furious and in retaliation informed her that he was suspending all construction until she gave in to his demands. The mother superior was thus forced to choose between the soul of her novice and the stones of her convent. The restoration took precedence, and the novice was yielded up to d'Argenson. (Whether the novice ever got her promised fortune is not known.)

Next door on the corner at **no. 60** is an unusual wall that masks a fountain built in 1624 (redone in 1671). The fountain exists because of Marie de Médicis. When Henri IV built the palace at the Luxembourg Gardens for her, she demanded a plumbing system that would be able to handle enough water for the palace and for the gardens. The only way to do this was to reopen and repair the ancient Gallo-Roman aqueduct. This brought so much water into the Left Bank, however, that fourteen new fountains had to be built along the aqueduct's route to pump off the excess. This remaining fountain on the Rue Mouffetard, now a classified historical monument, has been restored. Formerly it was black and smothered in posters; today it is clean and at the top a frieze of shells and flowers has happily reappeared.

Turn left down the **Rue du Pot de Fer** (the iron pot). This street is filled with attractive restaurants, including the first Taiwanese teahouse in Europe, **La Maison de Trois Thés** at **no. 5**. As you sit, perhaps at one of the outside tables, the waiter will serve you tea from China or Taiwan and will explain the complex steps involved in preparing and drinking your infusion. You will be given one cup for tasting and one cup for smelling. Connoisseurs from all over Europe order their tea here.

When you reach the corner of **Rue Tournefort**, look at the building across the street on the right, **no. 20**. Between the two street signs, you can see, etched in stone, the original name of the street, "rue Sainte-Geneviève." Once again, the "Sainte," a sign of the church, had been scraped out during the Revolution. Now return to the Rue Mouffetard.

A buried treasure was found inside the walls of the building that once stood at **no. 53**. In 1938 the building was condemned by the city for reasons of safety, and a crew of men was assigned to tear it down. On the first day of the job, a wrecker, Flammo Maures, ripped open a wall and was astounded to see "medals" pour forth. In no time at all the workers gathered around and divided up the booty. When Maures went home that night, he showed his discovery to his wife, who immediately recognized the medals as gold. A law-abiding citizen, Maures took his "medals" to the police, where they were identified as louis d'or. The treasure was reassembled, and the walls carefully searched, finally yielding a collection of 3,351 22-carat gold coins, in the form of double louis weighing 16.3 grams each, single louis weighing 8.7 grams, and half-louis of 4.7. With the gold, an identifying piece of paper was also found: *"moi, sieur Louis Nivelle, écuyer et secrétaire du*

Roy, légue ma fortune à ma fille, Anne-Louis Nivelle" (I, Sir Louis Nivelle, assistant and secretary of the King, bequeath my fortune to my daughter, Anne-Louis Nivelle). The paper was not dated, but it was not difficult to determine that Nivelle had been the secretary of Louis XV and had played a main role in a still unclarified mystery: he vanished in 1757 without a trace.

The police, searching for the descendants of Anne-Louise, finally found General Robert de Saint Vincent, who, although surprised, said that he had been brought up with a family tradition of a lost inheritance. It was not until 1952 that a legal division of the gold was arranged. Two hundred and fifty-four pieces had to be sold to pay the genealogists for their research, 538 were given to the city officials, and the original wrecking crew and the eighty-four descendants of Anne-Louis Nivelle split the remaining 2,559 coins. The gold was valued at 16 million old francs (about $32,000) at that time, simply as metal. Its historical value is untold. (One hundred old francs equals one new franc; in 1960, the franc was revalued, and new francs introduced.)

Today no. 53 is a **Comfort Inn**—inexpensive, modern, and basic.

Nos. 52, **42**, and **34** all have small gardens hiding behind their entry doors. It is amazing that one struggling tree in a slightly shabby courtyard can still lift the spirits in a big city. You can enter **No. 34** through the glass doors to see a streetlike hallway with apartments on the ground floor. A plaque says a cabaret called the Cabaret of Ragpickers existed here in 1803.

No. 23 is a very old house with bulging timbers in the hallway. Above, to the left of the door, plaster has been removed to show the original structure. Stop at **No. 16** for some excellent pastry.

Above the door at **no. 12** is a recent wall decoration that is quite surprising. The name of the building is Le Nègre Joyeux (the happy Negro), and the painting depicts a young black servant waiting on his mistress. Most people in America have long since rejected and condemned the image of the "happy black servant," but up till now in France few objections to the stereotype seem to have been raised.

Place de la Contrescarpe

To your right the street widens to form the **Place de la Contrescarpe**. In the past, you could sit in the center of the *place* and watch the singing and dancing, the flame throwers, and the like. It was too much for the neighborhood, for the police, and for the cafés. Now, a fountain and flowers has turned this hot spot into a good café hangout, especially on a summer night.

The name goes back to the Middle Ages, when the Porte Bourdelles, one of the gates in Philippe Auguste's wall around Paris, stood just beyond this point on what is now the Rue Descartes. Outside the gate and its guard towers was the moat, rising to another earthen wall or counterescarpment (*contrescarpe*). At this time the Bourg Saint-Marcel was not really populated above what is now the Rue l'Epée de Bois, and so the land outside the gates became a no-man's-land. It gradually developed into a spot where people naturally congregated, although no one lived there. During this early period in the fourteenth century, there were only three streetlights in Paris, none of them here; thus the Place de la Contrescarpe was a dark and dangerous area at night. Throughout the sixteenth century (in 1504, 1526, and 1551) hopeless ordinances were passed, ordering each house in Paris to burn a candle in the first-floor window from nine to twelve o'clock every night. Either this was ignored or the candles were ineffectual, for the police estimated an average of fifteen bodies every morning from the killings of the night before—a fantastic murder rate for what was by today's standards a small town.

Place de la Contrescarpe

In 1662 a priest, the abbé Caraffe, invented mobile lighting. Place de la Contrescarpe soon picked up this innovation, and lamp carriers, or *lampadophores*, would wait here for customers. The lamp bearer would offer to accompany you right to your door, whether it was on the first or seventh floor, for five sous per slice of wax on his torch, or three sous for one-quarter hour with an oil lantern. In the eighteenth century this practice spread to umbrella carriers, who would protect you from showers on a time basis, and chair carriers promising to keep you out of the mud. At the turn of the eighteenth century, lanterns attached to house fronts with a rope pulley were tried, but the candles blew out and the glass darkened. Besides, the city chose to save money by not using the lighting on moonlit nights or in the summers. It was not until the 1770s that any kind of effective street lighting was instituted, and the *lampadophores* were put out of business.

The actual *place* as it stands today was not created until 1852. By this time the area had the taverns and action that made it a logical site for a barracks of the Garde Républicaine. Today the Garde Républicaine is mostly decorative; the ruffians who used to inhabit the area were replaced by "winos" or *clochards*, who had long staked their claim here. For them this area offered every convenience: the Rue Mouffetard has the wine shops, the *marché* throws out spoiled food twice daily, the students and tourists are good for begging (a cigarette, if not money), and the Place de la Contrescarpe and the Rue Lacépède offer *métro* heating vents to sleep on. (The *clochards* are harmless and you need not fear them. They will call out for change or a cigarette as you pass, but you can refuse them or comply, whichever you prefer.)

Here is a prize comment about the homeless, made by an Englishman, F. Berkley Smith, in a book called *The Real Latin Quarter*, written about 1901: "That women should become outcasts through the hopelessness of their position or the breaking down of their brains can be understood, but that men of ability should sink into the dregs and stay there seems incredible. But it is often so."

French and foreign youth dominate the night scene. The restaurants and cafés put their tables out on the pavements, the food is cheap, and conversation is easy. On our last visit, on a sunny Sunday morning, flowers bloomed in the center of the *place*, the café on the sunny side of the square was packed, and an excellent jazz band entertained in the street.

The building at **no. 1** Place de la Contrescarpe has "La Pomme de Pin" (the pinecone, referring to an old café that once stood on the square) carved into its wall. The café however, was not in that building, which is modern, but in what is now a charcuterie on the corner of the Rue Blainville, behind you as you face La Pomme de Pin. It was here that La Pléiade came into being. This was a literary group begun in 1549 by Pierre Ronsard, Joachim du Bellay, and Jean-Antoine de Baïf. These young men had all come to Paris for their education and were engaged in studying the classics, which they did avidly, straight through the night. From their interest in classical poetry they felt a great need "to defend the French language and render it illustrious." These writers had a strong influence on the French language, and their stylistic theories are still in use today. To be published in the Pléiade edition of classics is still a great honor.

Rue Blainville

Turn left into the **Rue Blainville** to find a group of very old houses, **nos.** 1, **3**, **4**, and **5**. At no. 4 look at the cleaned rough beige stones and the long beam across the front. **La Truffière** is one of the very few French restaurants in the area with a serious menu and reasonable prices. The inside has been restored as carefully as the outside (note the iron gate). The front room welcomes you with comfortable seating and a blazing fire. You almost hope your date will be late so you can relax with a drink in this convivial room. The food is traditional French with a southwestern emphasis, and it is delicious. Small nibbles are offered to start, a basket of interesting breads is presented, and complementary petit fours arrive with the after-dinner coffee.

Our server told us that she thought the basements of this seventeenth-century building may have served to hide people in World War II. Behind the first vaulted basement set with tables is a second basement with exits that are now blocked off.

At **no. 6** enjoy Korean food at the **Restaurant de Corée**. Try their fried chicken with scallions and garlic and the caramelized noodles. Prices are very reasonable.

Return to the Place de la Contrescarpe and continue up the Rue Mouffetard. The **Crêperie de la Mouffe** at **no. 9** is a good way to manage a light meal in Paris. This restaurant is beautifully decorated with Breton yokes, sabots, Quimper dishes, photographs of Breton life, and a closet of colorful traditional Breton costumes. They offer almost eighty kinds of crêpes here, approximately forty of buckwheat, *sarrasin,* with main course–type fillings and an equal number of dessert crêpes made with white flour. Prices are comparatively low.

The *enseigne* on the upper windows of three medallions and two golden bulls announced a butcher shop in the eighteenth century.

Il Fiorentino at **no. 3** insists on using all fresh ingredients to make their excellent food. Angelo's wife does the cooking. The restaurant is open seven days a week in the summer. It is especially lively at night, and the price is right.

Rue Descartes

At the intersection with the Rue Thouin, the Rue Mouffetard becomes the Rue Descartes. Where you are standing was the emplacement of the Porte Bourdelles and its guard towers; they were demolished in 1685. There are still remains of Philippe Auguste's wall, however, at **no. 47** Rue Descartes. If the door is open, go into this historically classified building and notice the half-timbered walls.

Look closely at the stone slabs you are walking on. Two on the left have numbers carved into their faces. These are stones that were taken from the cemetery of Sainte-Geneviève when it was destroyed in the eighteenth century. Again, a little saving in construction costs has preserved history. The numbers probably refer to lists of the people buried in communal graves dating from the sixteenth and seventeenth centuries.

Continue back to the second hall with its huge stone building slabs. The third staircase on the left is unfortunately now locked. It winds up to a door that leads outside. Suddenly it was as though you were on a secret street, above ground. You were actually standing on the top of the medieval wall. The buildings along the old wall all made thrifty use of it as their fourth side. A curved building on the right was that way simply because, when the original house was built, that was the contour of the wall at that point.

This is one of the most charming secret spots of Paris and we are unhappy that more and more building owners close off their houses. Owners do receive financial aid from the government for some maintenance in order to preserve history and the general feeling is that these sites should be open to the public—even for non-paying tourists.

At **no. 39** there is a plaque stating that the poet Verlaine died here in 1896.

From here you are within walking distance of the Arènes de Lutèce, the remains of a Roman arena on the Rue Monge; the Jardin des Plantes, the botanical gardens with a small zoo; and on the same street, Rue Geoffroy-Saint-Hilaire, the Mosquée, what was long the only mosque in Paris. The building also includes a charming Turkish café. In the other direction, in the Place du Panthéon there is the Panthéon, a burial place of famous Frenchmen, and the church of Sainte-Geneviève, with its unusual architecture and famous rood screen.

Walk · 5

Place des Vosges

C'est le coup de lance de Mont-gomery qui a créé la Place des Vosges.

It's the blow of Montgomery's lance that created the Place des Vosges.

—*Victor Hugo*

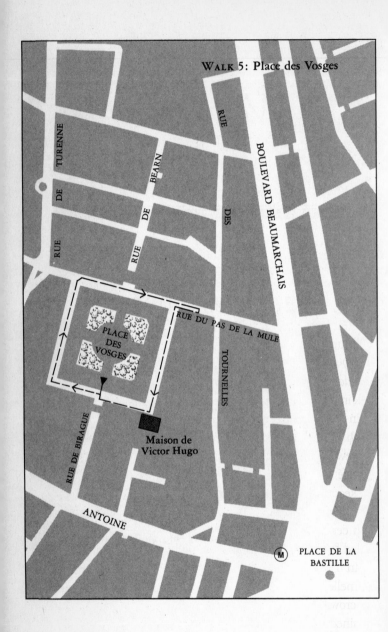

WALK 5: Place des Vosges

RUE DE TURENNE

RUE DE BEARN

RUE DE

RUE DES

BOULEVARD BEAUMARCHAIS

RUE

RUE DU PAS DE LA MULE

PLACE DES VOSGES

TOURNELLES

RUE DE BIRAGUE

Maison de
Victor Hugo

ANTOINE

Ⓜ PLACE DE LA
BASTILLE

Starting Point: Rue de Birague, the south entrance of the Place des Vosges
Métro: Bastille or Saint-Paul, 4th arrondissement
Buses: 20, 29, 69, 86, 87, 91, 96

Walk up the Rue de Birague (stop and look at interesting shops) and continue into the Place des Vosges (pronounced *plass day voge*) before you. The *place* is a square with a large park in the middle and symmetrical townhouses all around. Sit in the garden near the children's area so that you can watch the children play *à la française* (despite the mix of Hebrew, Yiddish, and Arabic you'll hear). If it is cold, try the café Ma Bourgogne on the northwest corner of the *place*.

Read the history of this *place* and some of its surroundings. While the Left Bank was inhabited as far back as the sixth century, the Right Bank, or Marais (marsh), was not settled for another five hundred years or more.

In 1407, a *hôtel* (grand private residence), known as Tournelles, for the small towers in its walls, came under the crown and replaced the previous royal residence. It remained the royal residence until 1559 and the fatal joust that cost Henri II his life. The king had fought and won two jousts already that day, but he insisted on a third against the captain of his Scottish Guards, Gabriel de Lorges, sire de Montgomery. At the first pass, both knights splintered their lances. The king wanted another run; Montgomery was reluctant. Of course, the king, savoring his success, had his way. Once again Montgomery's lance broke, but this time, by a freak accident, the point pushed up the visor of the king's helmet and entered his head above his eye. For ten days Henri suffered. The greatest doctors were called; Ambroise Paré and Andreas Vesalius came all the way from Brussels. Four criminals under sentence of death were decapitated so that the doctors could study their cranial anatomy, but to no avail. Henri died, of infection if nothing else, and his widow, Catherine de Médicis, persuaded her son Charles IX to demolish the palace with its unhappy memories.

Once royalty abandoned the palace, the ground on which it had stood was given over to a succession of improvised roles. The militia used it for its exercises. The city installed stables and used some of the buildings to store powder. For many years the interior courtyard housed an active horse market that attracted many rogues, posing a growing problem for the authorities. The answer was found by Henri IV. The horse market would be replaced by a development project, Paris's first. It would be a spacious, symmetrical public square to be known as the Place Royale, a *place* of respectable residence and assembly. The parceling of terrain began in 1605, and the first building finished was the large pavilion at the south end of the square. It marked the start of an epoch in domestic architecture and set the example for the remaining construction.

The Place Royale was only one of Henri IV's three urbanization projects. Another, a set of large avenues that would radiate out from the *place*, was never built, and the third, the Place Dauphine on the tip of the Ile de la Cité, was only partially completed. (Today at the Place Dauphine you will find the splendid statue of the gallant Henri IV on horseback looking out over the Seine.)

The Place Royale, however, was the king's pet project, and he visited the construction site daily to speed the workers along. In his plan for the large square, he reserved the south side for himself and the north for a silk factory *à la façon de Milan*. The east and west sides were to be sold in parcels to private owners.

The Duke of Sully filled 50 percent of the pavilions with his friends. The Duke of Guise did likewise. The result was one that pleased Henri, a convert to Catholicism: a mix of Protestants and Catholics.

The façades were to be all the same, built of brick with *pierre taillé* (cut-stone) trim. The ground floor, planned for shops was set back to create a covered walkway of four arcades per lot: Each building was to have two floors above that, the whole capped with a steep slate roof encompassing another two floors pierced with mansard windows. The style was known as *bleu*, *blanc*, *rouge* for the slate roofs, the white stone trim, and the red bricks. At the center of the south end would be a raised pavilion for the king. Within a year or two, when the silk project failed, the north end was given its own pavilion for the queen and private residences matching those opposite.

The open space in the center would be promenade, tournament ground, and stage for public events, functions that no street, however wide, could perform. There was no other public square in Paris at this time, and it was Henri's intention that all visiting foreign dignitaries arriving in Paris would enter by the gate just to the east of here at the Bastille, travel down the Rue Saint-Antoine, and then turn into the Place Royale from what is now the Rue de Birague, where you entered.

In principle, the buildings around the square were to be made of brick with stone trim. In fact, only the first structures, including the Pavillon du Roi, lived up to the plan. It took a long time to lay brick, and Henri was in a hurry. Bricks and mortar were also expensive, especially in a city that had never before (and has never since) considered brick to be fashionable. Nor did the local workers have the skills necessary for this huge undertaking.

In any event, the owners of the later buildings were

only too happy to construct them of plaster on wood framing and then paint them to resemble brick in colors ranging from dusty pink to dark red. Some of this trompe l'oeil is still visible. It is surprising that these masterpieces of French architecture, praised for concept, size, proportions, and colors, were mostly façade.

The artifice, however, does not seem to have dimmed the square's glory. Although no king ever lived here (the Pavillon du Roi was far too small to accommodate the king and his retinue), the square was inhabited in the seventeenth century by the best society. Before the Faubourg Saint-Germain-des-Prés became the chic neighborhood, the Marais, and especially the Place Royale, was the *place* where anyone who was anyone lived.

Unfortunately, Henri IV was assassinated shortly before the square's completion. The square was therefore inaugurated by the young Louis XIII. This is why the equestrian statue in the center of the square is of Louis XIII, and not Henry IV.

On April 5, 6, and 7, 1612, a fabulous tournament was held at the resplendent Place Royale. Jousting was forbidden, but five equestrian ballets were organized for the cavaliers, each with different exotic costumes—including one group dressed as American Indians. A description of one of the quadrilles will give you some idea of how elaborate these festivities were: the Duke of Longueville and his retainers were dressed in gray-violet satin with silver embroidery; the pages and the horses were dressed in red velvet; four winged horses pulled a chariot with two rhinoceroses harnessed to the back; and two giants in blue satin preceded the duke himself, who rode a horse draped with repoussé plaques of silver and gold. There were 150 musicians in the *place*, as well as games, continuous parades, and fireworks at night.

The square was packed with ten thousand people, some crowded onto viewing stands, some at the windows. Members of the royal entourage had been assigned different houses and balconies from which to observe the tournament. In fact, the residents had been required to make their balconies available to the noblemen assigned to them. It was the first time that houses had been built with real balconies; until then Parisians had had only small stone ledges to lean on. Once the Place Royale had shown the way, balconies quickly became de rigueur. The common people had to hang from the chimneys or squeeze into the recesses of the arcades.

The Place Royale was used frequently in the seventeenth century for tournaments and spectacles. Visiting ambassadors staged elaborate processions to show off the riches and costumes of their home countries. For many Parisians this was their only contact with a foreign culture, and dress and appearance were carefully scrutinized and criticized. Of one delegation Mme de Motteville wrote, after describing their rich clothes studded with jewels, "In general they are so fat that they give you heartburn, and concerning their bodies, they are dirty."

The Place Royale was also the favorite dueling ground for the hotbloods of the French aristocracy. The fashionable ladies of the *place* enjoyed the spectacle, and the swordsmen were encouraged by these ardent admirers. The fights were more than show, however. In 1614, three out of four antagonists were killed in one encounter, and over the years France lost some of its most valiant cavaliers in this square.

In 1626, Richelieu, first minister of Louis XIII, forbade dueling on pain of death. The very prohibition was a challenge to French manhood. Only one year later there occurred a six-man duel (two principals and four seconds, who were expected to do more than hold the combatants' coats) right in front of the Pavillon du Roi. Results: two dead, two fled to England, and two off to Lorraine. The latter two were caught en route, brought back to Paris, and decapitated, over the protests and appeals of the nobility of France. Richelieu was not a man to take insolence lightly. The incident cooled the ardor of the young blades, but only for a time.

Northwest corner of the Place des Vosges

In 1643, after Richelieu's death, the last scion of the Protestant Colignys dueled with Henri, duc de Guise, grandson of the man who had killed Coligny's grandfather, Admiral Coligny, in the aftermath of the Saint Bartholomew's Day Massacre (1572). The duel was supposedly fought to champion two quarreling women, but who is to say that old, unavenged grievances did not enter into it? Anyway, the ladies watched and cheered their men on. Guise was wounded first, but managed to grab Coligny's *épée* (sword), hold it, and simply finish him off. This time the king, hoping to end the enmity between Catholics and Protestants, chose not to punish the victor.

Not all the action in the place was outdoors. The Place Royale was the center of Parisian social life, and such fashionable ladies of the neighborhood as Ninon de Lenclos and Marion Delorme invented a new and durable institution. They met at intimate gatherings, *ruelles,* at which the elegant guests rivaled one another in wit, fine speech, and social finesse. Molière parodied their excesses in his play *Les Précieuses Ridicules*.

The predecessors of the fashionable salons of the eigh-

teenth century, these encounters took place in the hostesses' bedrooms, perhaps because an amazing number of
the hostesses were as renowned for their sexual as for their
social prowess. Several of the great ladies of the Place
Royale could hardly keep track of their lovers. We shall
meet them later as we visit each house individually.

The fashionable lifestyle of the Place Royale spread to
the rest of the Marais, and large *hôtels* sprang up everywhere
throughout this sparsely settled part of the city. Houses
here were larger and more elegant than anything Paris had
ever seen. One can imagine the constant visits and receptions of the nobility, the clergy, and the officials who
thrived here. The busy streets hummed with ladies carried
in their sedan chairs, beribboned soldiers strutting in high
boots, and clergy of all levels carrying out their errands.

It was also the era of great changes in interior decoration, brought about mainly by the women. Mirrors replaced
paintings above the fireplace for brightness, armchairs were
more comfortable than thinly upholstered straight chairs,
moveable torchères around the fireplace supplied both
light and heat. Wallpaper began to replace tapestries, and
ceilings, copied from Italy, were painted.

But there was misery in the streets. The poor lived in
the streets as much as possible to avoid their miserable
and dingy hovels. People wore big boots that were mud
encrusted. The joke was that the favorite color in Paris was
brown. When night fell, anyone with honest intentions
went home. There was no protection from those who
roamed the dark streets. Lanterns were lit on moonless
nights only, and one toss of a stone could throw an entire
area into total darkness. What guards there were, were generally not interested in losing their lives to some brigand,
so they chose to appear only after the battle was done and
the bodies lay dead.

Tallement des Réaux, a chronicler of the Marais,
reports one night an incident involving the Duchess of
Rohan, a member of the great aristocratic family that lived
throughout the quarter. She was returning from a ball when

she was stopped by thieves. "Immediately," he recounts, "she put her hands on her pearls. One of these gallant men, to make her let go, grabbed her where women ordinarily defend themselves best; but he was dealing with a tough lady: 'That,' she said, 'you can't carry off, but you can take away my pearls.' " Luckily someone happened along, and the duchess was saved.

Beginning in the eighteenth century, the Marais went into a decline. The center of Paris fashion and social activity moved steadily westward. The aristocracy moved to the Faubourg Saint-Honoré, where the Elysée Palace and the British and American embassies are now located. The decline continued into the nineteenth and twentieth centuries. The fashionable neighborhoods grew toward the west, in part because the prevailing winds came from the west and carried the unpleasant odors of central and eastern Paris away from the residents of these new fine neighborhoods.

Palaces were abandoned to manufacturing and trade. Heavy machinery was bolted to elegant parquet floors; paneled walls were stripped or covered over; large reception rooms were divided into two-floored work spaces; spacious courtyards were filled with homely utilitarian sheds and shops.

The whole area eventually grew into an industrial center of small enterprise and craft shops, running from the old market, Les Halles, in central Paris to the Faubourg Saint-Antoine east of the Bastille. (With each updating of this walk, we observe, with some regret, the steady disappearance of the small factories and craft shops. If not for these enterprises it would have been the Place des Vosges that disappeared. They kept the buildings heated, roofed, and occupied.)

In the years after World War II, the trend reversed. The newly elegant districts of Passy and Auteuil filled up, and well-to-do Parisians, unwilling to settle in distant suburbs, began to look again at the long-abandoned buildings of the older neighborhoods. The first areas to benefit from the new mode were on the Left Bank. Old residences came to have a new cachet, like old furniture and objets d'art.

Serious renewal of the Marais came later, with a special push from the law of 1962 requiring the cleaning, *ravalement,* of the façades of all buildings at least once every decade or so. The law created a massive new industry that transformed the appearance of Paris. Suddenly, black and gray structures took on the colors and details of their youth. Paris became once again a city of light.

The Marais was one of the areas that benefited most from the new cleanliness; the *hôtels* were spectacular once one could see their lines and details. Some of them were restored by the state; others by developers. There was no lack of customers waiting to pay small fortunes for apartments in renovated buildings. But there was also no lack of residents who were very happy to stay in their old quarters at low rents.

The result was a small, quiet civil war. French tenancy laws made removal hard enough; politics made it even harder. There were abuses on both sides. Tenants organized themselves into defense committees and solicited support. Some of them were eventually scared or bullied into leaving. Later, tenants held up badly needed improvements even when generous provision had been made either for their subsequent return or their relocation into what were often better accommodations. Militant denunciations and calls to resistance covered neighborhood walls. We found one petition in a courtyard and started to copy it down. The concierge came out and asked us what we were doing. She was furious at the "troublemakers" and tried to scratch out the poster as we stood there. She was no doubt on the side of the "improvers." They would bring in better and richer tenants and that would mean a substantial gain in status and income for her. Can't blame her.

Now the tumult has quieted down. The new procedures are fairer; the worst abuses are behind. The Marais has become the neighborhood of choice for intellectuals, professionals, and those who want the feel of old Paris.

Jacques Lang, the former minister of culture, lives in the Place des Vosges.

Before you begin a close look at the different houses in the *place*, take a look at the garden and the façades. The railings that you see today, surrounding the garden, are merely a poor imitation of the wrought-iron version with elaborate gold trim that originally stood here. The gate was locked at night, and residents had their own keys.

During the Revolution the railing was almost torn down to be made into spears but was saved because a depot for military equipment already existed in the *place*. The gate was inexplicably torn down, however, during the reign of Louis Philippe, despite the eloquence of Victor Hugo on its behalf. It was replaced in 1839 by the uninteresting grille that you see before you today.

During the Revolution the Place Royale was renamed the Place de l'Indivisibilité, after the new Republic, one and indivisible. Then in 1800 the name was changed again. It became the Place des Vosges to honor the region that paid its taxes first. Lovers of old Paris argue heatedly for the return of the original, historic name, La Place Royale. Imagine the confusion between the Place Royale and the Palais Royale.

At first glance you might think that all of the houses in the square are identical. But although the architectural plans for the square were strict, the individual owners still managed to put their marks on the buildings in discreet yet effective ways. As we noted earlier, the original plan for each dwelling or *pavillon* called for four arcades. Each *pavillon* was to have mansard windows, two round oeil-de-boeuf windows and two square windows, all framed by the roofline. Yet every set of windows is slightly different. Look to see how, with time, ownership has changed the original four-pavilion plan into any number of variations.

Today, the most noticeable difference between buildings is between those that have been restored and those

that have not. When you get inside the courtyards you will see that some with glowing façades are in terrible shape on the inside, and some with marvelous courtyards are in disrepair outside. By the time you read this there may be total restoration of the *place* with all signs of false brick and dilapidation gone.

The garden before you is the subject of great and ongoing controversy: to keep or not to keep the trees. To preservationists and purists, the large leafy trees are an intrusion. They weren't there originally, and for good reason: they block the view of the *place*. The French have always been devoted to vistas, which is one reason why Paris is such a beautiful city. Here in the Place des Vosges, the original garden was minimal—lawns with paths cut on the diagonals—in order to leave an unobstructed view of the whole square.

The trees that are here today are the second set of trees to be planted in the garden. The circle of trees that had surrounded the statue were stricken with Dutch elm disease and were replaced. The new trees obstruct more of the view of the entire *place*. When you visit the Musée Victor Hugo, look out of the windows from the second story onto the *place*. You will be astounded to see how magnificent the whole square looks when it is uninterrupted by the trees. You too may be tempted to side with the historical preservationists.

The children move about freely in a relaxed atmosphere that is unusual in a Parisian park. The older people sit on the benches in the leafy shade and converse, knit, and play checkers and chess while their children and grandchildren play happily. The park really fills with children between noon and 2 P.M. when those attending the three schools tucked away in these imposing houses—plus two more schools backing onto the *place*—come out to play. This park, once the social center of the seventeenth-century upper class, has now become a playground for the highly diverse neighborhood population.

Begin walking at the **Pavillon du Roi** at **no. 1 Place des Vosges**, the center of the south wing. As you face the pavilion, odd numbers are on your right, even numbers are on your left.

The pavilion was never occupied by the king but rather by his concierge, or gatekeeper, who was the first resident of the building. Since 1666 it has been rented to different tenants and today it is divided into apartments that are served by the unattractive stairs and lift built into the right-hand side of the entrance arcade. This blocking of the arcade, done in the sixteenth century, still rankles.

The building is a classified historical monument and therefore should be returned to its original condition. But how would the residents enter their building? Even more important, the stairwell blocks part of the vista from the Rue de Birague into the *place*, and, as we have already noted, vistas are serious matters.

As early as 1752, the writer Germain Brice said that these three arcades themselves should be torn down to leave the view of Louis XIII's statue unobstructed from the Rue Saint-Antoine. This is perhaps too much to ask, but he also wrote:

> It has to hurt to see one of the three arcades under the pavilion blocked to make a nasty stairway which defaces entirely the entrance from the side of the Rue Royale [Rue de Birague today]. But we have such little care for public embellishments in Paris that we do not hesitate to spoil a vista or an entire square for the minor interests of some private person who has influence with the officials who are supposed to look after the decorations of the city.

Looking up at the façade of no. 1 you will see that the balcony here is stone rather than wrought iron and that the building is adorned with a bust of Henri IV, which was added at some unknown time. Walk through the arcade and look at the other side of the building from the Rue de Birague.

On this side the pavilion is decorated with the arms

and initials of Henri IV just above the arches; these date from the original construction. In the spring and summer many of the residents fill window boxes on their balconies with flowers, and the building looks more as if it should be part of a narrow Mediterranean street, not a king's pavilion in Paris.

Re-enter the *place* and turn to the left at **no. 1 bis**. This four-arched residence, the Hôtel de Coulanges, is the last to remain in the hands of a single owner, Mme Cotin. More than twenty years ago she undertook the gigantic task of restoring the entire structure. She changed architects and contractors every few years, working first on the façade, then on the interior, then back again. It has been a source of wonder to the neighbors, who watch what goes on with great interest. One contractor, M. Sachet, of Sachet and Brulet, said in 1989 with some pride that this was a prestige job and therefore he had decided to face the building with real brick even though false brick was stated in his contract. He planned to make up the difference in cost himself. He has long since departed and work has ceased. Of the six arcades, the last two are in false brick, because each pavilion of four arcades must match and the first proprietor to restore sets the style of brick for the rest. The next two arcades had already been realistically restored in false brick.

The building has one of the oldest wrought-iron balconies in Paris, built in 1655. Its straight, plain support poles are the sign of its authenticity. There are more of these early balconies in the *place*, but most are more modern, with elaborately decorated supports. The rooms of this *hôtel* are reputed to have kept their seventeenth-century size as well as the painted walls and beamed ceilings that were so fashionable in the early days of the Place Royale. The last windows on the right-hand side of the second floor have seventeenth-century interior shutters (*pan clos*).

This grand house, the Hôtel de Coulanges, is famous as the birthplace, in 1626, of the Marquise de Sévigné, née Marie de Rabutin-Chantal. Note the plaque on the wall.

This was the home of her maternal grandfather, Philippe de Coulanges. Marie, orphaned at two, lived here for ten years. At seventeen she was married off to the Marquis de Sévigné. She had two children, one of them a daughter with whom she remained very close. After the death of her husband, who was killed in a duel in 1651, when she was still a very young woman, Mme de Sévigné lived in many different homes, always in the Marais. She was often courted and proposed to, but she chose instead to remain a widow, turning her aspiring lovers into friends.

Meanwhile, her daughter married the Comte de Grignan, who took his new wife to live in Provence, far from Paris and her mother. The separation was painful for Mme de Sévigné, who often disagreed violently with her daughter when they were together but missed her desperately when she was away. And it prompted one of the most famous collections of letters in French literature and a picture of high life during Louis XIV's reign. In her last years Mme de Sévigné lived in what is now the Hôtel Carnavalet (Walk 6). Much of her furnishings, personal belongings, and portraits can be seen there.

In 1627 the Count of Montmorency-Bouteville hid here in the Hôtel de Coulanges after the duel, described earlier, that so piqued Cardinal Richelieu. As soon as things quieted down, he took off for Lorraine, but he would have done better to have run immediately. He was caught and put to death. Montmorency was well known in the Place Royale; he had been the lover of many of the women who lived here.

Fashion has been coming to the Marais in the form of avant-garde designers. The first major designer, at **no. 3**, **Issey Miyake**, combines inventive and practical ideas with high but wearable fashion. This year his clothes, despite the price, were made of pleated washable polyester that looked like pieces of sculpture. They are easily recognizable, which makes it fun for the viewers as well as the wearers. Most of the customers are between thirty and thirty-five, but one customer, well-known but unnamed, is ninety-five. The door to the shop is locked. Ring to be admitted—or you can just look in the windows.

The entrance at no. 3 Place des Vosges is always unlocked. Push the door open and walk into a charming courtyard. This was one of the first buildings in the *place* to have been restored, and the owners are justly proud of their work. The door is open on principle: people should be able to see the interior courtyards as well as the façades. This is also the only building in the *place* with "brick" walls in the courtyard. If you look closely at the front façade of this courtyard you will see that the "brick" is painted, even down to the pipes in the corners. The pipes are painted pink when they are in front of "brick" and ivory in front of the stone trim. The color is bright, but it has a pleasing effect, especially with the small garden and the elegant glassed-in terrace on the second floor of the back section of the building.

Note the windowed arches on the ground floor below the terrace. They were originally the entrance to a stable; this house was built in 1613 on the remains of the stables of the Hôtel des Tournelles. Two huge bronze urns stand against the back wall.

The front staircase, on your right as you leave, is lovely, with wide stone steps and a wrought-iron railing. During the nineteenth century the banister had been remodeled with wooden inlays, which are handsome but, as a resident informed us, not authentic. They have plans to return the garden to a classic French pattern but to keep the stanchions that ring it now.

As you go past **no. 5** look at the pavement to see rails installed that used to facilitate the delivery of heavy loads to the factory inside. If you want to see what the factory-filled Place des Vosages was like, open the door here and look inside.

Next door, always open, leads you to the back garden of the Hôtel de Sully, described in Walk 7.

Just around the corner, an attractive shop called **Sifrène** carries antique and modern gifts.

At **no. 9** is the **Hôtel de Chaulnes**, where there is much to see and read about. Press the bell for Galerie N.D. Marquadt to enter the courtyard; it is always open because of the art gallery inside. This is one of the larger, more elegant *hôtels*, and it is part of a guided tour given by the Monuments Historiques (once a month only) that will take you inside this building and inside the Hôtel de Sully. The tour, given in French, is announced in *Pariscope* and *L'Officiel des Spectacles*. If you understand even a little French, it is well worth going.

The history first, then the present-day offerings. The Hôtel de Chaulnes, built in 1607, was one of the most luxurious houses in the Place Royale. Louis XIII stayed here when the tournament inaugurated the *place*. The Hôtel de Chaulnes was also the site of the royal reviewing stand during all the public events that were held here. In 1644 the building was bought by Honoré d'Albret, maréchal de France, duc de Chaulnes, and peer of France. The Chaulnes were a wealthy family, and much of the decoration was done by them. When the duke died, his widow remodeled the house to include a new dining room and an oratory in the left wing. In 1655 her third son, a man who was accustomed to living well, inherited the residence. He hired Mansart, the famous architect, to extend the right wing of the house back to the Rue de Turenne. Mansart designed a façade with a large triangular *fronton*, pediment, in the roofline.

Today this wing is partially obscured by a gallery that cuts into its center. Mansart also built a monumental staircase to serve this newly expanded wing, but the wrought-iron stair rail was sold to someone in England in the nineteenth century. In the expanded courtyard the new duke had a huge formal garden planted; it had a fountain and a trompe l'oeil perspective painted on the back wall. One of the few touches remaining today from the Chaulnes era is a room with a painted-beam ceiling in the left wing. This was the duchess's oratory, but it was later converted into a kitchen and plastered over. It was the thick covering of plaster that happily has preserved the wooden beams for us.

In 1695 the building was sold to the Nicolaï family. They restored it in a neoclassical style with stucco ceiling decorations, which were recently uncovered when layers of paint were stripped off. Legend has it that during the Revolution, Aimard Charles de Nicolaï hid in his wife's boudoir closet when the sans-culottes, working-class revolutionaries, came looking for him. He was discovered and led straight to the guillotine. The *hôtel* itself was seized and not returned until 1795, after the Terror had run its course. By that time only one of the four Nicolaï brothers still had his head.

Elisa Félix (1820–1858), better known as Mlle Rachel and one of France's most famous actresses, lived here in the mid-nineteenth century. She was renowned especially for her performance in the role of Phèdre, which she played for the first time in 1838. Rachel died in Egypt, but her body was returned to Paris, and a great funeral service was held in the synagogue at no. 14, on the other side of the Place des Vosges.

Today the entire second floor of no. 9 is owned by the Architecture Society, an élite group of one hundred members who use this center for conferences and reflection. They are responsible for the restoration of the building and the cleaning of the façade. They also did some marvelous work in the interior, which you should try to see.

The courtyard of this *hôtel* is very large. One of the first things you notice is a statue of a satyr. Viewed from the side, it has an amusing symmetry of profile. The right wing of the building still reflects the work of Mansart, despite the gallery at the back. Note the arched doorways with the *mascarons* above them. The large *fronton* gives a pale idea of how grand the newly designed wing must have been in the seventeenth century.

Look in the doorway of the right wing to get a feeling of the volume of the stairway Mansart designed, even though the railing is now gone. In the left wing, through the last second-floor window—if the lighting is right and the curtains are open—you can see the painted pink and green beams of Mme de Chaulnes's oratory. The beams, decorated with a *C* and a *D* for Chaulnes and Dailly (the duchess's maiden name), were painted in 1654, among the last in Paris to be thus decorated, for that fashion ended around 1650.

There is a second courtyard behind and to the left of the one we are in now. This is a charming, hidden corner of Paris, one that most visitors to the Place des Vosges never see. The houses here are privately owned and may have been the stables or servants' quarters of the original estate. In a tiny garden the statue of a girl holding a bunch of roses is surrounded by real roses.

Today, a huge warehouse-like gallery, Nikki Diana Marquadt, has moved into the courtyard after the retirement of the owner of a lighting fixtures factory that had been a fixture of the *place* since the beginning of the century. As busy and noisy and full of people as the factory was, and friendly too, this huge empty space contained only two twelve-foot-high, trophy-shaped sculptures. On the right wall there was a ten-foot-square tile mural, decorated with black-and-white photographs of small people pasted onto it. The last time we visited, a fashion house rented it for a fashion show. You will surely see something odd when you visit.

Visit **Plaisait**, the magnificent, almost hidden silver museum and shop in this courtyard. Enter the shop from the left side of the courtyard as you leave. As they describe their goal: "The precious objects which are created by their hands are faithful and delicate antique copies and contemporary creations with pure lines." Their clients include Puiforcat, Hermes, Cartier, the president of the Republic, and others.

In 1987 the museum became the repository for silver objects from all over the world. Plasait restores the long lost art of "artistic craftsmanship that makes silver the servant of a new decorative art." If you wish to have a copy made of a piece of silver in your collection, they can do it. If you like beautiful objects that are still being made, visit this shop/museum.

L'Ambroisie, also at no. 9, is one of the points of pride in the revitalized Place. A Michelin three-star restaurant, it is the only world-class restaurant in the Marais. Half of this writing team went there for lunch (dinner reservations were unavailable for at least a month) as an anniversary present from the children. Lunch cost $250 for two of us ten years ago. Today it costs $400.

The food is extraordinarily fine, in nuance and taste. The flavors are subtle, and yet the essence of each ingredient remains clear and distinct on the palate. The menu changes, but there are three standard and supplementary offerings that accompany each meal. The *trou normand*, a rinsing of the palate between courses, is a fruit sorbet set in a sabayon sauce. The *trou normand* was originally a shot of alcohol (calvados, no doubt) between two courses to clear the palate to make room for more. Maupassant writes (free translation) in his *Contes de la Bécasse*, "Between each serving, the norman hole was made with a glass of eau-de-vie that lit a fire in the belly and madness in the head." Custom continues, but in a much weakened form. The other additions to the meal are a feathery light warm chocolate mousse and a mix of citrus fruits in syrup to help cut the sweet but light desserts.

The décor here is sober and refined. The tables are far apart and the seating is luxurious. Service is, as to be expected, absolutely perfect. Closed Sunday and Monday.

Popy Moreni, an ultramodern women's shop, was the first clothing shop in the *place*. Their collection is avant-garde.

No. 13, **Hôtel d'Antoine de Rochebaron**, marquis de Villequier, was originally one of the most elegant houses of the square, and it is now restored to its grand state. According to a description of the house as it once was, it was a gem, with decorations by all the best artists of the time. Stucco ornaments by Van Obstal were painted by Vouet; an alcove was decorated by Buirette, the foremost wood sculptor of the time, who had *"epuisé tout son savoir"* (exhausted all his skill) in making it. There was a *salon à*

No. 13 Place des Vosges

l'Italienne with a huge fireplace decorated with silver and gold. The salon itself calls for elaboration. It was two stories high, with a ceiling in the shape of a lantern, and was lined with mirrors, a rare commodity in the seventeenth century. A chronicler writes:

> When reclining in this salon, if we look to the right, we see, through the two glass doors, opening on to the *place*, carriages, people on foot or on horseback, and all that is happening in the Place Royale. If we turn to the left, the same thing reflected in the mirrors is presented to our sight, so that, without getting out of bed, in summer as in winter, in sickness or health, we can enjoy the diversion.

After the marquis de Villequier, the house was owned by the ambassador to Venice, des Hameaux, who added to its luxurious appointments, installing precious paintings, furniture, and even more mirrors, brought from Italy. The stables were large enough to hold three carriages and seven horses.

Today we have new wonders of restoration to see here instead. The property was bought by the Société Française de Promotion et de Gestion Immobilière (SFPGI), which administers apartment houses, and the work was financed by the Banque de Indo-Suez. Elegant as the building looks now, the Société's first set of plans was rejected by the Monuments Historiques as being too pompous for a popular neighborhood.

To see the splendid courtyard of no. 13, look through the windows of **Antiquités Philippe Magloire**, specializing in Middle Eastern antiquities. The back wings in the courtyard were reextended all the way to the Rue de Turenne, which was how the building stood in the seventeenth and eighteenth centuries. The wings had been demolished by the twentieth century. The entire back section of the building is therefore new, though built in the style of the eighteenth century, while the front half has been redone in the seventeenth-century brick style.

The garden in the center is a copy of a classical French design, but here too, old and new merge; it is automatically watered every evening at eight o'clock by sunken sprinklers. Under the garden is a garage for the residents. This is the first underground garage in the Place des Vosges. A parking space in Paris is like gold. The entrance is just past the back grille on the Rue de Turenne, and looks like the entrance to an apartment building of grand standing rather than a garage door.

The apartments are fabulous: parquet floors in the Versailles pattern, restored or rebuilt; huge fireplaces of red marble in the living rooms; ceilings almost sixteen feet high. Many of the rooms have interior lofts accessible by spiral staircases. Elevators have been recessed into the thick walls because the stairs are classified as historical monuments and may not be touched.

No. 15, in contrast, is one of the last pavillons that desperately need restoration. We are told that the proprietor "talks good but won't spend." Let's hope our informants are wrong. Its condition does, however, allow us to see the state of disrepair before the restoration of the Marais.

At **no. 17**, the **Galerie de la Place**, replaces a previous one, which replaced a previous one. Since the galleries unfortunately change almost yearly, we will let you find what interests you as you walk.

At **Musatamo**, **no. 19**, the Japanese designer can sometimes be seen sitting at a small table, designing men's clothes. The store is spare. Each item stands by itself. Many of the clothes are black.

Next door, also at no. 19, is the very popular café **Ma Bourgogne**. Stop here for a cup of coffee with milk, a *café crème*, no matter what the time of day, and if it is lunchtime, have one of their charcuterie platters from Auvergne. They specialize in these and in wine from Bourgogne and Bordeaux, but they also serve excellent meals the price of which can add up quickly. The waiters here are characters and enjoy teasing; they offer advice whether asked or not. The café also has a good WC. There has been a café here since 1920. Note: Don't sit on the curb side. The pigeons will drop gifts from above. Open daily.

In the seventeenth century this building was owned by the *conseiller d'état*, Robert Aubrey, who lived here with his wife, Claude de Pretevel. Tallement des Réaux, the contemporary chronicler of life in the Marais, wrote astonishingly of this couple: "*Elle le méprisait beaucoup, de sorte qu'elle a pissé plus d'une fois dans les bouillons qu'elle lui faisait prendre*" (She hated him so much that more than once she pissed into the soup that she gave him). Hardly an appetizing legacy for a building that houses a café. Fortunately those manners are far behind us.

No. 21 is another one of the larger and more elegant buildings in the *place*, with eight arcades. It was given to Cardinal Richelieu by Henri IV, but no one knows for sure if he ever lived here. Possibly he stayed here briefly while waiting for the Palais Royal to be completed. He bequeathed it to his grandnephew, who then passed it on to his son. The son never lived here either, but he is rumored to have made good use of his pied-à-terre to know almost every woman in the *place*.

This *hôtel* was restored in the summer of 1978. Residents here have put a lot of money and care into the work. These arcades had originally been done in real brick, and the residents wanted to return them to their original condition. The Monuments Historiques was not eager to do it, but the owners insisted. They went to the brickworks in Versailles, which had made the original bricks in the seventeenth century, and they matched the missing parts as closely as possible. Compare this arcade with the fake paint and etched plaster of the others. The beauty of these arcades has now inspired other residents in the *place* to restore with real brick.

From out in the street, look at the façade of **no. 21** above the fifth pillar from the left, at some stones cut in little squiggles like vermicelli, the same kind used to decorate the Seine side of the Louvre. Some of these, the sharply cut ones, are new; the worn ones—the sixth to ninth squiggles on the left column—are the originals. M. Balmès, the owner of the antique shop here, says that the Monuments Historiques helped pay for the restoration of the façade and for the part of the roof that shows from the square and will also pay a small amount for any classified stairways or railings. Other renovations must be paid for by the owners of the building, which is one reason why the work goes so slowly and erratically.

Look closely at the sides of the arcade pillars right above the pediments, and you will find little square stone patches. These patches date from the Revolution, when this section of the arcade was used as a forge for making arms. They cover the points from which metal curtains were hung to close off the forge. As you walk you will notice many more of these patches in the sides of the pillars. Until around 1930 the arcades were filled with shops of all kinds—butchers, shoemakers, and so on—and each shop walled itself in by setting beams into cuts in the stone. There were so many little shops it was hard to make one's way through the arcade. The last survivor of this era was a shoemaker, who is said to have worked in the arcades as recently as the 1950s.

Go into the courtyard if you can. It is large and sunny, well maintained and charming. Face the entry and look up at the windows on the front portion of the building. On the second floor you will see the original *pans clos* that were used in the seventeenth century.

On the right is a small private garden (you may see a cat stalking the birds) and the entrance to a large staircase. The stair railing here was unfortunately sold to the United States in the last century. M. Balmès explains that Englishmen and Americans would come and ask the building owners to sell stair railings, offering them enough money to restore a whole building. The owners were thrilled then, but the current owners are sorry now.

In the back there is a kind of *orangerie*, dating from the latter half of the eighteenth century. No one knows what it was built for, but now it is a small factory with a small, carefully tended garden. On the left were the stables of the *hôtel*; today they make a sunny apartment with a terrace on top. The buildings in this courtyard all seem to vary slightly, which is partly explained by the fact that they were built at different times. But the layout has been the same since about 1750, as shown by Turgot's famous map of that time.

The **Richelieu** specializes in scientific instruments from earliest times to the twentieth century: clocks, optical devices, navigational aids. M. Balmès has a number of "masterpieces," the graduation projects that guild apprentices have made as a test of their skills and proof of readiness to work on their own. The guilds were all abolished in 1791, so these masterpieces are usually more than two hundred years old. (Today, artisans learn their trade at the Compagnons du Devoir described in Walk 7, page 241.)

We saw a small wrought-iron balcony or miniature stair-cases of exquisite detail. We also learned how lace was made by examining a *carreau*, a box with a square cushion overlaid with a paper pattern stuck with pins to weave the threads around. The threads were drawn from small bobbins, which in this case were still attached to the half-finished piece. M. Balmés is as much a collector as a dealer, and his shop often looks empty. But do try the door. He is usually upstairs, but his wife will wait on you. If you are interested in something special, he will come down to help you. He also knows the Place des Vosges very well.

At **no. 21** the owners of **Les Deux Orphelines** collect eighteenth- and nineteenth-century *art populaire*, or country handicrafts, mainly in wood: marvelous ox yokes, wooden shoes, religious statues, and metal objects such as candlesticks, sconces, and planters. The prices are reasonable, and the merchandise is amusing.

Next door is **Max Spira**, a jumble of old and new twenties-style bric-a-brac. They are open at night.

Saturday and Sunday from noon to 6 P.M. the Minor String Quartet plays to more than a hundred admirers in front of no. 21. The clarinetist is so good everyone applauds in the middle of the performance. They sell cassettes on the spot. Check with the storekeeper.

At **no. 23**, notice the heavy wooden door decorated with thick wooden plaques attached with metal bolts. There are several doors of this kind in the *place*, and each one has its own pattern. This was the Hôtel de Marie-Charlotte de Balzac d'Entragues. Not only her name was impressive; her career was as well. She lived here with her mother, who had been the mistress of Charles IX. Her sister, Henriette d'Entragues, had been the mistress of Henri IV. (Decidedly, these ladies did not bring good luck to their lovers.) Marie-Charlotte was the mistress of the maréchal de Bassompierre and gave birth to his son, Louis, in 1610. Their relationship was very stormy, and Marie-Charlotte kept pressing the maréchal to marry her. He refused, reneging on his written promise. So Marie-Charlotte consoled herself with a series of lovers of equal distinction or equal means, among them the archbishop of Paris, Jean-François de Gondi, and the financier Le Plessis-Guénégaud. We are told that there is a room in the house that still has painted beams dating from her residency, but we have never been inside.

At **no. 25** is the charming **Guirlande de Julie**. The restaurant's lofty goal is to "make the dining an inter-mission from the absurd, an instant stolen from daily drudgery." The reality is that the interior is decorated in a soothing bower of green and pink and the food is excel-lent, beautifully presented and served, bounteous, refined, and with all that, not too expensive. The name is from the history of the *place*. The *Guirlande de Julie* was a small book of madrigals, each surrounded by a different flower, that the Duc de Montausier offered to his wife on May 22, 1641. The restaurant, like Coconnas, also in the *place*, is owned by the colorful Claude Terrail, impresario of the two-star Tour D'Argent. Closed Mondays.

The courtyard and house on the right side of no. 25 are lovely. The ground-floor window just past the doorway is a large hemisphere of glass usually associated with a shop-front window. This building, however, is occupied as a pri-vate house. Formerly there was a trellis with plants rather than curtains, which permitted a glimpse of the living room. Under the frescoed ceiling, a huge stone fireplace on the right wall could hold three men standing upright.

Press the button marked *porte* and enter the courtyard. Pause for a moment to look around. Look at the nicely done modern glass door in the rear to the right; the *mas-caron* has been lost, but the stairs and their fine railing are still there. This whole right wing is owned by one family who live there with free-flying birds, animals (including chinchillas), and *very* large plants. The left side of the build-ing is much more conventional. The entrance at the back is modern, but the old *mascaron* is still intact above the door.

You have now gone halfway around the square and are standing in front of the **Pavillon de la Reine**, which is opposite Henri's pavilion where we started. This one is exactly the same except for the sun emblem of the Médicis on the façade and the very long iron balcony. The small street here, the Rue de Béarn, was the exit route for all the parades that passed through the Place Royale.

The **Hôtel Pavillon de la Reine, no. 28**, would please a queen more than the Pavillon de la Reine, the central north pavilion of the *place*. The hotel is set back from the street behind a classical French garden. It looks as if it has always been there. It has all the comforts and luxuries of new hotels, close to all the new goings-on in the Marais, and yet quiet and private. A double room costs $300, a duplex double close to $400, and an apartment for four with a loft almost $600. The clientele is largely European. Stay there if you can.

No. 26 was the *hôtel* of the first *précieuse* of the Place des Vosges, Charlotte de Vieux-Pont. Today the building itself is not very interesting, but the shops that occupy the ground floor are.

No. 24 has a fine wooden door, but the courtyard beyond is undistinguished. We will take a look at the shops here instead. The first, the **Jardin de Flore**, is an excellent print and engraving gallery. The remarkable doorway was made by the sculptor and jeweler Jean Filhos. He constructed the frame out of a special acrylic combination that turned out to be poisonous. The work made him quite ill, but he has since recovered, and the results, a fantastic combination of Gothic and Art Nouveau, have repaid his effort if not his illness. The Jardin de Flore sells all kinds of engravings and illustrated pages of antique manuscripts. This is a shop with excellent taste and knowledgeable service.

This *hôtel*, du maréchal de Geran, does not have as illustrious a history as some of the others, but it did have one famous or notorious resident, the wife of the maréchal de France, Duke of Bouffleurs. She was fourteen years old when she was married and she quickly became known for her beauty, caustic wit, and number of lovers. This verse was written about her:

Quant Bouffleurs parut à cour,
On crut voir le mère d'amour,
Chacun s'empressait à lui plaire
Et chacun l'avait à son tour.

When Bouffleurs appeared at court,
You would have thought you were looking at Venus;
Everyone tried to please her
And everyone had her in turn.

We are now at the end of one side of the *place*, at the corner where the Rue du Pas de la Mule joins the square. Originally there was a house here, and the street joined the square through the arcades of the house. The marks of the building are reportedly visible on the side of the wall of No. 22, but we have never found them. The building was torn down in 1823, making the northern side of the Place des Vosges a too-well-traveled route for cars headed toward the Bastille and the new Opéra.

Walk east out of the *place* to **no. 6 Rue du Pas de la Mule**. This is one of the most fascinating shops in Paris. It was called the **Boucherie** (the butcher's shop), but it now sells musical instruments. Note above the doorway the metal hooks from which the meat was hung. The tiled walls are original.

M. Bissonet comes from a long line of butchers, and this shop was his until his passion for musical instruments gradually won out. He began by hanging violins and trumpets alongside his sausages, but eventually the meat vanished, and now the shop is crammed from floor to ceiling with instruments. His cold-storage room has become a library of books on the topic, and his workrooms are now his office and a workshop to restore the instruments to their original playing condition.

An arcade in the Place des Vosges

He showed us a silver-etched guitar, a porcelain trumpet, and a tuba made of Venetian glass. He also played for us a Breton bombardon, a flutelike instrument that is only twelve inches long and less than one inch wide but makes an enormous sound. He drew quite a crowd. The store also had a player piano that made the sounds of twenty-nine flutes, a mandolin, and violins in addition to the piano; it was built for a merry-go-round in 1920. M. Bissonet is so agreeable that he might just play an instrument in the shop for you.

Return now to the Place des Vosges to continue the walk. On the corner at **no. 22** is **La Chope des Vosges**. This restaurant was once a café. The ground floor was lowered and a balcony installed in order to put in more tables. This is an excellent place for lunch, but get there early or reserve ahead of time; it is a popular neighborhood hangout. There is a table laden with hors d'oeuvres in front of you when you enter. Their plat du jour provides a hearty hot meal at a reasonable price. In winter eat in the restored seventeenth-century building; in summer sit outdoors under the arcades.

The enlargement and renovation of the restaurant about ten years ago cost the owner 3,000,000 francs (approximately $500,000). The rule is that the city pays a little more than 24 percent of renovations and the state pays 36 percent. The rest is paid by the owner. In this case, the owner got tired of waiting and did the work on his own. He is very proud of his restaurant, and justifiably so. He was wise because the *mairie* officials in the city hall of the fourth arrondissement have just decided not to pay for the cleaning of three of the last pavilions in the *place*.

Press the button above the keypad at **no. 20** to enter the courtyard, and face the front wall (facing the *place*). It is in the midst of repairs that were halted eighteen years ago. An architect, known for prefabricated constructions, lived here and wanted to restore the façade. He had wanted to finish a nineteenth-century addition: a glassed-in hall on the first floor and a covered passageway on the second floor. Originally the apartments in these buildings had been built without halls; each room opened on to the following. Halls were added later, by taking space from the original rooms, which were usually large enough for the purpose. In this building, though, these halls were built on to the outside of the building.

The architect's plan here was to build a new façade in the original seventeenth-century style that would encompass the hallways and incorporate them into the building. He began construction with hollow bricks, but when the authorities found out, they objected, saying that the original did not have bricks at all but rather plaster painted to resemble bricks. The decision? The building must remain in status quo, that is, the ugly glass balcony and the partially completed work would have to remain as they were.

Residents assure us that the work will be done this year, now that the architect has died. Not everyone is as lucky as M. Dhulster of the Auberge des Deux Signes, who was able to finish his excavation before anyone caught on (see Walk 1). Of course, the Monuments Historiques assures the authenticity and quality of the work it endorses, so perhaps it's better that unauthorized restorations are stopped. But is a building better in indefinite limbo?

The walls here do serve a purpose, however, in their present condition: they give us a good opportunity to see how these buildings were constructed. Look at the window frames on the right and left of this wall as well as the corners. You can see how the large stones were used as a frame, which was then filled in with small stones and rubble and covered with plaster. This is essentially the same *colombage* technique used in the sixteenth century, except that here stone replaces the timber framing.

L'Occitane, also at no. 20, sells fine natural bath products. The mural, the brick floor, and the decorations are splendid.

No. 18 was the Hôtel de Marguerite de Béthune, the duchesse de Rohan and the daughter of Sully, Henri IV's first minister. Married at the age of nine in 1604, she later had innumerable lovers, many of them residents of the Place Royale. Of her nine children, only one daughter survived her. Today the building has little to offer from the seventeenth century other than a frieze in the Greek key pattern on its façade, which can be seen from the street. A glance at the windows of the apartment on the second floor with their *pans clos* hints at what riches may lie inside. The courtyard has been restored only in the entryway. The walls have been lined with wooden cupboards on the right and with pillars on the left. It is all new and somewhat attractive. The rest of the courtyard has not been touched, but take a look at the bronze statue of the Gypsy in the stairwell on the left. She has lost the lantern from her left hand and one earring. The concierge proudly told us that Victor Hugo put the statue there, but we have not found mention of that anywhere else. We do know for a fact, though, that the Gypsy was stolen some years ago. A woman resident called the police and got immediate results. The statue was found minutes later at the light on a nearby corner. Her head was sticking out of the back of a pickup truck. She is now firmly attached to her red marble base, which is firmly attached to the floor.

No. 16 was owned in the seventeenth century by a royal counselor named François le Roux, who had the dubious distinction of marrying *"une petit garce qui se donnait pour un quart d'écu"* (a little bitch who gave herself for a quarter of an *écu*). That was slightly less than a livre, but in those days a livre was a day's wages for a manual worker, so Mme le Roux was not so cheap after all. Anyway, she had a lot of amateur competition in this area, as we have seen. Today the courtyard needs restoration, but take a look at its wrought-iron railing and the *mascarons* over the portal and entry.

A most pleasant place for lunch or afternoon tea is **Nectarine**. Lunch is mainly salads and vegetable pies, while a changing array of luscious cakes and tarts will tempt you either for dessert or as an afternoon reenergizer with a cup of tea. A dense chocolate cake is always appropriate; in the summer try their ice creams.

Short-lived art galleries have now been taken over by an appraisal office that will tell you the worth of your own valuables for free in the hope that you will sell to them. By appointment only.

The **Hôtel de l'Abbée de la Rivière, no. 14**, is now one of the best restored in the *place*. The six arcades have been redone in real brick and the wrought-iron balconies have been cleaned of rust. Notice the balcony and the campanile on the roof, which was added at a later date. Step back from the building to look at the roofline and see the arched back of the façade of the building's entrance on the Rue des Tournelles. Today this is a synagogue, and the half of the building that faces the Place des Vosges is used by the Ashkenazic community (the eastern European Jews who are mostly Yiddish-speaking); the half on the Rue des

Tournelles belongs to the Sephardic community (Jews who settled in Spain and Portugal; now most are from North Africa). The doors on the *place* are sometimes locked, but you can always enter on Friday evenings and Saturday mornings when services are being held.

. The walls are wood-paneled; the stairs are carpeted with Oriental rugs; plants sit in the entry. The interior resembles a Victorian home. Indeed, this half once was. The chief rabbi of France lived here with his wife and five children. There is an art gallery on the third floor, exhibiting Jewish artists. Visitors are welcome.

The Sephardic synagogue on the other side of the building, entry on Rue de Tournelles, serves the growing Oriental Jewish community. It has a large Moorish sanctuary; the stucco pillars are painted with words and designs, and the ceiling, high above the sanctuary, is rounded in a long arch.

No. 14 takes its name from one of its seventeenth-century owners, the abbé de la Rivière, favorite of the duc d'Orléans, tutor of the duke's children, and himself promoted to duke and bishop of Langres. This son of a tailor, a veritable model of social advancement through the church, never did realize his dearest ambition, however—to be made a cardinal. The best painters of the era, Le Brun and Mignard, created a fabulous interior that is now in the Hôtel Carnavalet.

When la Rivière died, a poet composed the following verse:

> *Ci-gît un très grand personnage*
> *Qui fut un illustre lignage*
> *Qui posséda mille vertus*
> *Qui ne trompa jamais, fut toujours très sage.*
>
> *Je n'en dirai pas plus,*
> *C'est trop mentir pour cent écus.*

Here lies a very great person
Who had an illustrious lineage

Who possessed a thousand virtues
Who never deceived, was always well behaved.

I won't say more,
That's too much lying for a hundred *écus*.

The hôtel was later used as a neighborhood city hall. That role is commemorated by a plaque that is barely legible. Later it was used as a school.

Next door to the synagogue, there is a public nursery school for children aged two to six.

No. 8, as the plaque tells us, was the home of the poet Théophile Gautier, who lent his name to the commercial high school next door. There is another small restaurant here, **Salon Victor Hugo,** serving quiches, salads, and coffees.

The **Musée Victor Hugo** at **no. 6** was Hugo's residence from 1832–1848. Before Hugo's time it was the hôtel of the princesse de Guéménée, Anne de Montbazon. She was the most famous *precieuse* of the *place*. She was married at twelve to her cousin, the prince, and like other premature wives of the day, never settled into monogamy. Anne was mistress of the coadjutor of Retz; of the financier d'Emery; of the count Montmorency-Bouteville, beheaded in 1627 for his famous duel; of the duke Henri II of Montmorency, beheaded in 1632; of the count of Soissons, who died tragically in 1641; and of the counselor of Parliament, Auguste de Thou, beheaded in 1642. She did not bring luck to her lovers, but she herself lived to be eighty-one.

The princess is representative of Molière's liberated *précieuses*. These women established a literary style and a new standard for excellence of the French language. They were also sexually liberated, conducting their many affairs with the grudging consent of their husbands. They seem to have thrived on this, marrying at puberty and living to a ripe old age.

Marion Delorme may also have lived here, in a small pavilion at the back, but most historians feel that it was unlikely that two famous women could peaceably have shared the same house, if only because of the traffic jam that would have resulted. Marion was a match for Anne in every way, in number of lovers and in the brilliance of her salon. She began her career as courtesan with Jacques Vallée, sieur Desbarreaux, a notorious "epicurean" (read hedonist) and, unforgivable at the time, an avowed atheist. Next came the Marquis de Cinq-Mars, a handsome, stylish courtier who made the mistake of plotting intrigue against Richelieu and lost his head, literally as well as figuratively. (The marquis may have died young, but his place in history and literature is assured as the protagonist of Alfred de Vigny's novel *Cinq-Mars*.)

After the execution of Cinq-Mars, Marion is said to have gone on to a long series of lovers, including George Villiers, the first Duke of Buckingham. (You may remember him in *The Three Musketeers*.) Also Louis II de Bourbon, Prince de Condé (called "the great Condé"), prince of the blood and the last of the great feudal barons. He was eight years younger than she and a great success with the ladies. Yet this great wencher had his own wife confined for her alleged unfaithfulness (which even the malicious gossips of the day refused to credit) and wrote his last letter to the king to ask that she never be released. Nice fellow. Last but not least, Marion is said to have gotten Cardinal Richelieu himself into her bed. Ironically, it was Richelieu's niece who was Condé's unfortunate wife, so everything was neatly kept in the family.

Marion, unlike the other great courtesans of her day, died early, in 1650, but as with other legendary figures, there were those who refused to believe she was gone. Some said she lived on to 1706, when she would have been ninety-three, or even 1741, when she would have been one hundred and twenty-eight. Victor Hugo wrote a drama called *Marion Delorme*, and G. Bottesini wrote an opera of the same name. In a sense, she lives on.

The property at no. 6 was large, stretching back to no. 17 Rue des Tournelles, with a discreet rear alley for quick exits, a feature that Hugo often used when visiting his mistresses.

Hugo lived here in a rented apartment one floor up until his disagreements with Louis Napoléon required him to flee into political exile on the isle of Guernsey. Today the museum is on the first, second, and third floors of the building. Start at the top with the history of Hugo's life, move down to his drawings and mementos on the second, and then visit a recreation of his apartment on the first. Each room is dedicated to a period of his life. The museum has restored Hugo's bedroom with his Louis XIII deathbed and his death mask. Don't miss the romantic and striking Chinese-style dining room that he built himself in his second home in Guernsey. The wall with its bright red chimney and lavish plate collection reveals in how many ways Hugo was remarkable.

Be sure to look out on to the *place* before you leave to get a good view of the whole square above the trees. The museum is open from 10 to 5:45 daily except Mondays and holidays. The fee is 27 francs.

On this last side of the square there are several galleries which change often. Stop in those that appeal to you.

Marc-Annibal de Coconnas is the restaurant at **no. 2** Place des Vosges, although its front door opens on to the Rue de Birague around the corner. This restaurant is owned by Claude Terrail, who also owns the Tour d'Argent, and it is no accident that both places provided locales for the movie *Who Is Killing the Great Chefs of Europe?* This restaurant is casual and moderately priced. Meals are prix fixe— no à la carte. The specialty is *poule-au-pot*. The menu no doubt commemorates Henri IV's promise of a "chicken in every pot." The restaurant is open daily.

You have now completely circled the Place des Vosges. The area is so rich, now the richest in history and monuments in all Paris that we have ended this walk here. But if you still have strength, the walk continues in Walk 6, right outside the *place*. Exit the *place* from the northwest corner by Ma Bourgogne, and turn left to the Rue des Francs-Bourgeois.

Walk · 6

Rue des Francs-Bourgeois

"Now the backbone of the Marais, it prides itself on the sumptuous homes endowed by prestigious institutions."

—Jacques Chirac, in his dedication to
La Rue des Francs-Bourgeois

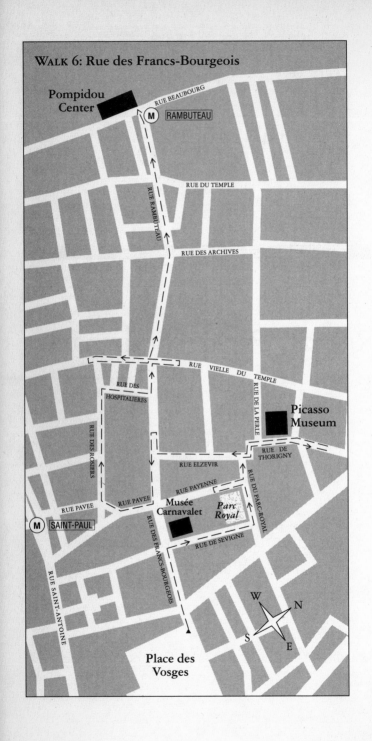

WALK 6: Rue des Francs-Bourgeois

Pompidou Center

RUE BEAUBOURG

Ⓜ RAMBUTEAU

RUE DU TEMPLE

RUE RAMBUTEAU

RUE DES ARCHIVES

RUE VIELLE DU TEMPLE

RUE DES HOSPITALIERES

RUE DE LA PERLE

Picasso Museum

RUE DE THORIGNY

RUE ELZEVIR

RUE DES ROSIERS

RUE PAYENNE

RUE DU PARC-ROYAL

RUE PAVEE

Musée Carnavalet

Parc Royal

Ⓜ SAINT-PAUL

RUE DES FRANCS-BOURGEOIS

RUE DE SEVIGNE

RUE SAINT-ANTOINE

W N
S E

Place des Vosges

Starting Point: No. 5 Rue des Francs-Bourgeois, 3rd and
    4th arrondissements
Métro: Saint Paul
Bus: 29

The Rue des Francs-Bourgeois stood just outside the limits
of the city against the encircling walls built by Philippe
Auguste, but reentered the city limits under Charles V's
later and wider wall around Paris. The street marks the different periods in the city's long history.

In the sixteenth and seventeenth centuries, the aristocracy installed itself along the length of this east–west
axis, parallel to the Seine, between the Place Royale, now
the Place des Vosges (see Walk 5) and the Palais de
Soubise.

The heart of the city drew the great lords and powerful
financiers to these free swampy lands. The neatly bound
parcels suited the time's architectural fashion of placing
the *hôtel* between the courtyard and the garden. This
allowed for a grand easy entrance for the horse and carriage, a view of the house, and privacy in the garden.

The rich competed in luxury and creativity in the
construction of these great houses. Among the products
of the pomp and circumstance of the society that flourished between the seventeenth and eighteenth centuries,

we have the sumptuous *hôtels* of Soubise, Carnavalet, Lamoignon, Albret, and others. Around them, similar residences planted themselves, less well known, but which have now recently come into their own thanks to intelligent restoration.

The street was first called the Rue des Poulies, named after a pulley, or wheel, on a loom, for the street was a street of weavers. Until twenty years ago it was still a street of fabrics. In the fourteenth century an almshouse was built here. The poor, too destitute to pay taxes, were called "free citizens," hence, *francs-bourgeois*.

When we first researched this walk, this street had potential but was still dark and, for the most part, seemed uninteresting. Today it is historically restored and booming. The very narrow sidewalks are crowded with shoppers and museum-goers, still mostly French. We are going to give you a description of the great houses and museums, and a limited rundown of the shops because there are so many and they change so often. You will be going back and forth across the street. Be careful in crossing.

This shopping street is jam-packed on Sundays. It claimed the right to keep open on Sundays because the Rue des Rosiers is open on Sunday, but closed on Saturday, the Jewish Sabbath. Legally, a store can open on Sunday if the owner is working but not the employees. This ruling was hardly taken seriously and eventually the shop owners received legal permission to open from 2 P.M. to 7 P.M. on Sundays.

In the last edition of this book, the trend was American Western. Today that is almost gone. Shoes came in, but are losing ground to ready-to-wear. Who knows what the trend will be when you walk today? Style changes often in Paris, though there are a few old standbys.

Hier pour Demain at **no. 4** has been here for fourteen years specializing in thirties Art Deco furniture, objects, and materials. **Et Vous**, next door, sells dresses and suits at stiff prices. **No. 6** is **Catimini**, an adorable, expensive children's clothing store.

No. 5, **Monic Bijoux**, is an Ali Baba's cave of costume jewelry. They have drawers and drawers of it. They say Americans particularly buy the garnet jewelry from Czechoslovakia.

At **no. 7** is a new and interesting French restaurant, **Un Piano sur le Trottoir**, a piano on the street. The name has a double meaning: the word *piano* is slang for the stove in a restaurant. Piano music, vocal performances, and group singing are offered every Thursday through Sunday night. This kind of evening is fun for tourists because you can join in conversations as well as singing.

L'Objet at **no. 9** sells bibelots and estate jewelry. **No. 11**, **Fugit Amor**, sells jewelry, as well as, as they say, "love and fantasy."

Enter the ivy-covered courtyard of **no. 8** to visit two wonderful shops. The right side of the shop, **Imex**, was originally the factory for the coats and jackets they specialize in. The left side of the store is **L'Entrée des Fournisseurs**, a ribbon and button, tassels and thread store—now a rarity in Paris. The final store in this building is **Autour du Monde/Country Furnishings/Home**, a remaining American-style store, this one with an overwhelming odor of potpourri.

Lipsic specializes in imaginative women's knitwear. Enter the courtyard of **no. 13**, **2 Mille et 1 Nuits**, to find a collection of decorating exotica. The place glitters. **Emet** sells very conservative expensive dresses and sportswear.

No. 17 is the address for **Archetype**, an architectural drawings gallery, and the street's old-timer, **Jean Pierre de Castro**. When there were only some musty men's tailoring shops here, savvy French ladies came to buy silver by the pound. Flatware, candlesticks, bowls, and serving pieces in hundreds of styles, some famous French and English marks, most of it plated, fill baskets on tables.

Crossing the street again, you come to **no. 12**, **Les Bourgeoises**, a small, dark restaurant that anyone who wants a long, private chat might find just perfect. **Anne Fontaine**'s collection of white blouses is, like **Big Ben**, part of the white blouse craze that has hit Paris. Also at **no. 12**, look at **Jeanne Cecile**'s creative jewelry. Her work has been chosen by the National Museum stores for sale at museums and the Opéra.

La Charrue et les Etoiles, at **no. 19**, is full of minia-ture figures, especially animals and Viennese bronzes. Bring home a souvenir of the small diorama scenes of Paris peopled with lead figures.

Up at the corner is the French version of Banana Republic, called **Autour de Monde**.

Rue de Sévigné

And now we come to one of the great houses of Paris, the **Musée Carnavalet**. Turn right on the Rue de Sévigné. The entrance is on the left at **23 Rue de Sévigné**.

As a result of the elaborate celebrations of the bicenten-nial of the Revolution, the museum has been changed from a storehouse for the cognoscenti to an educational institu-tion for the general public. Twenty million dollars were spent on this successful renovation.

The museum has doubled in size by incorporating the *hôtel* behind it, **Le Peletier de Saint-Fargeau**. Le Peletier houses the history of Paris from the Revolution to the twentieth century. Mme de Sévigné lived here at the end of the seventeenth century for twenty years. She was famous as a letter writer to her beloved daughter who married and moved to Provence. Her letters preserve a way of life full of gossip and stories. She was the epitome of luxury. It is said that doors had to be knocked down to make room for pyramids of food twenty platters high to enter the dining room. Guests passed notes to each other because they couldn't see around the food.

In the courtyard, look at the bas reliefs of the four seasons. Compare the central sculpture, *Winter,* by Jean Goujon in 1550 with *Diane* on the right, sculpted by Van Obstal a hundred years later. Compare them to similar sculpture in the courtyard of the Hôtel de Sully. (See Walk 7, page 241). Note the devilish *mascarons* above the side windows. The statue of Louis XIV, in Roman garb and French wig, was done by Antoine Coysevox, who created the horses at the Place de La Concorde.

Enter the museum through the bookstore. The first room holds a collection of amusing and historical rebus and shop signs. When your customer can't read, you have to show what you're selling. One of the rebuses shows three rats, which was the symbol for the phrase *mort aux rats*. If you wish to visit the rooms dedicated to the Revolution and La Belle Epoque, take the staircase in front of you and follow the long hallway to Le Peletier.

The Revolution is displayed in eleven rooms decorated in the style of the day. The exhibits combine paintings and documents with politically relevant porcelain, a model guillotine, and even a model of the Bastille made from the stones of the original.

After the passion and seriousness of the Revolution and the Paris Commune, the Belle Epoque is like a glass of champagne. With as much of the original furnishings as possible, the Carnavalet has reproduced several rooms from the period.

Proust's cork-lined bedroom is here, as well as a private dining room from the Café de Paris decorated in mauve with furniture by Louis Majorelle. The jewels that adorned the "Grandes Horizontales," as the demimondaines of that time were called, were purchased by their wealthy, ardent admirers at the famous jewelry store Fouquet, magnificently recreated here in all its Alphonse Mucha Art Nouvean glory.

Bust of the Patron of Commerce in the Parc Léopold Achille, taken from the old city hall

The final room from the twentieth century was a great discovery to us. We entered and immediately realized we had been in this room before. We were in M. and Mme Maurice de Wendel's Art Deco salon, with its "sumptuous and theatrical" decor. It was originally in their magnificent *hôtel* on the Quai de New York. The artist was José Maria Sert who completed the salon in 1924. Panels of metal (the Wendel fortune came from iron and steel) painted in crimson and white gold depict the Queen of Sheba's journey across the desert to visit King Solomon. The queen is accompanied by an enormous retinue, and her accou-trements include fireworks, a menagerie, and even palm trees to be planted every evening to provide her with an oasis wherever she might be.

The original building of the museum, Mme de Sévigné's beloved home, exhibits prehistoric, Merovingian, Carolin-gian, and medieval pieces that have been in storage for years as well as the entire pre-Revolutionary collection. Open 10–5:40 daily except Mondays; 27 francs.

Continue down the Rue de Sévigné. You may see a group of high school students fill the street from the Lycée Charlemagne. Push through the crowd of students dressed in black and smoking, or cross the street.

A funny American-style store, **Lyons Co.**, at **no. 38**, scours the United States for collectibles from the fifties to the seventies. You can be sure the cookie jar or poster you buy is not a reproduction.

Note the open courtyards of **nos. 46** and **52**. The mother-and-children fountain sculpture at **no. 48** was part of a larger display with water coming from a fountain flanked by two poplars.

The street ahead is **Parc-Royal**, a street of elegant houses and courtyards. **No. 4** in front of you dates from 1620 and flaunts the famous fake pink brick of the Place des Vosges (Walk 5).

Take a seat in one of the loveliest small parks, the **Léopold Achille** park, and watch society in action. There is a mix of Parisian-dressed kids and their chic parents with families from all over the world. The young boys, all of them, play at kung fu, turning and kicking and yelling, while the girls go up and down the slides. Nothing new. Seen scrawled on the slide: *"Mort aux Bourgeois"* and *"Une Seule Solution—la Révolution."* Nothing new.

A little farther down, adults sit and sun and read, facing a statue of a woman standing among flowers. It was originally the Hôtel de Ville, city hall, which was burned to the ground during the Commune in 1870.

Look out through the park's gate at the **Rue du**

Parc-Royal. **No. 8** (the German Historical Institute) also imitates red brick. **Nos. 10** and **12** house an inventory and archives of historic Paris. In 1960, **no. 10**, the **Hôtel de Vigny**, was saved from destruction by a coincidence. An old gentleman who lived there told his guest, who was an engineer, that his father had said there were painted rafters hidden under plaster. The following weekend, the engineer returned and uncovered the décor we admire today (if one can get in).

Not only did the old gentleman alert André Malraux, then minister of culture, to this find, but he, a puppe-teer, put on marionette shows in the courtyard to gather support to save the building. The hotel was saved, and this inspired Malraux to create the Sauvegarde et Mise en Valeur du Paris Historique (the organization to protect and value historic Paris—see Walk 7, page 241). It is one of seventy-seven restoration organizations now active in France.

Leave the park at the far end and turn up the **Rue Payenne** to the **Georges Cain** park, where it is more shady and quiet. There is a circular parterre of grass, also with a statue of a woman. The graceful seventeenth-century figure, *Flore et Son Char,* poses in the center. The back building is the back of the Hôtel Le Peletier.

The building between the parks was the original *orangerie* of the Musée Carnavalet and is now the stone museum of the City of Paris. Notice the collection of impressive remains of sculpture on the side wall opposite and the rocks on the ground near the gate. The tree with the biggest leaves, a fig tree, stands in the northeast corner.

Enter the courtyard of the **Swedish Cultural Center**, **no. 11**, the perfectly restored Hôtel de Marle, across the street on the Rue Payenne. Free exhibits and an interest-ing gift shop. Open Tuesday through Friday, 10–1 and 2–5. Free.

Return to the Rue du Parc-Royal and walk left to the **Place de Thorigny** on your right. There is a circle of benches there in front of a café and a wonderful decorative store, the **Comptoir de Shanghai**.

To your left, find the **Musée de la Serrure-Bricard, no. 1 Rue de la Perle**. This small, splendid seventeenth-century home of Libéral Bruant is now a museum of the most intricate and fascinating keys and locks. We dare you to put your hand in one of the locks, a lion's mouth, that promises to catch your wrist and hold it there. We found a note inside that read, "Help me." The locks are as complicated as a Rube Goldberg invention—a medieval trunk in particular—and as decorative as clockworks.

The façade of the building is classical. Note the four circular bays with Roman personages between, and the triangular pediment with two fat-winged angels surrounded by horns of plenty. Open Monday 2–5, Tuesday through Friday 10–12 and 2–5. Closed on the weekend; 30 francs, free for those under eighteen years old.

Directly across the street, the **Rue de Thorigny** leads to the **Picasso Museum**, which was the Hôtel Aubert de Fontenay. Pierre Aubert de Fontenay built this grand house in 1656. Fontenay was collector of the tax on salt, a tax mightily resented by the populace. They derisively called his *hôtel* the Salt House, *l'Hôtel Salé*. Fontenay's joy in the mansion, however, was short-lived. He was allied with the disgraced Fouquet of Vaux-le-Vicomte, and both were relieved of their property and their freedom by Louis XIV. (Visit Vaux-le-Vicomte for the whole story.)

The entry of this pleasing semicircular courtyard is flanked by two monumental sphinxes. Note the two pediments, one heavily sculpted with allegorical figures, under the mansard roof. The house has gone through many changes and uses. As a result, none of the original interior remains except for the main staircase, with its sculpture and intricate wrought-iron banister, a forerunner of the majesty of the one at the Opéra-Garnier. With its bare elegance, the seventeenth-century wrought-iron chandelier could have been designed today. Take in the whole splendid scene. Note the modern touches of open spaces in the walls to allow visitors to peer into parts of the museum. The house has now been completely renovated. There is a small room of photos that show what the *hôtel* was like before restoration.

The museum houses a collection of works given by Picasso's heirs as a means of paying off their inheritance taxes. The museum houses over two hundred paintings, sculptures, collages, and Picasso's own collection of Braque, Rousseau, Miró, and Renoir. The works are displayed chronologically, beginning with the famous Blue and Rose Periods, followed by cubism, a classical period, an eclectic period, much sculpture, and some ceramics. The collection completes a circle with a self-portrait done in 1901 and another painted in 1971. Closed Tuesday, open 9:30–5:30 from October through March, and 9:30–6 from April through September; 30 francs, free on Sundays and for those under eighteen years old.

Return to the Place de Thorigny and walk up the **Rue Elzévir** on the way back to Franc-Bourgeois.

Stop at the curious paper-making and jewelry shop, **Charta, no. 16**, where the artist creates different kinds of paper and coats some in gold leaf to make his jewelry. On the left, at **no. 10**, find the peaceful back garden of the Hôtel de Marle on the Rue Payenne. This is a favorite spot for fashion photos and television scenes. The trees are always festooned.

Eighteenth-century decorative art is the mark of the **Cognacq-Jay Museum** at **no. 8**. There are works by Boucher, Chardin, and Fragonard; pastels by de la Tour; and porcelain of Saxe. Cognacq and Jay, serious collectors, made their fortune as founders of the department store La Samaritaine. Open Tuesday through Sunday, 10–5:40; 17.50 francs, free to those under eighteen.

The **Compagnie Sénégal Afrique de l'Ouest**, at **no. 3**, represents artisan and artistic work from this area. They offer a variety of objects and materials. An artist in residence often gives courses to children. Look across the

*Entrance to the Hôtel d'Albret, now the
Center for Cultural Affairs of the City of Paris*

street at **no. 4**, **Lutherie Ancienne Moderne**, to see craftsmen at work making and repairing violins.

Continue down the street to Franc-Bourgeois. **Camille**,
on the corner, is a busy and happy neighborhood café that
serves typical French food.

Look to the right across the street at **no. 35–37**, the
Maison de l'Europe, now a center for international meetings. This was the **Hôtel de Coulanges**, built in the mid-
seventeenth century. It was nearly torn down in the 1960s,
but a media campaign saved it. Enter the courtyard to see
the arcaded façade, the *mascarons*—each one different—
and the wrought-iron staircase on the right.

Directly across the street is the **Hôtel de Sandreville** at
no. 26. It has a Louis XVI façade with wide fluted Doric
pillars and a frieze of garlands. The heavily sculpted door is
in disrepair. A wrought-iron key plate has been stolen from
this door, but the courtyard has recently been magnificently restored. The white stone walls now gleam.

Two doors to the left is **no. 30**, the **Hôtel Alméras**.
Pierre Alméras was a counselor and secretary to Henri IV.
He copied the brick-and-stone combination of the Place
des Vosges. Push the door button and stand at the grille to
see a beautiful courtyard, recently restored. The stones
glow. Henry IV's bust looks down from the third story, and
if the light is right, you will see the beams in the ceilings of
the apartments. The superb door and pediment are characteristic of the seventeenth century.

Turn back to Camille and walk right to **no. 31**, the
Hôtel d'Albret, which has recently been restored by the
city as offices for Cultural Affairs of the City of Paris. Originally built at the end of the fifteenth century for the
connétable (supreme commander of the royal army) de
Montmorency, it has been reworked repeatedly over the
centuries. Today it is a striking combination of preservation
of the past and twentieth-century design. Examine the fine
decorations of the façade and then enter the courtyard. On
the right side were the stables; today there is a Louis XIII

staircase that ends in stone on the top floor. The cellars have been restored for receptions. The left wing is called "the boat" because of the free-standing staircase that looks as if it came from an ocean liner. This wing has been painted the national colors of blue, white, and red to affirm the spirit of the city.

Space was lost in this wing because the building started tipping and needed support when a staircase was removed from the entry. The sculpture by Bernard Pagès in the courtyard was made for the Bicentennial. It recalls the tree wrapped in ribbons the colors of the flag of the Revolution. (See Walk 7, page 241.)

No. 29 bis still has factories in the courtyard. The **Paris Musée** reproduces objects from the national museums. **Jean Châtel** sells good men's clothes in an Art Nouveau setting, the historical remains of a bakery. Note the walls and the ceilings.

At **no. 20** is **La Chaise Longue**, selling reproductions of kitchen things used in the 1930s through the 1950s. **Marais Plus**, also at **no. 20**, is a fun tea shop and gift store. This was the cultural center for the Marais until the city cut funding, and now it is all privately run. The window usually has some odd collection of similar objects; once it was teapots. The store carries heaps of knickknacks especially interesting to children and adults who are young at heart. You can lunch on quiche and cakes and tea in a very casual atmosphere in the back. The shop is open until midnight every night.

Find more Art Nouveau panels on what was once a bakery, now **Le Garage**, on the corner of Rue Pavée. These are always classified as historical decorations.

The **Hôtel de Lamoignon** is on the corner of the Rue Pavée, one of the first paved streets of Paris. Before reaching the corner, look at the lovely garden that is part of the Hôtel de Lamoignon. The *hôtel* was originally built in 1555 by Robert de Beauvais, counselor to the king and comptroller general of the city of Paris. He died in 1568, and the property was purchased by Diane de France, duchess of Angoulême. She was the natural daughter of Henri II. It seems her mother, who was Italian, had refused the king's advances. Not deterred, he had her house burned down in order to kidnap her. Diane was legitimized and became one of the important women of her time, "wise in counsel, beautiful, and the finest woman on horseback."

Notice the square-windowed turret at the corner. A few other such turrets can still be found, one at the Hôtel de Sens. They are the last survivors of what was once a popular design that allowed householders to see what was happening in every direction. The initials *S. C.* carved into the stone on the base of the turret supports mark the limits of the property owned by the Culture of Saint Catherine, the largest religious settlement on the Right Bank. In the circular pediment of the entrance wall there are statues of two children. One, Truth, holds a mirror; the other, Prudence, a serpent. Today, the *hôtel* has been completely restored and enlarged. The right wing, built as recently as 1968, and in perfect harmony with the original section, houses the library of the City of Paris. Go into the courtyard, turn right and go up a few steps and then left into the reading room. Sit down, rest, and admire this beautiful room—its proportions, windows, and view, and the painted beams, with Diane in the middle of a back beam. There is always an interesting exhibition here. When you have finished browsing, take a look at the mausoleum in the courtyard to your left.

Continue down the **Rue Pavée** to the bookstore of the library. It displays historical exhibitions and carries a fine selection of books on Paris and its history.

At **no. 10** is the **Synagogue** built in 1913 by the famous Art Nouveau architect of the *métro*, Hector Guimard. The building is concave, which makes it look taller. The design recalls the shape of the tablets of the Ten Commandments.

Turn right into the **Rue des Rosiers**. Watch the dramas unfold among the cars that cram and jam and inch forward.

The coming of high fashion on the Rue des Rosiers was a kind of public announcement that the Marais and its beautifully renovated buildings had been discovered. Fifteen years ago, the real estate was some of the least valuable in Paris. Then it was some of the most valuable. Today, the real estate market is depressed and prices are down all over Paris.

Lolita Lempicka, a well-known designer, opened on both corners of the street, **nos. 3** and **2 bis**. No. 3 closed, as have some of these upscale fashion stores. A store with no name and curtained windows has moved in. A notice explains the curtains: "Ego. From a sexual point of view, we are not men and women, but shades of violet, orange, green, and brown—some of us are grey and undecided, others are black and have a dynamic gender complexity. Now, during life, we can all change our gender." No comment.

Across the street was a *hammam*, a Turkish bath, where the most chic, slimmest ladies came from all over Paris to keep thin and fit, the better to buy the clothes across the street. It was bought by the owners of the Chevignon stores. The beautifully tiled walls and pool were dismantled. The entire neighborhood mourned the loss of this establishment. Chevignon soon went out of business. The New Hammam Café, at **no. 4**, offers kosher dairy food, concerts, Internet activities, a radio station, and a publication. Friendly, lively.

L'Eclaireur, at **no. 3 ter**, is one of the high-fashion stores that sell ultramodern clothes and objects as well.

None of this, however, reveals the real history of the street. The Rue des Rosiers is the historic home and first stop for Jewish immigrants and refugees. It plays the same role for French Jews as the Lower East Side once did for Jews in New York. When Jews were forced to leave Eastern Europe on account of pogroms at the end of the nineteenth century, they came here. When Jews fled the Nazis, they again came here. This is also the street where the Nazis and the Vichy French marched through in order to drag 75,000 Jews away to concentration camps. A third wave of immigrants arrived as a result of the French exodus from Algeria. This time the newcomers included both Muslims and Jews, who live side by side in the area.

The corner of Rue des Rosiers and Rue Ferdinand-Duval, the center of the Jewish quarter, is marked by the restaurant **Goldenberg**, which serves all the typical Eastern European Jewish dishes. This was the scene of a terrorist attack by Palestinian sympathizers in which four people, including the Arab cook, were killed in the summer of 1982. A sign on your left as you enter reads in part: *"On ne cède pas au terrorisme"* (We don't give in to terrorism). The food at the take-out counter will give you an idea of the quality and variety of Polish-Jewish food. Try the blintzes and a cup of tea for a light bite if it's lunchtime.

This corner is a meeting place of the neighborhood. Sundays, when everyone is out socializing, there is no walking up and down the street, as in a *passeo*. People just stand and talk. Pity the poor unknown soul who starts down this street in a car. To add to the confusion, the street is lined with barricades to ward off terrorists. These barricades exist all over Paris where there is a school or a possible site for terrorist attack. The owner of the kosher market told us he didn't sell out to high fashion on principle a few years ago, and now he couldn't do it if he wanted to. This much of the ghetto is here to stay.

From Goldenberg's on down, the street is still Jewish. It is dotted with butchers and bakers and Sephardic fast-food *schwarma* and falafel places—especially **l'As du Felafel**, **no. 34**, bookstores, religious articles stores, and bakery and appetizer stores.

Two Finkelsztain shops, one bakery in particular, are worth a visit. **Finkelsztain**, at **no. 27**, sells all dairy food, the finest breads, cakes, and appetizers. The delicious dark rye slices easily and stays fresh indefinitely; not so with a

Excellent traditional Jewish food at no. 27 Rue des Rosiers

baguette. Cheesecake and apple cake are the favorites. The specialty of the house is a unique eggplant dip that is smooth and silky, topped with sesame seeds. The high quality justifies the very high prices. Try something.

Korcarz, up the street at **no. 29**, is an excellent kosher bakery and restaurant. Stop in for a meal or for tea and cake. The busy bakery offers a rich selection of cakes and breads—take home some goodies, even pretty good bagels.

Return and turn to the right up the **Rue des Hospitaliers** to the school on the right. This spot tells many stories. Originally a meat market stood here—thus the heads of the bulls on the walls. They were originally the decorations of two fountains, no longer here. Then it was a Jewish public school—boys on the right, girls on the left. Read the startling plaques on the walls to relive the horror of the Nazi occupation.

> One hundred and sixty-five Jewish children of this school were deported to Germany during World War II and were exterminated in the Nazi camps. Lest we forget.

The second plaque is an acknowledgment from former students:

> To Jean Mignaret, teacher and director of this school from 1920 to 1944, who by his courage and at peril of his life saved tens of Jewish children from deportation.

Today the right side of the building is a school for special needs students and the left is a regular mixed public school. Continue up the street to the Rue des Francs-Bourgeois.

Rue des Francs-Bourgeois

Directly in front of you is the **Swedish Cultural Center** at **no. 38**. The seventeenth-century houses lean toward each other and almost meet at the top. The old-fashioned pharmacy next door, at **no. 36**, is worth entering. Note the back wall of blue medicine bottles, the etched lady in the mirror, the clock in the wall, and the old-style scale.

A l'Image du Grenier sur l'Eau (the picture of the

hayloft on the water—a street name near the Seine) at **no. 45** across the street is a one-of-a-kind postcard store. Here two brothers have assembled postcards from the last quarter of the nineteenth century to 1945 in hundreds of drawers classified by every possible subject. The cards range in price from $1 to $100. If you can bear to mail them, they make a great change from the typical tourist cards you have already sent home.

Cross again, turning left to an excellent knitting store, **Anny Blatt** at **no. 40**, famous for its wools. The **Villa Marais**, next door, is a mixture of modern and antique gifts and furniture.

Continue up the street to the corner of Francs-Bourgeois and Vieille du Temple. You will immediately notice the flamboyant Gothic tower at **no. 54**. This is a reconstruction from the manor house of **Hérouét**, which was destroyed by the last German bombing of Paris in August 1944. For years the crumbling building was supported by heavy railroad-type buttresses extending out into the street. Restoring this house became a serious issue. Oddly enough, it was said that it had no historic interest, was extremely ugly, a disturbance to the city and its aesthetic sense. Fortunately, someone found a statue that led to classifying the building as a historic monument. Fortunately this lovely round tower with its flamboyant tracery is still here.

Do go up the Rue Vieille-du-Temple to **no. 87** and enter the courtyard of the **Hôtel de Rohan**. Turn right into the next courtyard. The Rohans were one of the most important noble families whose members lived all over the Marais. On the wall to your right you will see the famous and fabulous horses of Apollo, riding out of the stone they were sculpted from. The more you look at these horses the more detail you see. They were done in 1738 by Robert Le Lorrain.

Return to the Rue Vielle du Temple, retrace your steps, and cross Francs-Bourgeois. On the left, see if there is an

The collector's postcard shop at no. 45 Rue des Francs-Bourgeois

exhibition of food or books or art or antiques in the flag-bedecked former covered food market.

Across the street is **Ordning and Reda**, a Swedish stationery store. They have wonderful notebooks, pens, and pencils, all arranged by color. To your right try the very pleasant and reasonable restaurant **Au Gamin de Paris** at **no. 51**. Come here on the early side (before 7:30 and before the lines—people wait in the street) for an excellent bistro-style dinner. They have two superb desserts, a chocolate cake (a passion for some members of the family) and a tarte Tatin, sitting in the front window.

Continue down the street to a grand house, **no.47**, the **Hôtel Amelot-de-Bisseuil**. It is also known as the **Ambassadeurs de Hollande**. Its remarkably ugly door is reproduced everywhere. Two large and evil Medusa heads stick their tongues out at you. Peace and War are figured in the pediment. The door to the first courtyard is always open. Note the four sundials on the left wall.

The house has a long history, six centuries, but one that is particularly interesting to Americans. It was here that Beaumarchais wrote the comedy on which the libretto for Mozart's *The Marriage of Figaro* was based. Beaumarchais also created a business here called Rodriguez, Hortolez et Cie, which was a front for the exportation of arms to the American colonies in their fight against the English. The French and English had a long-standing enmity, not all of which is resolved. Beginning with the Revolution, the *hôtel* was left abandoned. Paneling and gold decorations were removed and a dome was covered up. Industry moved in, continuing the destruction. The hotel was divided into stores and small factories; false floors and ceilings were put in place; woodwork disappeared, as well as paintings on ceilings and friezes. Buildings, porches, and barracks in the courtyard hid all the wall decorations. Much has been restored, beginning only as recently as 1926. Painted ceilings and the dome were recuperated.

Further up on the left of this interesting street is a popular café, **Le Petit Fer à Cheval** (small horseshoe). The street is full of surprises, but we are heading back to Francs-Bourgeois to finish up near the Pompidou Center.

From the Hérouet house walk left down Francs-Bourgeois to one of the most architecturally interesting restaurants in Paris, at **no. 53 bis** on the left. **Le Dômarais** was originally the chapel for the religious order of the

Blancs-Manteaux and then was used as the auction room of the municipal pawnshop. The combination restaurant and music room is behind a very small courtyard with tables. It is a large round room encircled by a high balcony. The ceiling is a spectacular glass dome (hence the name). On our last visit, we found a new chef and had a superb meal at a reasonable price. If you are cigarette-smoked out of small, cozy restaurants, this is the place for you. The ceiling is so high you will breathe freely regardless of your neighbors. Be sure to visit the clever and pretty WC at the balcony level. The restaurant now has musical evenings with varied offerings.

Enter **no. 55**, the courtyard of the **Crédit Municipal**, the government-run pawnshop, known as *mont-de-piété*, or colloquially known as "my aunt" (*ma tante*). The wall surrounding Paris, begun by Philippe Auguste in about 1190 (see the plaque on the wall), cut across this yard and occupied the space traced on the ground. If you are on the entry side, you would have been outside the boundaries of twelfth-century Paris.

Walk through the far door on the left to see if there is a showing or auction going on. They specialize in jewelry and silver. It's fun to watch and if you can count fast enough in French, you might bid. Add 15 percent tax.

Walk right through the second courtyard to a large tower at the corner of the building. The base is a section of Philippe Auguste's wall, and the building opposite is decorated with *mascarons* of women, lions, and a satyr. Today the building is Munigarde, a storage and security facility for works of art. Turn right toward the street to see a doorway, the remains of a house that once stood there, and an antique column. If you cannot enter this second courtyard, return to the street, walk left, and stand across the street facing the end of the Crédit Municipal building. There, behind the iron door, you can see the tower of the wall. It is considered unfair to close off these historic sites, especially since taxes pay for part of the upkeep, but security is the excuse offered and accepted.

You are now standing next to the largest and most elegant palace in Paris. The **National Archives**, at **no. 67 Rue des Francs-Bourgeois**, is the entrance to a large complex including two of the most beautiful *hôtels* of the old regime, the **Palais de Soubise** and the **Palais de Rohan**, both visitable. Until recently the Palais de Soubise, in front of you, was used for research in the national archives. The great reception rooms that once heard the rustle of silks and the music of dance heard the whisperings of researchers and the scratching of pens.

The Prince de Soubise, who once lived at 13 Place des Vosges, found much wider scope here, as can be seen from this most grand colonnaded courtyard and the large gardens behind and to the side. The beautiful rooms, decorated by designer-architect Boffrand in the rococo style, give onto the interior garden. The sun fills these rooms, painted in gold and pale pastels with white sculpted ceilings and panels covered with scenes such as Venus at Her Toilette and the Education of Love. The palace is closed Tuesday. Hours are 1:45–5:45.

The oldest construction in the complex is the medieval gate with its two round towers and escutcheons on the walls on the **Rue des Archives** about a hundred yards to your left around the corner. This is all that the Prince de Soubise left from the fourteenth-century fortress that was originally built by Olivier de Clisson. But this remnant is a great boon, especially for the residents who have the pleasure of seeing a piece of the Middle Ages illuminated at night.

The national archives themselves have now moved to an electronically up-to-date building on the Rue des Quatre Fils around the corner. Among the archives are a letter from Joan of Arc and Napoleon's will. The palace is now used for receptions—a kind of republican return to royalist elegance.

The shop on the corner sells mementos of French history—medals, seals, facsimiles, and the like. They make wonderful gifts.

Rue Rambuteau

At the corner of the Rue des Archives, the Rue des Francs-Bourgeois changes its name to the **Rue Rambuteau**. This is a market street, and after two blocks of typical neighborhood food shopping, it leads right into the pedestrian zone that comprises the **Pompidou Center**, commonly known as Beaubourg; the **Quartier de l'Horloge**, and the **Fontaine Igor Stravinsky**.

Enter the pedestrian zone. Note the sweet-smelling baked goods and sandwiches (17 francs) at **Tout Chaud**, near the movie theater. You can snack while you wait on line at the cinema. Movies labeled "v.o." are in the original version—they are usually American movies with French subtitles.

Turn right after the cinema to the Quartier de l'Horloge, a combination of apartments and shops named for the huge brass clock in the heart of its interior courtyard. The clock, made of hammered and polished lead, was built by Jacques Monestier, and inaugurated here in 1979. The sculpture represents a man, the Defender of Time, in his victorious struggle against attacks by a dragon, a crab, and a rooster. They symbolize the earth, the sea, and the sky. Rumblings of the earth, stormy waves, and blustering wind accompany the attackers. At noon and at 6 and 10 P.M., the man is attacked by all three. At all other hours he has the easier task of fending off only one of the three. The *automate* weighs one ton and is about twelve feet high. Worth seeing.

Pompidou Center

Return to Rambuteau. Directly across the street is the entrance to Beaubourg, the Pompidou Center. Go right up the caterpillar escalator to see Paris spread out all around you. This will also give you a bird's-eye view of the musicians, magicians, and fire-eaters, *cracheurs de feu*, in the plaza below. Then visit the museum.

Six hundred and eighty-one designs were submitted for the Pompidou Center, and much to their surprise, two young architects, Renzo Piano and Richard Rogers, from Genoa and London respectively, were chosen. The fact that their French was limited made it easier for them to disregard the heated and constant criticisms surrounding the construction. When the center finally went up, with all its color-coded entrails of ducts and pipes (water, gas, air, and electricity) on the outside, most Parisians were horrified. Twenty years later, the center is undergoing drastic restoration and reaction is still sharply divided.

It is, however, the most visited attraction in the city, surpassing the Eiffel Tower, which was also maligned. When you consider the metal Lego effect of the Eiffel Tower, the ultramodern glass pyramid of the classical Louvre, the glass walls of the New Grand Library that let the sun shine on the books, the huge stone hulk of the Bastille Opera, the towering Arch of the Defense, you must credit the French with courage.

The museum houses a free exhibit area, the largest open-stack library in the city, special exhibitions, a bookstore, and the rich Museum of Modern Art.

Free entry to the museum was inspired by the idea of making this museum a people's museum. It succeeded. But there are drawbacks. The museum is a hangout for the down-and-out and for the avant-garde of pop culture. The inhabitants are not happy with the noise, crowds, and late hours. The place is somewhat seedy but always lively and fascinating.

The building's renovation will be finished for the

year 2000. In the meantime, you can enter a huge "ti pi" set up in the plaza for exhibits, auditorium, and bookstore. Open weekdays, 12–10 P.M., weekends 10–10; closed Tuesday.

Walk up the hill of the plaza to the street. **La Librairie Galerie** has an immense collection of posters and postcards. Continue straight to the left to the **Rue Saint-Martin**. The goodies on the street are a jewelry shop, a pen and paper store, a Quimper pottery shop, and warm fresh-made croissants.

To find the **Stravinsky Fountain**, turn left off Saint-Martin before the church of Saint-Médard. Kids love this spot. The brightly colored sculptures are by Nikki Saint-Phalle and intricate and mechanical metal automatons by Jean Tinguely are inspired by Stravinsky's music and are an expression of the New Realist movement. They bob happily in the large rectangular fountain. Find the different elements in the fountain: the key to the sun, the nightingale, the serpent, the firebird, the spiral, the heart, life, the elephant, death, ragtime, and love. Playing children surround the fountain in the daytime; the restaurants are filled at night. Try the outdoor tables at the red-painted **Brise-Miche** for a two-course, reasonably priced *menu*.

For reasons of space we have not detailed all the streets in this area, but that does not mean that you should skip them. They are laced with historic buildings, interesting shops, and restaurants. If you continue on the Rue Saint-Martin, you will pass several good restaurants, in particular, the one-star **Benoit**. This first-rate restaurant dates from 1912, and has passed from grandfather to grandson. The grandfather, like his friend, the famous chef Ferdinand Point, weighed well over three hundred pounds. The bistro used to serve the workers at Les Halles, the old Paris market. Now the bistro borders on becoming a restaurant with twenty-two employees instead of the usual ten to twelve. They still serve typical bistro food, cassoulet and soups, adapted but keeping the old spirit.

Continue down to the Rue de Rivoli, to Marks and Spencer, the English department store, and the Tour Saint-Jacques on your right; on your left, the Hôtel de Ville, city hall, and the Bazaar de l'Hôtel de Ville, a famous French department store.

Walk · 7

Bastille to Eglise Saint-Gervais

"Today, nothing happened."

—Louis XVI in his diary,
July 14, 1789

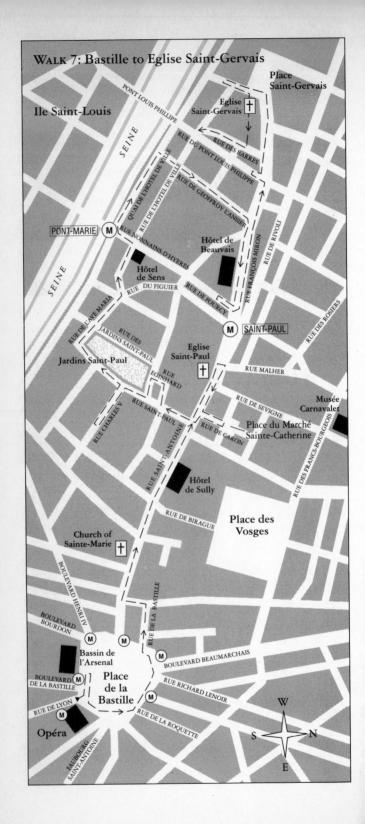

WALK 7: Bastille to Eglise Saint-Gervais

Place Saint-Gervais

Ile Saint-Louis

Eglise Saint-Gervais †

PONT LOUIS PHILLIPE

SEINE

RUE DES BARRES

RUE DU PONT LOUIS PHILIPPE

QUAI DE L'HÔTEL DE VILLE

RUE DE L'HÔTEL DE VILLE

RUE DE GEOFFROY L'ANSIER

PONT-MARIE Ⓜ

RUE NONNAINS D'HYERES

Hôtel de Beauvais

RUE FRANÇOIS MIRON

RUE DE RIVOLI

SEINE

Hôtel de Sens

RUE DU FIGUIER

RUE DE FOURCY

RUE DE L'AVE MARIA

RUE DES JARDINS SAINT-PAUL

SAINT-PAUL Ⓜ

RUE DES ROSIERS

Jardins Saint-Paul

RUE EGINHARD

Eglise Saint-Paul †

RUE MALHER

RUE CHARLES V

RUE SAINT-PAUL

RUE DE SEVIGNE

Musée Carnavalet

RUE SAINT-ANTOINE

RUE DE CARON

Place du Marché Sainte-Catherine

RUE DES FRANCS-BOURGEOIS

Hôtel de Sully

RUE DE BIRAGUE

Place des Vosges

Church of Sainte-Marie †

BOULEVARD HENRI IV

RUE DE LA BASTILLE

BOULEVARD BOURDON

Ⓜ Ⓜ

Ⓜ

Bassin de l'Arsenal

Ⓜ

BOULEVARD BEAUMARCHAIS

BOULEVARD DE LA BASTILLE

Ⓜ

Place de la Bastille

Ⓜ

RUE RICHARD LENOIR

RUE DE LYON

Ⓜ

Opéra

Ⓜ

RUE DE LA ROQUETTE

FAUBOURG SAINT-ANTOINE

W

S   N

E

Starting Point: Place de la Bastille
   4th arrondissement
Métro: Bastille*
Buses: 20, 29, 65, 87, 91

The **Place de la Bastille** stands today on what was the site of the fortified door known as the Porte Saint-Antoine in the protective wall of the city. Etienne Marcel, the provost of the merchants of the City of Paris, had this fortification built in 1356 as quickly as possible as part of his campaign against the imprisoned king, Jean le Bon, and in support of the English. This new portion of the wall was attached to the older wall of Philippe Auguste (see Walk 6, page 211), enlarging the enclosed, and thereby protected, area of the city. The entry at the Porte Saint-Antoine had a drawbridge and two huge towers called a *bastille* which was the term for a detached fortification.

   Etienne Marcel's treachery included attempting to deliver the keys to the gate to the king of Navarre and the

---

* Note: There are historical artifacts inside the *métro* station that relate to the history of the Bastille. To fully understand their significance you should read the history here before visiting them. However, if you leave the station to follow the walk while you read the history, you will be required to pay again to get back into the tunnels where the artifacts are located. The decision is yours—the description of the interior of the station is on page 247.

English on July 31, 1358. However, the men guarding the gate refused to turn over the keys, and instead hacked the provost to death with axes and threw his naked body in the Seine. Subsequently, Charles V regained control of Paris and had the wall completed. The Porte Saint-Antoine was enlarged, first by the addition of two more towers to create a fort, and then with two more; together, these established the structure that would become known as the prison of the Bastille.

The prison was a huge, oblong structure with thick, high, crenelated walls, eight round towers, a drawbridge, and a moat. In the seventeenth century, Richelieu turned it into a prison. Members of the aristocracy were often committed by a family member or rival politician. A secret letter, *une lettre de cachet,* sent to the king for his signature could put someone away.

The reasons for imprisonment were often peculiar. Voltaire was in the Bastille twice, once for writing malicious verse, another for challenging the Duc de Rohan to a duel. The prison was not for brutal criminals, and being locked up was not considered a disgrace. Quite the contrary. Prisoners could keep a servant, bring their own silver and porcelain, and make arrangements for receiving lovers. The Marquis de Sade draped his walls with fabric, Cardinal de Rohan had a dinner party for twenty. The prison was looked down upon as an expense to the state and unnecessary. And yet it became the symbol of the French Revolution.

The price of bread had gone up and on July 14, 1789, a mob gathered at the Palais Royale, prepared to make trouble. But the revolutionaries were short of powder for their guns. There was a rumor that there were 125 barrels of gunpowder in the Bastille, so off they went to storm the Bastille to get the gunpowder to start, in effect, the French Revolution. There were some intermittent shots during the day, but at about four o'clock an assault on the main gate began. (That is now 5 Rue Saint Antoine, the bakery Flo Prestige.) Six hundred thirty-three revolutionaries attacked thirty-two Swiss guards and fifty-two pensioners. Eighty revolutionaries and only one Swiss guard were killed.

The revolutionaries forced the governor of the Bastille, the Marquis de Launay, to give up the gunpowder and release the prisoners. He gave up the keys and was rewarded with being cut to pieces along with six Swiss guards.

Who were the prisoners? Four forgers, one accomplice to an attempted murder, a count accused of incest sent there by his family, and a madman. Hardly the makings of revolutionary symbolism, but that doesn't matter to an angry mob. This was the start of the Revolution. On that day, Louis XVI wrote in his diary, "Today, nothing happened."

General Lafayette eventually gave the key to the Bastille to General Washington. The eighteen-inch key is now on view at Mount Vernon.

Today, the location of the ancient walls of the Bastille is marked in the pavement of the *place* in brown bricks. There are many of these bricks in the roundabout, but they can be hard to see because of the constant traffic. Those at the entrance to the Rue Saint-Antoine are usually easy to find.

July Fourteenth became a national holiday in 1880. Bastille Day is celebrated July thirteenth with a grand ball at the Bastille from 8 P.M. on, with fireworks at the Eiffel Tower, and with a military parade on the Champs Elysées on the Fourteenth at 10 A.M.

Five years after the Bastille was torn down, in June 1794, the revolutionaries, ever vigilant in their campaign against the enemy, brought the guillotine from the Place de la Révolution, better known today as the Place de la Concorde, to the Place de la Bastille for three days. It was far from idle—seventy-three victims were beheaded in that time.

The *place*, however, was more frequently used as a location for large, symbolic public monuments. In 1793 the first fountain was erected, a colossal plaster figure of the goddess Isis spouting water from her breasts. In 1808,

Napoleon's minister of the interior placed the first stone for a new statue of an elephant that would commemorate the arrival of water through the subterranean canal from the Ourcq river into the city. Napoleon wanted the statue to be so monumental that one could enter through a leg and climb an interior spiral staircase to a viewing platform in a tower on the beast's back. The bronze was to come from cannons liberated from Spain, and the pachyderm's trunk would spray water.

The wood-and-plaster model was over sixty feet high and nearly fifty feet long. The project was abandoned though, and the model stood for thirty-five years, serving as a nesting place for millions of rats. Victor Hugo used it as a hiding/living place for Gavroche in *Les Misérables*. You can see what the elephant looked like in a fascinating copy of an engraving on a wall of the Bastille *métro* station.

In 1830, a law was passed to create a monument to commemorate those who died in the *Trois-Glorieuses*, July 27, 28, and 29, 1830, the three days of fighting that marked the end of the reign of Charles X. A column was designed to stand on the foundation that had been built for the elephant, with the bones of the honored dead laid to rest inside. The Colonne de Juillet is divided into three portions to represent the three days, with the names of the dead inscribed in gold in each section. It is topped with a statue of the golden spirit of Liberty breaking his irons and scattering light. The monument is dedicated, *"A la gloire des citoyens Français qui s'armèrent et combattent pour la défense des libertés publiques dans les memorables journées des 27, 28, 29 Juillet, 1830"* (To the glory of the French citizens who armed themselves and fought to defend the public liberty on those memorable days of July 27, 28, and 29). The column was completed in 1840 and soon became a favored site for suicides. As a result, the interior was closed.

There are several things to see in and around this hectic traffic circle, and we advise that you walk around only in the crosswalks and with the light. If you arrived on the *métro* there are a number of things to see in the corridors before you leave the station. If you came by bus you should invest in a *métro* ticket to enter the station. Use the entrance on the Rue de Lyon, on the right of the Opéra if you are facing that building. Go down the stairs, pay, and take the hallway to the right marked with the sign "Sortie Rue de Lyon—Opéra Bastille, Blvd. de la Bastille, Jardin du Bassin l'Arsenal." This leads you to a hallway with copies of historic engravings of the Place de la Bastille. Among the panels is the famous Fragonard drawing of the interior of the Bastille prison with the elegantly dressed women arriving to visit their wealthy imprisoned relatives, the elephant statue, and the demolition of the Bastille. These panels will help you understand the history of this area by providing the images of what is no longer here.

The *quai* for *ligne* 1, direction Château de Vincennes, is an elevated *quai* with glass windows offering a view of the canal below and the houseboats docked in the marina. On *ligne* 5, direction Bobigny, is the remains of a piece of the protective wall, the *contrescarpe*, that once surrounded the Bastille. Find the picture of a tree wrapped in blue, white, and red, colors of the Revolution, that is reinterpreted in a modern sculpture in the courtyard of the Hôtel d'Albret (see Walk 6, page 211).

Back outside in the *place*, go down to the banks of the canal if the weather is nice. Known as the **Bassin de l'Arsenal**, it was built to connect the Canal Saint-Martin with the Seine. It is a marina and, in the summer, is charming, with flowers and fantasies of life on the river in a neat little houseboat.

Back on the *place*, the most notable building is the new **Opéra**. It is built on the site of a small Jewish ghetto known centuries ago as the Cour de la Juiverie. The Opéra de Paris-Bastille opened in 1989 to celebrate the bicentennial of the French Revolution. It could not be more different from the Opéra-Garnier, built in 1875. That, however, is not a surprise because Paris in the last twenty years has been choosing a bold approach to modern architecture.

The Bastille Opéra is almost four blocks long, a huge hulking building, sectioned alternately in glass, metal, and stone, free of any decoration. The building takes on a different aspect each night as the lighting magically changes its appearance. The Garnier, in contrast, sits on a small island of land, and it is sculpted, pillared, arched, and decorated to the very top of its famous copper, gold, and stone dome.

The wide high steps of the Bastille, called *les grandes marches*, take you inside, where there is another staircase, geometrical, unadorned, curving high as it reaches the top. The Garnier's doubled, marbled staircase, illuminated with chandeliers sitting on caryatids, was made for a different time—a time for beautiful people in their grand clothes to descend and be admired. The Bastille, however, has a different function. Like the Pompidou Center, it seeks a wider more popular audience.

The main auditorium, narrow and high with few side balconies, is centered directly on the stage. The seats are made for comfort, with individual heaters underneath. Other auditoriums are used for smaller musical performances.

New technology makes it possible to perform several operas in one week. A series of elevators allows an assembled stage set to be brought up from below with the push of a button. We saw this remakable feat with our own eyes. For rehearsals, there is a second stage that is an exact duplicate of the main stage. Eight opera sets are made each year for both the old and new opera houses by teams of painters, tapestry workers, carpenters, sculptors, seamstresses, milliners, and designers in a work area of 75,000 square feet in the bottom of the Bastille.

Unfortunately, buying tickets is complicated. The automatic telephone service never connects to a real person and the voice is French. The best method is to ask your travel agent to reserve ahead for you. Tickets range from $20 to $100. Good luck.

Sunday-morning discussions at the Café des Phares

Next door to the Opéra is the brasserie, **Les Grands Marches**. Until 1990 the restaurant was known as the Tour d'Argent in recognition of one of the eight towers in the Bastille known as the Tour du Trésor, where Henri IV kept his savings. According to his minister, Sully, Henri had nearly 16 million pounds—quite a treasure. The *place* used to be graced with a large, highly visible red neon sign of a tower and the restaurant's name. Apparently this less-than-sophisticated display of the name was more than the world-famous Left Bank restaurant of the same name (until recently a three-star establishment) could stand. Claude Terrail, owner of that Tour d'Argent, sued for exclusive rights to the name and won.

The décor of the Grandes Marches (named for the uninspiring steps) is an eclectic mix of Art Nouveau, Art Deco, and whatever. Its drama makes you feel as though you have stepped onto a stage set for a movie. The restaurant is known for its shellfish and special "menu allegro," dinners that can be arranged ahead of time to be served during the fifty-minute intermission at the Opéra. Many of the stars of the opera stage have dined here and signed the guest book.

Continuing around the *place* to your right, at the entrance to the **Rue Richard-Lenoir** is the clock that counts down the seconds to the new millennium. The atomic clock used to be at the Pompidou Center, but that building is being restored. This street is known for its food market on Thursday and Sunday mornings. This is one of the least expensive food markets and people come from far to shop here. Even though prices may be lower than other markets, the quality remains high. A short walk down the street takes you to another Wallace fountain. (See Walk 4, page 133 for information on these.) Notice the complete Art Nouveau *métro* entrance on the **Rue Beaumarchais**.

Between the Rue de la Bastille and the Rue Saint-Antoine is the **Café des Phares**, a neighborhood hangout. The café hosts a philosophy debate every Sunday morning at eleven, drawing people from all over Paris. This was the first of about twenty *cafés philos* in Paris, many of which are near the university on the Left Bank, and many more all over France.

At the corner of the Rue Saint-Antoine is a plaque commemorating Charles de Gaulle's famous World War II motivational speech: *"La France a perdu une bataille! Mais la France n'a pas perdu la guerre!"* (France has lost a battle! But France has not lost the war!) France, he insisted, had to continue to fight in order to be present when the German enemy was crushed and, thereby, recover its liberty and grandeur. *"Notre patrie est en péril de mort. Luttons tous pour la sauver!"* (Our fatherland is in danger of death. We must all struggle to save it!)

Rue de la Bastille

Leave the *place* on the **Rue de la Bastille**. This small street came into being when the Bastille turned the Rue Saint-Antoine into a dead end, and Parisians needed a way around the fortress and out of the city. Today, the street's attraction is its good restaurants. The chief example is the brasserie **Bofinger**, at **no. 7**. Outside, the *huîtrier*, oyster opener, arranges and opens his fresh oysters in brimming bins; inside, patrons dine in luxury in magnificent Art Nouveau rooms. A colored glass skylight dates from the restaurant's restoration in 1919. For reservations in this nonsmoking room, ask for the Coupole. The restaurant's specialties are the *fruits de mer* and *choucroute* (an Alsatian mélange of sauerkraut and sausage cooked in beer). Bofinger is very popular for late-night meals after the opera. Reserve in advance and have a quintessential French experience. Across the street at **no. 6** is its little sister restaurant, **Bistrot de Bofinger**, with a simpler menu, lower prices, a less elegant but still comfortable setting, and the same good food.

At the corner at **no. 2** is **Le Bistrot du Dôme**. Under the same ownership as the famous Dôme in Montparnasse, this location specializes in very fresh fish. We began our lunch with a plate of tiny gray *crevettes* (shrimp) that had been lightly fried and which we ate whole like gourmet popcorn. Our meal was delicious, the prices were moderate, and the staff was friendly.

Turn right on the Rue des Tournelles into a tiny island at the junction of the **Rue Saint-Antoine** and Tournelles. This triangular intersection boasts a bench and a statue of

Art Nouveau at Bofinger, nos. 5–7 Rue de la Bastille

Pierre-Augustine Caron de Beaumarchais, watchmaker and author of the comedies that inspired Mozart's *The Marriage of Figaro* and Rossini's *The Barber of Seville*. Beaumarchais lived in this neighborhood in the eighteenth century. Behind him is **Flo Prestige**, a fine foods store owned by the same company that now owns Bofinger and several other Paris restaurants. This shop fills a social need created by a custom that is still de rigueur in France—you do not go to dinner at someone's house empty-handed. Flo sells food gifts that range in price from under $10 to $1,000 and will deliver them anywhere in France and even across the world.

Rue Saint-Antoine

You are now ready to explore the **Rue Saint-Antoine**, which at first glance appears to be a busy and uninteresting commercial street. While the Left Bank was inhabited as far back as the sixth century, the Right Bank, or Marais (marsh), was not settled for another five hundred years or more because the area was too wet to be habitable. Even at the height of the Middle Ages, in about the thirteenth century, this land was still largely field and meadow, much of it church lands. The major buildings were churches, chapels, convents, and monasteries, with smaller dependent structures nearby. The only built-up street was the Rue Saint-Antoine, which was the major road into Paris from the east.

One hundred years later, the Marais was to become the center of fashionable Paris. The Rue Saint-Antoine, because of its width from what is now the Rue de Sévigné to the Place de la Bastille, offered the best site in the city for the jousts and games that were the delight of the court and for the solemn processions, arrivals, and *cortèges* that were the public pageants of the day. When the center of Paris—that is, the Ile de la Cité—became dangerous for Charles V in the fourteenth century (a very troubled time, complicated by war with England, civil conflict, and urban uprisings), he moved to the Palais Saint-Pol (Saint Paul) near the Bastille, where he could take care of business and pleasure and yet still be able to get out of town in a hurry. The king's presence drew to the neighborhood wealthy courtiers, who built large residences that, with their fields and

Beaumarchais, librettist for The Marriage of Figaro *and* The Barber of Seville

gardens, towers and walls, seemed like so many chateaux in an urban setting. One of these, called the Hôtel des Tournelles because of the small towers that marked its walls, came under the crown in 1407 and replaced the Palais Saint-Pol as the royal residence. Tournelles was on the north side of the Rue Saint-Antoine and included the area that is the Place des Vosges today. See Walk 5 for information on the Hôtel des Tournelles.

The custom of games, processions, and spectacles in the Rue Saint-Antoine continued throughout the sixteenth century with the addition of autos-da-fé at which heretics (that is, Protestants) were burned for the salvation of their souls and the edification of the populace. It was here that Henri II, in June 1559, engaged in the joust that cost him his life and ended the role of Tournelles as royal residence, a story recounted in Walk 5 (page 174).

Across the **Rue Saint-Antoine** on the right side, **no. 5** was the location of the entry courtyard to the Bastille prison and was the entry used by the revolutionaries on July 14, 1789. **No. 7**, **La Bastoche**, is a small prerevolutionary house remarkably like the Petit Châtelet in Walk 1, page 17.

The large church at **no. 17** is the reformed church of **Sainte-Marie**, open only during Sunday service at 10:30 A.M. Originally this was a mansion owned by several illustrious people in the fifteenth century, including Charles VI and his brother Louis d'Orléans. In 1554 the *hôtel* was bought by Diane de Poitiers, Henry II's favorite mistress; in 1566 it went to the renowned architect Philibert Delorme.

In 1572 in Dijon, Jeanne Frémiot was born. This young woman married the Baron de Chantal and gave birth to a son who married Marie de Coulanges and fathered the future Marquise de Sévigné. Jeanne, who was widowed at a young age, devoted her life to the religious order of the Visitation Sainte-Marie (also known as les Visitandines). She became the mother superior of this order devoted to the education of young girls and care for the sick. A century after her death, Jeanne became the only married woman to be canonized by the Catholic Church.

In 1618 the religious order came to Paris, and in about twenty years the convent owned a vast property just inside this eastern edge of the city. The famed architect François Mansart built the chapel in the form of a huge rotunda inspired by Santa Maria Rotondo in Rome. Many of Mme de Sévigné's relatives and other aristocrats were laid to rest in its chapel.

In 1637 Mme de la Fayette sought shelter in the convent to escape the attentions of Louis XIII. He continued to visit her, but she succeeded in maintaining the relationship on a platonic basis. On the other hand, Cardinal Mazarin's niece Hortense Mancini was locked up in the convent to terminate her less than virtuous behavior. She took her revenge by putting black ink in the stoup (the receptacle for holy water in the church) and watching the nuns smear their foreheads with the ink.

During the Revolution, the convent was demolished, leaving only the chapel, which became a revolutionary club. In 1803, Napoléon, in an effort to equalize all religions, gave the chapel to the Protestants. Today the exterior is not very attractive and needs cleaning.

Next door to the church stands one of the more impressive *hôtels* of the Marais. The **Hôtel de Mayenne**, at **no. 21–23**, has been partially refurbished, and it demonstrates the vast difference between restored and unrestored buildings. The school in the center is dark and depressing. The office buildings on either side are glorious. Eventually the school will be demolished. The *hôtel* was built in the classic seventeenth-century style of the Marais—combined brick and stone capped with a steep slate roof.

The school was added above the rounded pediment in the center portion over what was once the grand entry to the *hôtel*, built in the style known as *entre cour et jardin*, between courtyard and garden. This architectural plan called for a wide entry flanked by two taller façades that formed the wings of the main building, which was centered between the courtyard and garden. The wings were used for the horses and servants, while the center of the house held the reception rooms and living quarters of the noble residents. The restored Hôtel de Sully at no. 62 Rue Saint Antoine, farther on in this walk, is built on the same architectural plan.

Originally the Hôtel de Mayenne was the Hôtel du Petit Musc, bought by Charles VI in 1378 and given to his brother, Louis d'Orléans. In 1562, it became the Hôtel de Boissy under the ownership of the Marquis de Boissy. Henri III's *mignon* (homosexual friend) Quélus was brought here after he suffered nineteen stab wounds in a vicious duel, along with two other of Henri's *mignons*, against three supporters of the Duc de Guise. At 5 A.M. on April 27, 1578, the six men met in the Place des Vosges. After the dust settled, two were dead on the spot, one died the next day, two survived their wounds, and Quélus lingered for thirty-three days in the Hôtel de Boissy before expiring. In an effort to save him, Henri ordered straw be strewn on the Rue Saint-Antoine to muffle the noise of the traffic and then further ordered the street closed to all.

Ironically, in 1613 the property came under the ownership of the nephew of the Duc de Guise who had incited the fatal duel thirty-five years earlier. Henri de Lorraine, son of the Duc de Mayenne, asked architect Jean Androuet to design his new *hôtel*. Androuet was only twenty-three years old at the time; eleven years later he was also the architect for the magnificent Hôtel de Sully, farther down the street. After passing through many aristocratic hands, the *hôtel* was leased to the Christian School of the Rue des Francs-Bourgeois—hence the name on the present façade.

Today, the Rue Saint-Antoine is primarily a commercial street, as this section attests. Stores selling inexpensive kitchenware are popular. No. 32 has an amusing façade based on *Alice's Adventures in Wonderland*. Tiles portray characters from the children's book, including Alice, the Dodo, and the White Rabbit, along with a bottle labeled *"bois-moi,"* drink me. Originally this was a children's dress

shop called "La Petite Alice," but today the shop is an unrelated tanning salon. The next street on your right is the Rue de Birague, which leads into the Place des Vosges, the subject of Walk 5.

Across Saint-Antoine, on the next block, **no. 53** is nicely restored with different styles of iron balconies. Back on the right side of the street at **no. 52**, in the front of the natural foods store Naturalia, is an example of the building beams that were used to make seventeenth-century houses. The employees here have no information on the history of the building, but go inside anyway and see how massive these support beams were.

The **Hôtel de Sully** at **no. 62** is one of the finest *hôtels* of the Marais. Built between 1624 and 1630 by the architect Androuet, it was not actually owned by the Duc de Sully until 1634. Sully was already seventy-four years old and was married to a much younger and faithless wife. She was so blatant in her affairs that apparently when he gave her housekeeping money he would say, "Here is so much for the house, so much for you, and so much for your lovers."

For a good view of the façade, cross the street to get some perspective. In typical early seventeenth-century style, the street façade was built to impress, something it does admirably, especially compared to its tasteless neighbors. Two two-story pavilions are divided into three windows each and are crowned with stately pyramid-shaped roofs with an ornate semicircular window. Between the pavilions is the spacious courtyard's entry for horse-drawn carriages. During the Revolution, this center section was filled in the same way as the Hôtel de Mayenne is today. The splendid interior was crowded with workrooms and the gardens were covered over with sheds and lean-tos. In 1951 the building was restored.

Enter the courtyard. The two wings leading to the main body of the house (the section straight ahead of you) were used for stables, a garage for carriages, the kitchens (noise and cooking odors were kept far from the reception areas, guaranteeing cold meals in drafty rooms), and housing for the vast staff required to maintain a home of this magnitude.

Look up at the sculptured bas-reliefs above the doorways. On the body of the *hôtel* are male figures representing two of the four seasons. Fall holds a bunch of grapes and has a hunting dog frolicking at his feet, and Winter is a balding old man with a serpent wrapped around a staff. Spring and Summer are in the back on the garden side of the principal building. The wings of the building are decorated with four female figures representing the elements. On your right are Water with a rainbow behind her and a dolphin at her feet and Earth with a lion; on the left, Air in wind-swept draperies with a chameleon (reputed to live on air) and Fire with electrified hair and a salamander (a mythical animal said to be able to withstand the heat of fire). The fashion for these symbolic sculptures dates from the end of the sixteenth century, and you will see more of them in the courtyard of the Carnavalet Museum in Walk 6. We had always admired these allegorical sculptures in the Carnavalet, but, in comparison, these are carved with more depth and greater detail.

Pass between the two sphinxes with broken noses and enter the building. A little off-center, to the right, is a staircase that was already dated by the time it was built. It consists of two straight runs of stairs parallel to each other and covered by a vaulted ceiling. An apocryphal story has the Duc de Sully reprimanding his wife for letting her lovers use the main staircase. She could have her lovers, but they were to stay off the staircase he used. Inventories show, however, that her rooms were, contrary to tradition, on the ground floor and he was on the *étage noble*, or our second floor.

On the left is the portion of the *hôtel* that is open to the public. The large room with painted beams is a bookstore. It stocks an excellent collection of books on Paris, including books in English. The other rooms are only open once a year in September as part of *le jour du patrimoine*, heritage day. Passing back into the gardens, remember to look up at Spring and Summer over the doorway. Spring holds a bird in one hand and a cornucopia in the other. A vase of flowers stands next to her. Summer also holds a cornucopia; hers is filled with wheat, while her other hand holds her scythe.

At the back of the garden is the *orangerie*—a large, formal greenhouse that all self-respecting noblemen had in order to grow their own supply of fresh fruit in the winter. This is one of the two remaining *orangeries* left intact in Paris. In the back right corner of the garden is an entrance to the Place des Vosges. (See Walk 5, page 171.) Sully enjoyed entering the square and promenading under the arcades. Today if you enter the *hôtel* from the *place* it is like stepping through a magic doorway and being transported back in history to a private seventeenth-century home.

Return to the Rue Saint-Antoine. A little farther down on the left side of the street are several food stores. At **no. 75** note the three gold horse heads, the required standard for a horse butcher. Horse butchers have become rare in Paris and are generally located only in working-class neighborhoods. **No. 77** houses a cheese shop that will mail vacuum-packed cheeses to the United States. When we stopped in, they had a wheel of Comté cheese that was nearly two and one-half feet wide in the front display case. On the façade of **no. 83** is a lovely modern standard of a sailing ship.

Nos. 101 and **99** Rue Saint Antoine are the addresses for the **Lycée Charlemagne** and the **church of Saint-Paul-Saint-Louis**. This was the location of the first Porte Saint-Antoine in the Philippe Auguste wall in the twelfth century. We will see traces of the wall behind the school later in the walk. The door was one of the four principal entrances to the city and stood here until 1382, when it was replaced by the door at the Bastille.

In the mid-sixteenth century, two *hôtels* were built here. In 1580, the Cardinal Charles de Bourbon, the uncle of the future Henri IV, gave one of these *hôtels*, no. 101, to the Jesuits. The Jesuits made it a retirement home for the superiors of their order. In 1594, however, a graduate of a Jesuit college made a failed assassination attempt against Henri IV, and Henri, in a rage, expelled the Jesuits and gave the property to the Hiéronymites (a Spanish order of priests who took Saint Jerome as their patron saint). They stayed only three years, to be replaced by artists favored by the king. In 1603 the Jesuits regained control of the *hôtel*, and this time they firmly entrenched themselves by buying the neighboring properties.

The Jesuits built the church of Saint-Louis between 1627 and 1641. It was the preeminent church of the Marais and provided the confessors for Louis XIII and Louis XIV. Mme de Sévigné was baptized here. During the Revolution, the *hôtel* became a repository for over a million books taken from convents that were suppressed by the regime. Many of the volumes were stolen or sold by weight—three sous a pound. The *lycée* (high school) that now occupies the site was begun in 1804, and the buildings of the school look as though they have hardly changed since that day. Although closed to the public, the school is said to have some very fine wrought-iron stair rails and an important frescoed ceiling painted by Gherardini in 1690 in what was the Jesuits' library.

The church, Saint-Paul-Saint-Louis (commonly called the *église* Saint-Paul—its official double name was given to commemorate the original *église* Saint-Paul, which was destroyed in the Revolution) was built during the reign of Louis XIII. Saint-Paul lacks the delicacy of earlier Gothic churches that inspire a feeling of spirituality. Information provided by the church states that "this façade, inspired by Saint-Gervais, was little appreciated in its time and was found too heavy. Today, it seduces you with her nobility." To most, its baroque façade still appears heavy, dark, and over-ornamented. Divided into three sections, the statues are modern (the originals were broken during the Revolution), while the clock dates from 1627 and was rescued from the original church of Saint-Paul.

The interior is also oppressive with sculpture, although

most of its treasures were lost in the Revolution. During the Revolution, the church's religious relics were also sold. The hearts of Louis XIII and Louis XIV were sold to the painter Saint-Martin. He wanted to use them to make a paint pigment called "mummy," which required mixing ground organic material with oil to achieve a brown glaze unavailable from any vegetable or mineral. This pigment was rare and highly sought after. Saint-Martin used part of Louis XIV's heart because it was the larger of the two. At the Restoration he returned the hearts and received a gold snuffbox from Louis XVIII in thanks.

In the seventeenth century this church was the site of awe-inspiring ceremonies for which no excess was spared. In his *Guide de Paris*, written in 1685, Germain Brice described the interior: "There is no altar in the kingdom that is more richly decorated and where there are more reliquaries, vessels, candelabras, chandeliers, lamps, and other similar things unknown to our ancestors, who liked simplicity in the house of God, and that the new orders have invented to warm the cooling devotion of the last few centuries." The church is still heavily decorated with an elaborate altar surrounded by paintings, arches, Corinthian pillars, chandeliers, and balconies and is capped with a heavily sculpted rotunda. One of the more charming decorations is the two huge shells for holy water given by Victor Hugo on the occasion of his daughter's marriage. Contrast this interior with the simplicity of the interior of Saint-Gervais later in the walk.

Retrace your steps on Saint-Antoine. Across the street, at the level of **no. 84**, is the entrance to the **Rue Caron**, which leads to the **Place du Marché-Sainte-Catherine**, one of the most charming squares in Paris. In the thirteenth century this area was the priory of Sainte-Catherine. In 1767, when the Jesuits were driven out of their property at 101 Rue Saint Antoine (and out of France), the religious order of Sainte Catherine took over the Jesuits' property and demolished their own to make room for a market.

Today the *place* is a picturesque spot to sit quietly on

the benches or to have a meal in any one the several restaurants that line the square. These include Le Marché de la Place; Ariang, a Korean barbecue restaurant; and Pitchi Poi, a Polish-Jewish establishment that specializes in smoked fish and blinis. We enjoyed a meal at the French **Bistrot de la Place**, which, at the time, was festooned with chandeliers waiting to be shipped down to the owner's newest venture—an inn in the South of France. If you are lucky enough to have good weather, take a table outside and relax.

Rue Saint-Paul

Return to the Rue Saint-Antoine, cross the street, and backtrack to the **Rue Saint-Paul**, known for its Village Saint-Paul, an antiques center. Turn right into this street which was named for a seventh-century church that disappeared with the invasion of the Norsemen in the ninth century. The street led to a busy harbor on the Seine that was also a swimming and washing area. Henri IV swam here accompanied by his subjects, while the ladies of the court were tucked away in a nearby tent where they could spy on the naked and cavorting men. The scene inspired this verse:

> *On y accourt pour voir l'homme en son naturel*
> *Et tel qu'il est sorti des mains de l'Eternel.*

> We came running to see man in his natural state
> And as he came from the hands of the Eternal.

No. 44 is an old one-window-wide building with an exposed beam over the door. **No. 47**, the **Cygne Rose**, is owned by an Englishwoman who serves as an unofficial helper to English-speaking tourists in the neighborhood. Her shop specializes in antiques and unusual gifts. **No. 31** is actually the arched entrance to the tiny pedestrian **Rue**

Eginhard. This street makes a 90 degree turn in the middle and ends up on the Rue Charlemagne. A few steps in on the right is a small gated and locked garden. In the center is a memorial that was recently placed here to commemorate a Jewish family that once lived on this spot. The inscription states:

Ici ont vecu Monsieur Elias Zajdner
mort pour la France a l'age de 41 ans
ancien resistant déporté à Auschwitz par les Nazis
en Mai 1944 avec ses trois fils. Albert, âgé de 21 ans
Salomon et Bernard âgé de 15 ans
morts dans le bloc des expériences.
Nous n'oublierons jamais.

Here lived Mr. Elias Zajdner
died for France at 41 years old
resistance fighter who was deported to Auschwitz by
    the Nazis
in May 1944 with his three sons. Albert 21 years old,
Salomon and Bernard 15 years old
who died in the medical experiments.
We will never forget.

We got the whole story from the daughter, Mme Sarah Yalibez, a Holocaust survivor. She was one of nine children living here with her parents when they heard rumors that Vichy officials were gathering Jews and taking them away. Where, they did not know. Mme Yalibez's mother left Paris, and some of the younger children had been sent to live with Catholics in the country. On the day the rest of the family was to follow them into hiding, the twins opened the door to the Vichy officials. One brother jumped out the back window and survived the war in hiding. Albert considered jumping too, but he stayed because he said he was needed to carry his grandmother's suitcases on the journey. Mme Yalibez, who was fifteen and a half when she was taken, survived Birkenau, but the others did not survive at Auschwitz. The twins were killed in Mengele's medical experiments on twins.

Mme Yalibez was very pleased that the French government finally let her put up a memorial fifty years after the war. Her requests had been rejected since after the war, but Mme Yalibez was determined. When she applied yet again in 1995, the government had a new policy and had begun making public gestures to atone for the crimes of the Vichy government. The neighbors were not happy when the memorial was placed and immediately planted a row of trees to block the view. Mme Yalibez pulled up the trees and asked the city to plant grass. It did, and locked the gate.

Return to the Rue Saint-Paul. On the left side of the street note **nos. 28**, **26**, and **20**. They are all old and attractively restored.

On the right side of the Rue Saint-Paul is a treasure trove of antiques and collectibles. **No. 27** to **no. 1** is known as the **Village Saint-Paul**; it is an enclave of antique shops selling everything including postcards, paintings, furniture, Art Nouveau glassware, keys and locks, and rustic farm tools. Some of the shops have a folder with a list of the participating stores and a map of the interconnecting courtyards that will help you uncover all of this charming complex.

In the twelfth century the basements under these buildings were used as dormitories by the religious orders and as a hospice for travelers. The property was just outside the city walls and served those who arrived when the gates at Saint-Antoine were closed. We have not seen, but have been told that the vaulted cellars under nos. 21 and 9 have been restored.

The Village Saint-Paul sells more affordable, less elegant antiques than those sold at the Antiquaires du Louvre or the Village Suisse. Here the stores are generally open from 11 A.M. to 7 P.M. from Thursday through Monday. Take time to wander through stores. Meet Annie at **Le Puceron Chineur** (a flea market prowler) in her shop that sells solid silver and silver-plated items. She is very friendly and will help to orient you to which shops are open and what to see. Wander down the Rue Saint-Paul and through the courtyards of the Village to appreciate antique dolls, Art Nouveau and Art Deco objects, kitchenware, keys, lamps, paintings, and knickknacks of all kinds and prices.

In the courtyards pause to enjoy the old buildings that have been renovated for reduced-price housing. In 1996 the media revealed that some of these coveted apartments were occupied by relatives of high city officials who enjoy the prime location and low rents. At the far side of the courtyard, exit to the **Rue des Jardins Saint-Paul**. In the sports terrain across the street is the largest surviving piece of the Philippe Auguste wall and two stone towers. To your right, at the end of the street, is the back of the Lycée Charlemagne and the church of Saint-Paul. To the right of the Village's center exit from the courtyard is a lovely trompe l'œil door painted to look like the flower-draped entry to a private garden. It is the back door of the atelier Un Autre Regard, a painting gallery on the Rue Charlemagne. (If you have not been wandering in the courtyards, go in the entrance from the Rue Saint-Paul marked 15-17-19.)

After you have taken the time to wander through the courtyards and found a few treasures to carry back home, return to the Rue Saint-Paul. At **no. 20** is the **Thanksgiving** restaurant and its associated food shop around the corner on **Rue Charles V**. The two are owned by an American woman, who does the cooking, and her French husband, who does the buying. They supply Americans and the French who admit to liking American products with foods from all regions of the United States. Their Sunday brunch is especially popular, serving pancakes, lox and bagels, and other American breakfast foods. Reservations for brunch are required.

On the corner of Saint-Paul and Charles V at **no. 25**

Rue Charles V is another good restaurant, **L'Enoteca**, an Italian wine bar. The restaurant offers delicious Italian food paired with a choice of about 360 Italian wines chosen by three sommeliers. We were assured that this was actress Claudia Cardinale's favorite restaurant in Paris. (She has an apartment in the neighborhood, but we weren't lucky enough to see her.) Make reservations for dinner.

Detour down the Rue Charles V with its nicely restored buildings (no. 23, for example) to **No. 12**, the **Hôtel de la Marquise de Brinvilliers**, also known as the Hôtel d'Aubray. Today only the doorway capped with a *mascaron* of a man has been restored. But it is the story of one of its residents that is so remarkable. The Marquis de Brinvilliers, Antoine Gobelin of the famous tapestry family, married Marie-Madeleine de Dreux d'Aubray in 1651. A worse marriage choice was never made. The marquise turned out to be astonishingly immoral and evil, even for her era, when the nobility were allowed considerable latitude in eccentric behavior.

By her own account, she "deviated from virtue" at seven and was a regular partner of her younger brothers. (Contemporary historians would probably reexamine her history for indications of sexual abuse.) Her father gave her an extremely generous dowry of 200,000 pounds when she married at twenty-one. She had three children, although their parentage was uncertain because she did not restrict her attentions to her husband. She became the mistress of the knight Sainte Croix, a man introduced to her by her husband. Her husband said nothing, but her father objected, and he had Sainte Croix arrested as he rode in her carriage on the Pont Neuf. Sainte Croix was imprisoned in the Bastille, where he made use of his time by learning about poisons from an Italian named Exili.

When Sainte Croix was released, he and the marquise established Exili in a laboratory to make poison for them. His concoction included venom of toad, arsenic, and vitriol. The marquise had, by now, spent her considerable dowry, and she set her sights on her inheritance. As a result of her charity work, she had access to patients in the city hospital, the Hôtel Dieu. She used this opportunity to experiment with proper poison dosages, and when she thought she had it right, she poisoned her father. He was evidently stronger than the sick hospital patients because it took ten tries to do him in. Four years later, in 1670, the marquise killed the older of her two brothers and attempted to poison his wife. Her younger brother was next, although she failed with her younger sister, a Carmelite nun. Next she set her sights on her husband, but Sainte Croix thwarted her because he was afraid that if her husband died, he would be obliged to marry this dangerous woman.

Not content with just her family, the Marquise persuaded Sainte Croix to assassinate the tutor of the two illegitimate children she had conceived with Sainte Croix. She had had affairs with the tutor and two of his cousins, one of whom fathered her sixth child. The assassination attempt failed because the lucky tutor, on the balcony across the courtyard, had seen the marquise hide Sainte Croix behind the fireplace.

In 1672, Sainte Croix died suddenly of natural (!) causes. As soon as the marquise heard the news she rushed to his house to retrieve the box that contained her letters. She made such a scene that the authorities became suspicious and confiscated the box. In it they found thirty-four letters detailing her crimes and twenty-seven recipes entitled "curious secrets." She fled, taking asylum in a convent in Belgium. She was lured out of the convent, however, by an agent of the head of the Paris police and was arrested.

She wrote a confession that admitted to having set fires, to losing her virginity at seven, to having poisoned her father and brothers, to having attempted to poison her sister, to incest, to adultery, and to attempted abortions. On July 15, 1676, she was condemned to make a confession at Notre-Dame and to be beheaded and then burned in the Place de Grève, her ashes scattered to the wind. She was exempted from having her hand cut off for her patricide.

Mme de Sévigné witnessed the execution and wrote up the events in a letter to her daughter. The executioner spent a quarter hour preparing the woman for her death, but "finally, it's done. Brinvilliers is in the air: after the execution, her poor little body was thrown in a very big fire, and her ashes are in the wind. . . ."

Return to the Rue Saint-Paul, pausing to peer in the nameless shop at no. 25 to see if the gentleman within is repairing violins and cellos, and head down the street to the left toward the Seine. Downstairs at **no. 11** is the **Musée de la Curiosité et de la Magie**, the museum of curiosities and magic. Normally the museum is open Wednesday, Saturday, and Sunday afternoons. During school vacation periods, children are offered a tour and an introductory lesson in performing magic. The last time we were here during a vacation, the line of children spilled into the street.

Note the façade of **no. 10** and its freize below the top floor. Go into the very pretty courtyard of **no. 8**. When we visited in the spring, the trees were flowering and a cat picked its way through the little gardens. Notice the wrought-iron stair rails on the left, in the square tower marked "entrance 8D," and supporting the balconies. Apartment 8D also has a small section of wall that is cantilevered out. This was the privy in the days when apartments did not have private water closets. 8A and 8B have beautiful wrought-iron balconies, in contrast to the cast-iron balconies of 8C.

There are a few more antique stores as you go. Turn right on the **Rue Ave Maria**. At the corner on the right are two stores selling old lace. **No. 2**, **Fuschia Dentelle**, sells blouses and skirts and cloths. Next door, **Francine Dentelles** carries dresses remade with lace. She also has a stand at the Marché aux Puces.

Continue down the street to the **Hôtel de Sens** at **no. 1**

Rue du Figuier. This striking *hôtel* is one of the oldest nonchurch buildings in Paris built in an architectural mélange of Gothic and Renaissance, military and civilian. The building was commissioned in 1475 by Tristan de Salazar, the tenth archbishop of Sens, and completed in 1519, the year of his death. Until 1622, Paris had only a bishop who was under the direction of the archbishop of Sens. This situation called for suitable housing in Paris for the archbishop, although because he had six other bishoprics to manage, he was rarely in residence. This infrequent use protected the building from being renovated over the years by succeeding archbishops.

In 1605, Henri IV asked the current archbishop for the use of the *hôtel* to lodge his ex-wife, Margot, who had been banished from Paris for the preceding eighteen years because of her unseemly behavior. (See Walk 3 for Margot's story, page 107.) She did not live there long, but when she did, the sober *hôtel* was transformed into a gambling den while Margot was locked up for days at a time with her very young lovers. She left precipitously for her property on the Left Bank after the murder of her eighteen-year-old lover and subsequent beheading of his assassin, her twenty-year-old lover.

When the Revolution came, the *hôtel* was sold, and a series of commercial tenants defaced and destroyed the original architecture. These included a laundry, a rabbit-skin wholesaler, and a jam factory. The City of Paris finally bought the *hôtel* in 1911 and, for decades, restored it in bits and pieces.

The turrets on both sides of the façade, while decorative, served the military purpose of permitting the residents to see down the streets on either side of the *hôtel*. Before you enter the courtyard stop to appreciate the flamboyant Gothic details of the mansard window flanked by angels, in contrast to the plain façade. Don't miss the gargoyles. Also find the hole above the portal that was intended to permit the residents to drop boiling oil on unwelcome visitors. Enter the courtyard to see the portions of the *hôtel* that are open to the public. On the left is a bookstore selling cards and posters of old advertisements and an exhibition space with changing exhibits. Straight ahead in the back of the courtyard is the **Bibliothèque Forney**, a library of art, decorative arts, and art techniques. Take the recreated staircase to the main reading room on the first floor, pausing to look at the photographs of the building before it was restored. The reading room is lovely and light and packed with students hunched over worktables and lined up to wait for books to be fetched from the stacks. In the back left corner behind the door is a corkscrew staircase, one of the few original portions of the building to survive. The rest of the building is a recreation in the style of the period. The library is open from Tuesday through Friday from 1:30 P.M. to 8:30 P.M. and on Saturday from 10 A.M. to 8:30 P.M.

Turn right as you leave and take Rue de l'Hôtel de Ville. This side of the building has beautiful flamboyant Gothic mansard windows that match the front window. There are also figures of dragons, musicians, and animals, and another turret to allow residents to see in both directions of the curved street. Behind the *hôtel* are formal French gardens and two more beautiful mansard windows.

You are now on the **Rue Nonnains-d'Hyères** and facing you is the **Jardin Albert Schweitzer**, a playground for children. Sit for a moment on the benches and watch the children play table tennis and climb on the equipment. Continue along the edge of the Seine on **Quai de l'Hôtel de Ville** to the back garden of the **Hôtel d'Aumont**. The *hôtel* was owned by Michel-Antoine Scarron, uncle of the poet Paul Scarron. In 1629, Michel-Antoine's daughter married up socially to the Duc d'Aumont. In 1648, the Duc d'Aumont sold his *hôtel* in the Place des Vosges and moved in with his father-in-law. When the father-in-law died in 1656, the duke enlarged the property by buying four surrounding houses. The architect Mansart was hired to transform the main building, while the interior was turned over to Vouet and Le Brun.

The duke died at sixty-nine of apoplexy. (It apparently

ran in his family—his son and his son's son both died of it. The third duke was taken ill at his mistress's; she hastened to send him home half dead in his carriage so that he would expire at Aumont rather than in her bed.) When the first duke died, his wife sought consolation in a new marriage, to which her son took offense. He had her confined to a convent, but before she was exiled, she managed to get back at him by burying a large sum of money, which was never recovered.

This second duke apparently did not control his wife as well as he did his mother. His wife, the duchess, lived a gay life that preceded her marriage and did not end with it. The story is told that one lover, surprised by the sudden return of the duke, was forced to hide in an armoire all day before he could make his escape. While his wife collected lovers (including prominent members of the clergy), the duke collected furniture and art. He collected so much that, at his death, the public sale of his possessions took several months.

Today, only the garden façade by Mansart and a ceiling by Le Brun remain. The ceiling survived only because it had been covered over with a false plaster ceiling and forgotten, perhaps for centuries. The garden façade is a classic French construction with *mascarons*, oeil-de-boeuf windows, tall windows and French doors on the ground floor, and wrought-iron balconies. The garden is mostly bare save an inappropriate and rusting modern sculpture that resembles perhaps a broken seesaw. This elegant façade by Mansart is a sharp contrast to the heavy, graceless façade of the *hôtel* on the Rue de Jouy. Return at night to see Aumont and Sens dramatically illuminated, rising out of the darkness like a stage set.

Walk along the Seine with the river and the *bouquinistes* (see Walk 1 for information on the bookstalls) on your left and the **Cité International des Arts** on your right. The Cité provides 180 apartments for artists from all over the world to come and study in Paris for a year. More than three thousand artists, musicians, and performers have come from seventy countries. Turn right on the **Rue Geoffroy-l'Asnier**.

Rue Geoffroy-l'Asnier

No. 17 is the **Mémorial du Martyr Juif Inconnu**, memorial to the unknown Jewish martyr, and the archives of contemporary Jewish documentation. Outdoors in the front of the building is a memorial to those who died in the concentration camps. Inside and downstairs is the crypt dedicated to the memory of the French deportees who never returned. It is a somber, below-ground-level room with a large Star of David with an eternal flame burning in the center. Two hundred thousand tiny lights burn in memory of the 200,000 French dead in concentration camps. A sculpture, *Despair,* by artist Michael Goldberg, is reminiscent of a Virgin Mary with the martyred Jesus across her lap; it represents the universal pain of the loss of a child, a parent, a sibling. It is dedicated to the six million who died in the Shoah. The crypt also contains a model of the Warsaw ghetto.

When we visited, the center had a temporary exhibit upstairs on the experience of the French Jews. France was unique during World War II in that it was the only country to deport Jews from territory not yet occupied by the Germans. It is only recently that the French have begun to acknowledge their official collaboration in the Holocaust.

No. 20, directly across the street from the center, has lovely *mascarons* of a lady. **No. 26** is the **Hôtel de Châlons-Luxembourg**, built in the early 1600s. One of the early owners was Antoine Le Fèvre de La Boderie. He was the French ambassador to England and returned to Paris with a gift of 150 horses. He was unable to stable them and so distributed them to his friends, keeping the best one for himself. Alas, Henri IV heard about the equine gifts and remarked, "Well pal, am I the only one of your friends not to get one of your horses?" Reluctantly, Le Fèvre was forced to give away his prize horse.

Above the door is the head of a magnificent lion with a luxuriant mane framed by a sea shell. The finely carved door knocker of horses recalls Le Fèvre's gift. Go inside the courtyard to see the interior façade with its double row of *mascarons*. The top row represents "real people" contrasted with the bottom row's grimacing faces. Two pairs of French doors are reached by a double staircase with a wrought-iron railing. On the right courtyard wall is a fountain with a marvelous man/fish head. Above is a classical cast-iron plaque depicting a mother nursing.

Rue François-Miron

Return to the street and continue on to the **Rue François-Miron** and turn right to **no. 68**, one of the more depressing architectural sights in the Marais. The **Hôtel de Beauvais** is in limbo, with plans to restore this unusual *hôtel* but no funds to accomplish the work. Renovations are funded on a yearly basis, and some years there is money, other years there is none. While the building is to be returned to the condition of the last known plans of the eighteenth century, no one knows when that will happen. The façade sports a sign explaining that the *hôtel* is the subject of an extensive study before the upcoming restoration.

There has been a residence here since 1200 and the Gothic remains are still found in the ogival arches of the cellars. The *hôtel*'s name, however, is due to its seventeenth-century owner, Catherine Bellier. Known as Cateau, this woman was reportedly ugly and blind in one eye, but she was the confidante and main chambermaid of Anne of Austria, wife of Louis XIII.

As a reward for intimacy (she listened to the details of Anne's romance with Mazarin and administered her enemas), Cateau and her husband, Pierre Beauvais, originally a ribbon seller, were given a baronetcy. Anne was especially thrilled when, after she told her maid her fears for the sexuality of her son, the future Louis XIV, Cateau (forty at the time) relieved the sixteen-year-old of his virginity so that he would not be frigid like his father.

The Baroness de Beauvais received such a large sum of money for her service to the crown that she purchased this piece of property and hired Antoine Lepautre, the king's first architect, to build her *hôtel*. The property was irregularly shaped and required creative use of the space. The resulting building is a polygon with the principal residence in the façade on the street rather than behind the courtyard as, for example, in the Hôtel de Sully. In addition, the architect designed the street level with stores, unheard of for a noble residence but revenue-producing for nobility of humble origins.

The façade, which is presently in a mutilated state, had a magnificent balcony that was topped by a triangular pediment decorated with reclining allegorical figures. On August 26, 1660, the famous balcony was the choice spot to watch Louis XIV and his new bride make their triumphant entry into Paris. Anne of Austria, Queen Henrietta of England and her daughter shared the Persian-carpeted balcony, shaded from the sun by a red velvet canopy as the royal procession made an honorary stop in front of the Hôtel de Beauvais.

The *hôtel*'s courtyard is a graceful oval with its very tall *première étage*, *mascarons,* and a staircase on the left with its original wrought-iron stair rail. The *hôtel* is decorated with intertwined **B**s for Beauvais and Bellier and the head of a ram (*bélier* means "ram"). Today the *hôtel* is filthy, the windows are broken, the balconies and pediment are gone, and the building is blocked off.

More than a hundred years after Catherine Bellier, Wolfgang Amadeus Mozart, his father, and his sister stayed here for five months. Mozart, only seven, was the breadwinner for the family. Although he was a great success at the court of Versailles, he was apparently unhappy that, after his concert, Mme de Pompadour did not embrace him.

To the right, **nos. 72** through **78** have nicely restored eighteenth-century façades. **No. 82** is three arcades wide, with a different *mascaron* on each arcade. The center one is the head of a Moor with a turban. Notice also the elaborate balcony and the wrought-iron railings. On the window above the center balcony is a pediment with another *mascaron*. Go around the corner on the **Rue de Fourcy** to see the garden and wing of this *hôtel*. In order to widen the street and still have a sidewalk, this side of the building is cantilevered out and held up by pillars.

Cross the Rue de Fourcy and continue on the same sidewalk (at this point François-Miron merges into the Rue Saint-Antione) to the second building from the corner. The **Hôtel de Séguier** at **no. 133** was built in 1626 and owned by this family until the Revolution. Note the balcony supported by fantastic chimeras.

Retrace your steps back down the Rue François-Miron to **no. 44**, the **Maison d'Ourscamp**, home of Sauvegarde et Mise en Valeur du Paris Historique (the organization to protect and value historic Paris). This nonprofit group, which is staffed by dedicated and educated retired volunteers, seeks to promote and protect historical Paris. The offices are open daily from 2 P.M. to 6 P.M.

In the twelfth century, abbeys across France were rich and powerful. They found that they needed a pied-à-terre in the city for the abbot and a dormitory for their students at the school of Notre-Dame. Ourscamp was originally one of these houses, as the vaulted medieval cellars attest. The house owes its name to the Sire de l'Ours, an unfortunate man who lost his head in the early fifteenth century for conspiring against Charles VI's wife. The building went through many owners and commercial tenants until, in 1941, it was declared insalubrious and was scheduled to be torn down. Almost nothing was left of the original building and the cellars had become a rubbish dump.

In 1963 the association was founded and their first project was to save nos. 44 through 46 Rue François-Miron at the association's expense. Work began, with young volunteers who gave their weekends to emptying the rubbish in the *caves* with shovels and buckets. They made a chain up the stairs to pass heavy buckets of stones up to the Dumpsters. They manually cleared out two thousand tons of gravel. Upstairs, they broke down walls, uncovered walls, and tore out floors. They made so much dust that billowed out the windows that the fire department came several times, called by alarmed neighbors. In 1970 the money ran out, and work stopped for fifteen years. The tarpaulins finally came off the façade in 1987, revealing the beautifully restored façade for the first time in fifteen years.

Take the time to visit the interior, which is like a museum of ancient construction. The floor of no. 44 is much lower than that of no. 46. The former has a thirteenth-century stone floor, while the latter has sixteenth-century hexagonal tiles except where a glass panel reveals a below-ground medieval column. The reception area is in the left half (no. 46), while most of the artifacts are on the right. On the wall a Gothic window tracery displays items discovered at the bottom of wells that were on the property. No. 44 also displays wrought-iron balconies and a wooden stair rail, a spiraling wooden pillar, and painted beams. The beams in the ceiling and one propped up vertically were recuperated from the Hôtel de Lamoignon. There are two staircases in no. 44. The stairs to the cellar are very steep stone stairs and must be descended cautiously. The cellars are medieval vaulted stone, and on one visit, the room had been transformed for a movie set in a Russian nobleman's castle.

At the base of the stairs that lead upstairs is an exposed wall of chimney tiles marking the site of an old fireplace. If someone is available to accompany you, go up the stairs to look out the window into the courtyard. The interior façades have been restored with the exposed beams. The rounded protuberances were the privies. Each floor had

one privy fitted out with a pot for wastes. Most likely, when the pots were full, they were dumped in the sewers or the river.

The association offers excellent guided tours of historic Paris, conducted in French. They can, however, with advance notice, organize an English-speaking tour for a minimum of ten people.

Directly across the street is the café **Chez Raymond**. Here men, mainly from North Africa, spend the day smoking and playing cards or backgammon. When we asked where the women were, one gentleman smiled and responded, "The women are in the cellar." Next door at **no. 19** is **Amadéo**, named for Mozart's stay in the Hôtel de Beauvais. This small restaurant has an inventive menu that features an unusual use of herbs and spices even in the desserts. For instance, the tarte Tatin is made with rosemary. On Tuesdays they offer a simpler, less expensive menu, and on the first Tuesday of the the month there is live classical music. On other nights, opera music plays discreetly in the background.

Back on the even-numbered side of the street, **no. 42** has a lovely double balcony and a *mascaron* of a man with lion paws. **Nos. 40** and **36** also have *mascarons*, including the eighteenth-century ladies on no. 36. Across the street, on the odd side, **nos. 11** and **13** have been remodeled to represent how an average house used to look in the seventeenth century. The buildings used to be in deplorable shape and were propped up with huge wooden crutches to keep them from crumbling into the street. No. 13, known as "at the sign of the sheep," has a fine fourteenth-century gabled roof. No. 11 is known as "at the sign of the reaper." The researchers at the Association de la Sauvegarde de Paris told us that the exposed beams are not full-sized, but are thin wood pieces put on the façade for effect.

Nos. 36, **34**, and **13** are Japanese stores selling pottery, fabrics, and all kinds of sleek, beautifully designed objects. **No. 30** is **Izrael**, **Epicerie du Monde**, an Ali Baba's cave of foodstuffs. This is the way stores used to be or perhaps the way we would like to remember them. As you enter, the odor of curry and pickling brine hits you in the face and you begin to salivate and your stomach begins to grumble. When you enter an American supermarket, the food is carefully packaged and beyond reach to maintain sanitary conditions. Here everything is exposed and the mingled scents are an inspiration to the pleasures of eating. The store is lined floor to ceiling with shelves overflowing with packages, cans, and jars. You have to pick your way around the aromatic barrels of olives and pickled vegetables and bags of beans, nuts, and grains. The store is an excellent source of all kinds of exotic spices that are doled out at your request into little plastic bags. There is a second room with tea, jams, mustards, and even some American mixes like brownies. They also sell cooking tools, bowls, baskets, posters, and all kinds of treasures.

The shop is owned by a husband and wife. Françoise Izrael's father originally opened the store when he came out of hiding after World War II. He had managed to avoid the Nazis by living in the woods in the Dordogne. M. Izrael, who was from the Balkans, stocked the shop with foods from that region. When Françoise married a man with the first name of Israel, she brought him into the business. She has worked more than forty years in the store, and her husband more than thirty. Now their son helps out. Monsieur, with a big white beard, is the friendlier one, but Madame can be drawn out and even gave us recipes that use some of the spices she sells. We left with a bag of candied kumquats, Moroccan preserved lemons, and some Hungarian paprika. Note: this store keeps traditional French hours—it is closed for a long lunch from 1 to 2:30 except on Saturdays and is closed all day Sunday and Monday.

When you leave the store, go around the corner to the black glass door of what appears to be a modern building at **22 bis Rue du Pont Louis-Philippe**. Once in the courtyard that lies behind the Izrael store, you will be surprised to see the restored wall to your right. It is of brick and stone and has a wooden mansard at the top.

The interesting and pricey shops on this street include several clothing and paper shops and even a lute maker. Return to François-Miron and turn left. **Nos. 14** to **4** are decorated with elegant wrought-iron balconies that run across the building at the third-floor level. They are decorated with an elm tree in the center to recall an elm that once stood in the Place Saint-Gervais at the end of the street. From medieval times, people met under the huge tree saying, "Attendez-moi sous l'orme" (Wait for me under the elm). It was pulled down during the Revolution, and although a new one was planted in 1912, the new tree does not have the significance the ancient one had. At no. 4 is a plaque to recall the home of the musical Couperin family who played the organ in the church next door.

Walk to the **Place Saint-Gervais** and pass in front of the church of Saint-Gervais (we will return here shortly) to the **Compagnons du Devoir** at **no. 1**. This is a training school for twenty-one different trades. Here students follow a five-year course of study to become masters of carpentry and building, shoe-making, iron working, and *les métiers de la bouche* (the mouth trades) of pastry- and bread-making. The students, who are sixteen to twenty-five years old, live in this building under the watchful eye of a head mother.

To become a *compagnon* you must complete a *chef d'oeuvre*, a masterpiece, some of which are displayed here. Go inside, past the wooden model of a cathedral tower and down the stairs with their wrought-iron railing. Go out the door to the courtyard and in the first door on your right to see a showroom of examples. We especially liked a fantastical wooden dome supported by several kinds of pillars poised over an elaborately inlaid floor, and a pair of women's red-and-black lace-up boots with a cancan dancer inlaid in the leather sole.

Return to the church. When we were here last, there was scaffolding on the façade and a plywood roof covered the steps to catch falling stones. The history of the church is as old as civilization on the right bank of the river. This spot was one of the few hillocks rising above the marsh and was the first to be settled by fishermen and boatmen. This became the path for the Roman road northward as well as the site of a pagan cemetery. A chapel was built to serve the cemetery when it became a Christian burial ground dedicated to the twin martyrs, Saint Gervais and Saint Protais.

There is little record of this church—it was probably destroyed in the Norman invasion. In 1190, the wall of Philippe Auguste enclosed this plot of land, making it very attractive to the residents. The church became too small to serve its parishioners, and a new one was begun in 1213, not to be completed until 1420. All that remains today of this church is the first two levels of a bell tower that stood outside the body of the building. When the new church became too small, the third (and current) church was begun in 1494. This engulfed the bell tower, whose dimensions set the plan for the size of the whole building. The church was built in the flamboyant Gothic style despite its construction in the Renaissance, but it took so long to complete (sixty-three years) that the façade was built in the style that was then current, hence the heavy baroque style copied by the church of Saint-Paul.

Paris was so taken with the façade with its three sections in the Ionic, Doric, and Corinthian styles that Voltaire (an anti-Catholic) remarked perhaps sarcastically, "this is a masterpiece, lacking only a square to hold its admirers." The nineteenth-century statue of Saint Gervais is on the left, one of Saint Protais on the right. The evangels, above, date from the early twentieth century. The original statues were demolished during the Revolution.

Saint-Gervais was an important church of the Marais. Mme de Sévigné was married here and innumerable prominent people were buried here. In modern Paris, however, the church has become isolated from its congregants, surrounded as it is on one side by administrative buildings including the city hall, l'Hôtel de Ville; the non-church-going students from the Cité des Arts on another; and the predominantly Jewish and Arab neighborhood on a third.

Humorous wood scenes under the stalls at the Church of Saint-Gervais

On Good Friday, 1918, the church suffered the disaster of being hit by a German shell of the type known as Big Bertha; the shell killed fifty and injured two hundred. As a result of the damage, the stained-glass windows are all modern.

Enter the church, which is in the process of restoration, and appreciate the freshly brightened Gothic pillars, especially the flamboyant ones behind the altar. The nave is furnished only with stools because the church's monastic order, the Communion de Jerusalem, believes in simplicity. In contrast, the organ is elaborately carved with garlands, ribbons, and cherubs.

The treasure to discover in this church is the miséricords carved in the pews of the choir. There are animals, faces, and scenes representing trades. Find the lion, the man and the woman sharing a bath, and the lady dancing with a jester. These small sculptures were tucked under the brackets on hinged seats that permitted the priests to perch their bodies during portions of the service that required prolonged standing. In addition, there are different faces carved on the armrests between the seats. This decoration expresses the humor and vitality of the anonymous tradesmen who built these massive churches.

Leave the church by the back door at the end of the left aisle. You are now on the **Rue Barres**. To the left and down two doors at **no. 15** is the remains of a building and a room with a beamed ceiling. Through the back, the church gardens are visible. Across the street, at the corner of **Rue Grenier Sur l'Eau**, a building shows its exposed beams and sags from age. This building, **no. 12**, has been beautifully restored as an inexpensive youth hostel. This was once a convent and now houses students from all over the world. Peek in the lobby to see the fine antique furniture.

The Rue Barres offers a dramatic view of the flanks of the church and its attractive roofs and gargoyles. Across from the church is **Artisanat Monastique**, which sells products from monasteries all over France—primarily jams, honeys, soaps, candles, and religious articles. The monks and nuns from Saint-Gervais are the salespeople.

In good weather, a small restaurant, **L'Ebouillanté**, serves meals under the wings of the church in the pedestrian street that dips down to the Seine. The outdoor tables are highly sought after in their peaceful and attractive surroundings. The restaurant is inexpensive and serves generously. It specializes in teas, salads, and hot sandwiches called *brik*.

If you continue to the end of the street you will be at the Seine across from the tip of the **Ile Saint-Louis**. If you are not too tired, walk over to visit this unique community within Paris. Until the twentieth century, it was not uncommon for residents of the Ile to be born and die there without ever having left the island. Today it is famous for Berthillon ice cream. Pay high prices for precise, small scoops of highly flavored ice creams and sorbets.

Berthillon is on the corner of the **Pont Louis-Philippe**, a meeting place for the French and for tourists. On summer nights and on Sundays, singers, mimes, and all kinds of performers line the pedestrian bridge and pass the hat.

Another option would be to retrace your steps to the front of Saint-Gervais and from there to the Place de l'Hotel de Ville. The elegant city hall always has interesting exhibits on some aspect of the City of Paris, and the department store across the street, the Bazaar de l'Hotel de Ville, commonly referred to as the BHV, has a good stationery department and the best hardware department in Paris. After a fruitless search through antique stores all over the city, we found the ideal solid brass lion-faced door knocker in the basement of the BHV for a very reasonable price.

Finally, behind the Place de la Bastille, from **9** to **129 Avenue Daumesnil**, is the **Viaduc des Arts**, an old train viaduct that has been restored with gardens planted on the top and artists' ateliers and shops under the arches. It is a lovely walk on the top and the bottom.

Cafés, Restaurants, and Hotels

Cafés and Restaurants

The following is a list of restaurants and cafés in or near the area of the walks. Each group is arranged in order of expense. Meals cost 40 to 50 percent more in Paris, but the quality is worth it. These are the places we have frequented, but there are many more for you to discover. If we have not included the phone number, the restaurant is casual and you can just stop in. We have listed restaurants as inexpensive, moderate, or expensive just as a general guideline. Food is expensive in Paris, although you can modify the price of your meal by how you order. Appetizers can be as expensive as the main course, and aperitifs, wine, and bottled water can easily send the bill in a modest restaurant into the expensive category. To save money in a café, order standing at the counter. It's much cheaper, but lacks the advantage of permitting you to sit and rest your feet.

Cafés, Restaurants, and Hotels

Saint-Julien-le-Pauvre and Saint-Séverin

Les Bouchons, 12 Rue de l'Hôtel Colbert, tel. 01-43-54-15-34. Excellent food. The wine is sold at cost. Expensive.

La Bûcherie, 41 Rue de la Bûcherie, tel. 01-43-54-24-2. Excellent French food in a comfortable setting. Expensive.

Allard, 4 Rue Saint-André-des-Arts, tel. 01-43-26-48-23. A famous classic French restaurant. Expensive.

La Rôtisserie Galande, 57 Rue Galande, tel. 01-46-34-70-96. Roasted meats and fish, simple and good. Moderate.

Hippopotamus, 9 Rue Lagrange. The French version of an upscale hamburger joint. Very popular and inexpensive.

Chieng Mai, 12 Rue Frédéric-Sauton, tel. 01-43-25-45-45. Thai food. Pleasant service and tasty meals. Inexpensive.

Le Départ, Place Saint-Michel. A large, busy café good for people-watching. Inexpensive.

Latin Mandarin, 4 Rue Saint Séverin. Small, good, and inexpensive Chinese.

The Tea Caddy, 14 Rue Saint-Julien-le-Pauvre, tel. 01-43-54-15-56. Light lunch, afternoon tea, and cake. Inexpensive.

Tentations, 21 Rue Saint-Jacques. Lunch and tea. Tasty and very informal. Inexpensive.

Saint-Germain-des-Prés

Brasserie Lipp, 151 Boulevard Saint-Germain, tel. 01-45-48-53-91. Alsatian food. Reserve ahead as it is popular with writers and publishers in the area. Moderate to expensive.

Le Petit Zinc, 11 Rue Saint-Benoît, tel. 01-42-61-20-60. Flowing Art Nouveau decor. Good food and service. Moderate to expensive.

Armani Café, 149 Boulevard Saint-Germain. Modern; inside the Armani boutique. Moderate.

Vagenende, 142 Boulevard Saint-Germain, tel. 01-43-26-68-18. Fabulous original Art Nouveau setting. The décor is more impressive than the food. Moderate.

La Grosse Horloge, 22 Rue Saint-Benoit, tel. 01-42-22-22-63. Classic French food. Moderate.

Restaurant des Beaux Arts, 11 Rue Bonaparte, tel. 01-43-26-92-64. Busy lunch spot. Classic food, moderately priced.

Café les Deux Magots, 170 Boulevard Saint-Germain. Busy, popular, great for people-watching. Moderate.

Café de Flore, 172 Boulevard Saint-Germain. Same as the Deux Magots. Moderate.

Art O'Leary's Pub, 73 Rue de Seine. Quiet, dark pub. Inexpensive.

La Palette, 43 Rue de Seine. Arty casual café and restaurant. Inexpensive.

Table d'Italie, 69 Rue de Seine. Italian deli and restaurant. Inexpensive.

Così, 54 Rue de Seine. Inexpensive, quick lunch.

Mouffetard

La Truffière, 4 Rue Blainville, tel. 01-46-33-29-82. The best restaurant in this neighborhood. Serious restaurant specializing in southwestern French food. Moderately expensive. Reserve.

Restaurant de Corée, 6 Rue Blainville. Korean food. Inexpensive.

Crêperie de la Mouff, 9 Rue Mouffetard. Light meals. Inexpensive.

Il Fiorentino, 3 Rue Mouffetard. Simple, good Italian food. Inexpensive.

Jardin de la Mouff, 75 Rue Mouffetard. Casual restaurant with a small garden in the back. Inexpensive.

The Marais

Place des Vosges
L'Ambroisie, 9 Place des Vosges, tel. 01-42-78-51-45. The

only three-star restaurant in the Marais. Exquisite food. Reserve months ahead. Very expensive.

Coconnas, 2 bis Place des Vosges, tel. 01-48-87-94-07. Set menu specializing in stews. Moderate to expensive.

La Guirlande de Julie, 25 Place des Vosges, tel. 01-48-87-94-07. A bower of flowers and fine food. Eat outdoors in the summer. Moderate to expensive.

La Chope des Vosges, 22 Place des Vosges, tel. 01-42-72-64-04. Very popular lunch spot. Good classic French food. Eat outside if weather permits. Moderate.

Ma Bourgogne, 19 Place des Vosges. A popular café in a great location. Good food and wines. The price can add up for a café meal. Moderate.

Nectarine, 16 Place des Vosges. A light lunch of salads and vegetable pies. Try the dense chocolate cake. Inexpensive.

Salon Victor Hugo, 8 Place des Vosges. Another light lunch spot. Inexpensive.

Francs-Bourgeois to the Pompidou Center

Ambassade d'Auvergne, 22 Rue du Grenier-Saint-Lazare, tel. 01-42-72-31-22. A one-star restaurant. Expensive.

Benoit, 20 Rue Saint-Martin, tel. 01-42-72-25-76. Michelin one-star restaurant. A classy bistro with excellent food. Expensive.

L'Alisier, 26 Rue Montmorency, tel. 01-42-72-31-04. Excellent classic French food in a comfortable setting. Moderately expensive.

Le Dômarais, 12 Rue des Francs-Bourgeois, tel. 01-42-74-54-17. A beautiful dining room worth seeing. Live music. Moderate to expensive.

Marriage Frères, 30 Rue Bourg Tibourg, tel. 01-42-72-23-11. The finest tea store in Paris. Hundreds of teas from all over the world weighed out from large black tins for a line of customers. Tea shop in the back specializing in food made with tea. Expensive for a lunch/tea shop. Tea museum upstairs.

Camille, 24 Rue des Francs-Bourgeois, tel. 01-42-72-20-

50. A busy moderately priced restaurant. Classic French food and nice service.

Au Gamin de Paris, 49 Rue Vieille-du-Temple, tel. 01-42-73-97-24. Good classic French food. Don't miss the chocolate cake. Moderate.

Goldenberg, 7 Rue des Rosiers, tel. 01-48-87-20-16. Jewish, but not kosher, Eastern European food. Meals and deli take-out. Moderate.

Le Grizzli, 7 Rue Saint-Martin, tel. 01-48-87-77-56. Good French bistro food. Eat outside in good weather. Moderate

Un Piano sur le Trottoir, 7 Rue des Francs-Bourgeois, tel. 01-42-77-91-91. Live music. Moderate. Closed Mondays.

Korcarz, 29 Rue des Rosiers. A bakery and restaurant. Tasty and kosher. Buy your bagels and strudel here. Inexpensive to moderate.

L'As du Felafel, 34 Rue des Rosiers. Street food. Inexpensive.

Au Petit Fer à Cheval, 30 Rue Vieille-du-Temple. A very busy café. Inexpensive.

Brise Mich, near Stravinsky Fountain. Inexpensive.

Hammam Café, 4 Rue des Rosiers. Kosher dairy restaurant. A neighborhood hangout. Inexpensive.

Marais Plus, 20 Rue des Francs-Bourgeois. Tea shop and light lunches. Inexpensive.

Bastille to Saint-Gervais

Bofinger, 7 Rue de la Bastille, tel. 01-42-72-87-82. Beautiful Art Nouveau decor. Alsatian food and shellfish are specialties. Reserve. Expensive.

Les Grandes Marches, 6 Place de la Bastille, tel. 01-43-42-90-32. Large traditional restaurant serving the Opéra. Comfortable setting. Expensive.

Bistrot du Dôme, 2 Rue de la Bastille, tel. 01-43-35-32-00. Fresh fish. Friendly service and serious food. Moderate to expensive.

Le Petit Bofinger, 7 Rue de la Bastille, tel. 01-42-72-05-23. Less formal and less expensive than Bofinger. Traditional, quality food.

Pitchi-Poi, Place du Marché-Sainte-Catherine, tel. 01-42-77-46-15. Kosher Polish food and blinis. Moderately expensive.

Amadéo, 19 Rue François-Miron, tel. 01-48-87-01-02. Very small restaurant specializing in the interesting use of herbs and spices in traditional food. Reduced-price menu on Tuesdays and musical evenings. Moderate.

Ariang, Place du Marché-Sainte-Catherine. Korean barbecue. Moderate.

Bistrot de la Place, 2 Place du Marché-Sainte-Catherine, tel. 01-42-78-21-32. Moderately priced. Eat outside if you can.

L'Enoteca, 25 Rue Charles V, tel. 01-42-78-91-44. An Italian wine bar with weekly menus. Very good food at moderate prices.

Thanksgiving Restaurant, 20 Rue Saint-Paul, tel. 01-42-77-68-28. When you need an American food fix. Reserve for weekend brunches. Moderate.

Le Coude Fou, 12 Rue du Bourg-Tibourg. A small eccentric restaurant with painted murals. Inexpensive.

L'Ebouillianté, 6 Rue des Barres. Light lunches, teas. When the weather is good get a table outside. Generous servings and inexpensive.

Café des Phares, Place de la Bastille near the Rue Saint-Antoine. Popular café with a philosophy debate every Sunday morning. Inexpensive.

Hotels

Saint-Julien-le-Pauvre and Saint-Séverin

Les Rives de Notre Dame, 15 Quai Saint-Michel, tel. 01-43-54-31-16. Elegant, especially for this neighborhood. Moderate to expensive.

Hôtel Colbert, 7 Rue de l'Hôtel Colbert, tel. 01-40-46-79-50. Elegant small hotel, recently redone. Moderate to expensive.

Hôtel Parc Saint-Séverin, 22 Rue de la Parcheminerie, tel. 01-43-54-32-17. Nice hotel tucked away in this neighborhood. Great view from top floor. Moderate to expensive.

Hôtel Esmeralda, no. 4 Rue Saint Julien le Pauvre, tel. 01-43-59-19-20. Very small but cozy. Great location. Inexpensive.

Hôtel du Mont Blanc, 28 Rue de la Huchette, tel. 01-43-54-49-44. Recently redone; noisy street. Inexpensive.

Saint-Germain-des-Prés

This neighborhood has many charming, moderately priced hotels. You are safe booking a room in any of them.

L'Hôtel, 13 Rue des Beaux Arts, tel. 01-43-25-27-22. Highly decorated, with fabulous atrium. Some rooms are very small. Expensive.

La Villa, 29 Rue Jacob, tel. 01-43-26-60-00. Sleek, modern hotel with a popular jazz club. Moderately expensive.

Hôtel des Deux Continents, 25 Rue Jacob, tel. 01-43-26-72-46. Popular. Moderately priced.

Hôtel des Maronniers, 21 Rue Jacob, tel. 01-43-25-30-60. Nice courtyard. Moderately priced.

Hôtel Millisime, 15 Rue Jacob, tel. 01-44-07-97-97. Nicely decorated and friendly. Moderate.

Hôtel Saint-Germain-des-Prés, 36 Rue Bonaparte, tel. 01-43-26-00-19. Charming lobby, updated rooms. Moderate.

Hôtel de Seine, 52 Rue de Seine, tel. 01-46-34-22-80. Up-to-date. Moderate.

Mouffetard

Comfort Inn, 53 Rue Mouffetard, tel. 01-01-43-36-17-00. Modern, basic, inexpensive. Book directly with Comfort Inns in the United States.

The Marais

Hôtel Pavillon de la Reine, 28 Place des Vosges, tel. 01-42-77-96-40. Elegant, charming hotel tucked away in the *place*. Expensive.

Hôtel Caron de Beaumarchais, 12 Rue Veille-du-Temple, tel. 01-42-72-34-12. Eighteenth-century décor, modern amenities. Friendly service. Moderate.

Index

Index

Index

Index